MENE MENE TEKEL UPHARSIN

Rich Alliston

Copyright © 2019 Rich Alliston

Mene Mene Tekel Upharsin Rich Alliston Mene Mene Tekel Upharsin
Copyright © 2019 by Rich Alliston Printed in the U.S.A.
ISBN-13:978-0-578-48947-6 ISBN-10:0-578-48947-3
Cover art by Rich Alliston
The characters and events portrayed in this book are not fictitious. Any similarity to real persons, living or dead, referenced in the Holy Bible is not coincidental and intended by the author. Any references to individual church ministers, or ministries individually is coincidental and not intended by the author.
Any references to 'Babylon' are generic. The terms 'Babylon,' 'Babylonian' references the perpetuation of a centuries old carnal system of ruling that incorporates religious worship. This system is headed up by the Prince of the Power of the Air and includes each and every system of worship, which operates independent of the Lord, Jesus Christ personally. This reference is intentional.
References to those who appear to be alive apart from God, but are dead is intentional as apart from God, they are deceased. The references to those who are actually living before God, yet have been physically deceased for centuries is intentional. For those believers who intentionally identified being buried with Christ in baptism? There are references to them as being alive with God with those afore referenced as being dead for centuries. This reference is intended as they are dead to their 'old man' whom they buried in baptism.
Unless otherwise indicated, all Scripture quotes are either from the King James version of the Bible, or from the Holy Bible, New Living Translation, copyright @ 1996,2004,2007 by Tyndale House Foundation. Used by permission of Tyndale House Publishers, Inc, Carol Stream, Illinois 60188. All rights reserved.
Anytime a scripture reference is made bold, italicized, or underlined, it represents emphasis added by the author. Portions of this book limited to individual chapters may be reproduced for the purpose of instruction, teaching, exhortation, and debate as long as the entire subject context is included.
However, the book in its entirety may not be reproduced, or stored in a retrieval system, or transmitted in any form or by any means, electronic, mechanical, photocopying, recording, or otherwise, without express written permission of the publisher.
r.calliston@yahoo.com
Library of Congress Control Number: 2018675309
Printed in the United States of America

Final Revision 9/29/2024

Dedication

The child in prayer went before God and stated; "You say if you raise a child in the way he should go, when he is old he will not depart from it. You are my heavenly Father, and I hold you to your word, to do whatever is needed in this life to make me your forever child."

I wish to dedicate this book to my loving heavenly Father, who has taught me the difference between what is important, what is to be valued, and what is to be discarded. In the darkness, He has been my light, in the abyss, He was present with me. In times of my foolishness, and blatant stupidity, He was my protector and as a blind man's guide to His child. He has been my counselor, my teacher, and His words are spirit containing life. His corrections at the time seemed severe, yet afterwards yielded an amazing place IN Him. There will never be enough time to express my appreciation to Him, for His unfailing love.

I ask of you Lord, that whoever reads these chapters, that in them you will find a willing heart to reveal your plans and purposes to them...

CONTENTS

Title Page
Copyright
Dedication
Author's Note 1
Why This Book? 10
The More Things Change... 27
The Struggle 36
The Seat of the Flesh and Blood... Soul ... 54
Obtaining God's Soul 70
Born Again, and Unconverted 86
Choosing God 107
Ordained 125
The Beast 143
'Mustard Seed Faith' 175
The Temple... 198
White Cane Blind 211
King-Pleasing 228
The Heart of God 243
The 'Sin' Issues 255
The Reality of Love 273
Tithes 282

Equality is Never Wholeness	292
Church Ministry	313

AUTHOR'S NOTE

Years in coming, this is a prophetic word to the Body of Christ. In 1982 I saw church leaders exposed and uprooted as weeds laying in the sun. I did not understand what I had seen, and I kept it to myself, locked away in my heart. In 2019, I was directed to write this book, and as I did was informed to *'tell it like it is'* without being concerned with how it came across. That is paraphrasing, as the word I heard was personal and much more direct.

The reader will be presented with a decision.

That decision is this,

>"Is this writing accurate?"
>"Is this what the Lord is telling pastors and those involved with the 'ministry' to His body?"

Frankly, the messenger of God never picks his message. It is NOT his word, nor his choice of messages.

As the author, I will speak what I am given without apology, nor will I couch it in pleasing terms. It is a direct word, it is a heart-breaking word, and it is delivered in the vernacular received.

This writing will not appease your dead soul, it will not minister grace to those in willful sin. It will however reveal a strait gate, a narrow path that can only be walked by following hard after the One who gave His all to make this path available. This is a direct word to every individual, every person involved in the leadership of *their* church. It is also a word to every person who has believed on the Lord Jesus Christ as their personal Savior.

The word is this,

>"Judgement has begun at the House of God."

Judgment is imputed sin or iniquity, resulting from repeated warnings being ignored.

Judgement results from ambivalence towards the word God is speaking.

In Genesis 4, men had begun to 'call on the name of the Lord'. Yet their calling on the Lord did not work out to good for them. The message is simple, because then as today flesh and blood will not inherit the Kingdom of God.

In Noah's time the *end of all flesh had come before God.* It was through Noah's faith that God judged sin in the flesh and the resulting destruction, we have the record, amen?

Through His Son, the Last Adam the *end of all flesh has again come before God.* Now we see God has condemned sin in the flesh through the faith of one man, Jesus Christ.

Man-approved pastors, and ministries with their degrees and certifications declaring they are man-approved are the focus of this writing. Jesus stated unequivocally that we could not please man and please God. Now we understand why these ministerial miscreants are absent the power that is the witness of God's approval of His ministers.

God told the Israelites in Isaiah, and in Jeremiah that those who led them caused them to err. In Amos God stated he was pressed under them like a 'cart laden with sheaves'. God offloaded those who were a burden to Him then, and God is offloading those who are a burden to Him this day.

Today, the message that God's grace covers a life lived in the flesh likewise has *'laden'* a holy God with the dead weight of those who preach and teach these lies. God is *'off-loading'* these dead weights who believe the call to walk holy before God does not apply to them.

This is not a fun word.
This is not even a word to sell books.

To read this writing all the way through will be difficult. Everything presented in this book, regardless of how offensive it is to the impotent professional pastor, will be backed up in this writing. There will be pages, references that will be so repulsive initially, it will be difficult to believe it is really God's word. Just as the seventy walked away when told they had to eat Jesus' flesh, and drink His blood, the truth was available then as it is today for those whose heart is humble and dependent upon God.

Before God, reading this book brings the reader into accountability before God as God watches over HIS word to perform it.

If you have believed the grace of God covers your carnal religious life, I have news for you...

The grace for this has been non-existent.

There has been patience as the Heavenly Father waits for a child to come to their senses. As understanding enters, that patience departs as the child's heart is exposed.

The choice, and the resulting blessing or consequences are yours.

Disagree?

As Noah built the ark, was God's patience with sinners? Or was His patience with Noah?

This book was tough to write, as accountability landed hard in my heart, and in my time here. It has been revised from its first edition. The revisions are in response to my Father revealing His word, making it more personal, more direct.

This writing is as offensive to social, cultural Christian church '*leaders*' as Jesus' words were to the religious descendants of Abraham.

Jesus' word to them was that their self-righteous circumcised Abrahamic flesh and blood would never inherit God's kingdom.

To those who get offended, no problem.

I serve a holy and righteous God, His judgements are indisputably righteous and eternally true...

The terminology God uses, along with the Gospel of Jesus Christ is spoken apart from the filters of cultural Churchanity. What God calls adultery and fornication?

It will be revealed as church leaders and their followers being *physically* involved with the god of this world, spiritually from within their *own* souls.

You will read of those who changed themselves into the image of servants of God, masquerading as God's messengers. These are Satan's ministers of righteousness, just as the Apostle Paul referred to them.

God is no respecter of persons, right?

Peter likewise was addressed as Satan when he took Jesus aside and then told Jesus His upcoming death was not to be. Peter was not demon-possessed and to Peter?

His intentions were good.

But he was being used by Satan, nonetheless.

What will we do when our self-pleasing religious ways are revealed as being from that same source?

When Peter was rebuked, he took that rebuke, and corrected his heart.

Today's cultural man pleasing ministers that echo Satan's words as though they were Jesus' words? Those who declare taking up our cross is unnecessary?

These man-pleasers will be addressed for who they are, just as Peter was.

Just as the Jerusalem which is above is the mother of the believers, Babylon will be revealed as the mother of Satan's ministers. Their self-righteousness will be exposed as them being 'one' with their mother, *in bed* with the woman described by God as the 'Great Whore'. The clarity, this adultery in its most disgusting form will be seen just as my Father sees it.

As you now understand, the anger in my Father's heart is expressed in tempered words.

Babylon's sins are as Sodom, and this '*woman*'? Those who are involved with her are under God's laser-focused judgment.

Babylon has been described as an enigmatic power, or a metaphoric spiritual city or kingdom. This lie is finished...

She is going to be revealed for who she is and the place we have given her in the dead soul of our flesh and blood living. Her diabolical work exposed in Christianity will bring both

understanding and accountability.
Again, this is a direct word to each individual involved in church leadership.

> *As you operate as the head of your church with your service planning, you personally are opposing the true head of the body, Jesus Christ.*

Disregarding the words of our Lord, is not without consequence. When we read Deuteronomy 18:18-19, we understand that God takes this despising His Son seriously... as in you have just challenged God on a personal level.

This is a warning, just as the Pharisees received from John the Baptist to flee the wrath to come.

To the believer this is a call to get personal with God. We will identify Babylon and understand God's redemptive word to us is for us to leave her. We are to separate ourselves from her seduction, her world system, her politics and her harlot daughter's ministries which have pleased our carnal souls.

There will be understandings that reveal church leaders doing Satan's work from their pulpit. Their lack of understanding is not being accepted as an excuse.

> *That lack of understanding is not being accepted as an excuse.*

Instead the words of Jesus to Nicodemus echo down through the years,

> *"Are you the teacher of Israel, and do not know these things?"*

If we believe Jesus' words are to another, not applicable to us we are blind, and our darkness is great darkness. If understanding can be received, sincere repentance, a real turning this moment is being required before God.

The Bride of the Lord of Hosts

As Abimelech with Sarah, there needs to be an understanding of God, God's authority and a restoration of God's people to God from *your* heart.

> *This is for your benefit.*

They are *not your* sheep, they are not to be *your* followers, it is *not your flock.* They are God's heritage, and you are in the wrong place at the wrong time.
God's word to Abimelech as he took another man's bride as his own plaything?
> *That word is God's word is to you.*

How you respond to this understanding, how you receive it, is on you...
> "Behold, thou art but a dead man, for the woman which
> thou hast taken; for she is a man's wife..."

Abimelech's response to God regarding Abram reveals Abimelech's wisdom.
The question to the church leadership is this, "*Who told you they were yours?*" You have taken their finances, their support as though it were being given to you for your kingdom. Again, you are in the wrong place at the wrong time. Abimelech's response to God was,
> "...He is my brother: in the integrity of my heart and
> innocency of my hands have I done this."

The church is my brother Jesus' bride.
How can you not see this?
Or were these just words you read?
Or can you grasp how your response determines the reality of your future?
God's grace has been removed from church leaders who preach and teach their doctrines instead of the Holy Spirit's words. There is an anger that is burning in the heart of God as this season of patience in man's stupidity and willful ignorance is ending. Strong words? Understand this;
> *God has not respected one person, one man above*
> *another.*
> *God will not regard one person over another that seeks*
> *Him in spirit and truth.*

It is impossible for God to lie, amen?
Since we know God absolutely does not regard one man above another, our excuse of '*I did not know*' is now exposed as our

evil heart of;
> *'I did not seek you. I had better things to do than spend time with you'.*

The man that will walk in the power of the Holy Spirit has paid a price the man who prefers his self-righteousness has not. One loved my Father in totality, the other?

The self-righteous knowledgeable leader?

In his arrogance he has told my Father he had more important things to do than humble himself and spend time with Him. To say otherwise is calling my Father a liar. If that describes you, God is totally finished with you. Repentance, genuine repentance from the heart is needed, immediately.

This book is written with multiple references to the Bible. Some of these identify book, chapter, and verse. Some may identify book and/or chapter only. The reader will be charged to abandon the doctrines of men, and cleave to the Lord abiding in His tangible Holy Spirit.

The stronghold of *'what I believe'* based on man's intellect and *'bible teachers'* personalities will be torn down as God's word infused by the Holy Spirit is revealed.

The *'church'* built on the personality of its charismatic pastor will be exposed as the gateway to hell, with that being an exceptionally nice way to put it.

Strong words?

It is the Lord Jesus we at this very moment stand before. Focus on HIM! He is the only One we are to be concerned about.

This is not an anti-church book.

The Rock that Jesus builds His church on? The Gates of Hell do not, *they cannot prevail against it.*

This church has Jesus Christ as its head. Jesus is the head of each of His servants, rich or poor, Jew or Greek, male or female. Among those who are His, Christ is the head of the man, as the husband is also the head of his wife. This is the *'even as'* spoken of in Ephesians 5:23 reflecting Christ as the head of the church. We will see the age we are in is not what man has called *'The Church Age'*. We will actually see this as the *'Age of Restitution'*.

The disciple's focus will be seen as becoming the place of God's rest so the consummation of the '*Week of Creation*' can occur. Just as the woman was returned to the first Adam, Jesus the Last Adam is seated at the right hand of God waiting for the restitution of ALL things.

In the Gospel of John, chapter 7, Jesus told us that those of us who are willing to do His Father's will would understand His doctrine. As the Holy Spirit IS the teacher, this writing will offer paths the Holy Spirit can expand on, and increase the child of God IN Christ.

How to walk in the conscious awareness of the Holy Spirit who is tangible, will be explained. How to walk as a son of God will be laid out clearly.

Life or Death

The Tree of the Knowledge of Good and Evil is the diet of the carnal man. Even with his seminary degree and his religious airs coupled with his false humility, tucked or untucked, that spiritually uncircumcised bastard is dead.

The Tree of Life will be revealed, it is accessed through a gate called Strait.

This path is so narrow it requires counting the cost, as it takes intense commitment to ascend it. The sons of God WILL ascend it. The foolishness of walking after the flesh while claiming authority with God in this world will be exposed as being deceived, cooperating with Satan just as Adam did.

It IS a *different* kingdom Jesus brought.

It IS a *different* realm.

It is a *different* city we receive life from.

The false gospel that flesh and blood is saved by God's grace through our mental assent will be exposed as Satan's ministers producing the '*child of wrath*'.

A student of God's Word will recognize some references merely by the terms and words used here, and there may be no reference to their biblical location. This is intentional. I encourage you to search the Scriptures and determine the validity of what is written.

When you sense the Holy Spirit '*quickening*' His word, please stop reading... Go before your Heavenly Father and wait on Him...

> *It is because of His inheritance IN you, His heart to you, that I encourage you to check with Him on the matters that follow.*

WHY THIS BOOK?

An industry, a business has sprung up in America and like cancer has spread to other countries. In the USA a new and virtually tax-free market has been realized, and entrepreneurs have seized on the opportunity to cash in on its rewards. It is a *'non-profit'* business model legally run by false prophets for the purpose of personal profit.
The more supporters they attract, the more luxurious lifestyle they are able to enjoy. This is their business selling the promise of carnal prosperity both to the believer and the government as the blessing of... God.
This *'for profit'* entity grows through targeting the souls of men, marketing a false gospel of Jesus Christ obtaining finances, gifts and accolades from man.
God is not part of this charade whatsoever.
Welcome to *'Mystery, Babylon the Great'*, the woman that amazed the apostle John. Pulling the veil back, we are going to take a look at this *'woman'* and understand who she is, where she sits or is at rest. We will see how she works through the unbeliever, and the believer alike. This message is part of the Revelation of Jesus Christ to us, amen? This IS God's word to us,

> "Blessed is the one who reads aloud the words of this
> prophecy, and blessed are those who hear it and take
> to heart what is written in it, because the time is near."
> Revelation 1:3
> "Write the things which thou hast seen, and the things
> which are, and the things which shall be hereafter."
> Revelation 1:1

In Revelation 17, Jesus reveals this *'woman'* who is anything but His bride. She is not in heaven, but as with Sodom, her sins have reached into heaven as a stench. She is the epitome of everything God hates, and ironically her presence is found '*at rest*' in the earth from Genesis to this very day.

Her identity along with her demise is found in Revelation.

> *"...Come hither; I will shew unto thee the judgment of the great whore that sitteth (at rest) upon many waters: With whom the kings of the earth have committed fornication, and the inhabitants of the earth have been made drunk with the wine of her fornication.*
>
> *So he carried me away in the spirit into the wilderness: and I saw a woman sit upon a scarlet coloured beast, full of names of blasphemy, having seven heads and ten horns.*
>
> *And the woman was arrayed in purple and scarlet colour, and decked with gold and precious stones and pearls, having a golden cup in her hand full of abominations and filthiness of her fornication:*
>
> *And upon her forehead was a name written, MYSTERY, BABYLON THE GREAT, THE MOTHER OF HARLOTS AND ABOMINATIONS OF THE EARTH.*
>
> *And I saw the woman drunken with the blood of the saints, and with the blood of the martyrs of Jesus: and when I saw her, I wondered with great admiration..."*

Later in the same chapter we find,

> *"...And he saith unto me, The waters which thou sawest, where the whore sitteth (is at rest), are peoples, and multitudes, and nations, and tongues."*

This '*woman*' is seen as '*being at rest*' upon the earth which we will see is the '*wilderness*'. Her '*sitting upon many waters*' is exposed as her being at rest upon those souls who have their home in the earth. These are the children of wrath who are quite content in this wilderness.

The description of this woman by God is the '*Great Whore*'.

This disgusting reference used indiscriminately is not this writer's definition, I do however accept and wholeheartedly share my Father's view and sentiment of her along with her vile daughters.

It is extremely important for the believer to understand this woman will *never be redeemed*. This is put here so that when you find your soul being pleasured in her, you will know it is time to break off your relationship with death. We will also understand who she is and if we prefer our soul being pleased in her, we get to share in her judgement.

The application, the understanding of *'Babylon'* is likewise applied indiscriminately in exposing Satan's work through her harlot daughters, her religions and/or churches.

Stick with me, and an understanding of Babylon will cause you to understand your entire life lived in or after the flesh, is being her citizen. She is the one the carnal man, believer or not draws their life from, she *spiritually is the dead flesh and blood soul's mother*.

Again, God's definition of her, His viewpoint, and His sentiment is embraced by this author.

Love God or Love Your Church?

We will see the *'harlot church'* ministers of righteousness as her sons physically involved in fornication with her. Again, she is identified as the Great Whore, not metaphorically but literally. It is in their souls, identified as their mind, will, and emotions they physically writhe with her in spiritual adultery.

Disgusting? Abstract?

This *'woman'* is also seen as drunk with the blood of the saints, the *'martyrs'* of Jesus Christ.

Should not we be asking, *'How could this be'*?

As cultural church teachings define martyrs as those who have died for the testimony of Jesus Christ, how could this scripture be applicable?

This intentional misdirection has removed any *'present-tense'* accountability of the believer. Yet, we absolutely know she could not be drunk with those who are absent the body and present with the Lord, amen?

Now we see the definition of an actual martyr as misunderstood and misrepresented.

A martyr is a witness.

A martyr not only describes an individual killed for the testimony of Christ, but also a living witness. Jesus told His disciples if a brother trespasses against them and will not hear them, to...

> *"...take with thee one or two more, that in the mouth of two or three witnesses (martyrs)..."*

We now see this vile *'woman'* is drunk with AND IN the souls of those who present-day bear witness, or testify that Jesus Christ is their Lord.

Remember, she is *'drunk with the blood of the saints'*. The identification of *'saints'* being intoxicated with her does not exclude them from partaking of her judgement. A person who declares Christ as their saviour, believes on Him but stays in Babylon will experience her plagues just as a Hebrew that rejected putting the lamb's blood on his doorposts would have lost his first-born.

God's word.

While this sounds abstract, what is stranger is this *'woman'* that God hates, is unknown. She remains hidden in plain sight as her revered respected ministers, her sons, her lovers wrapped up in fornication with her in their ignorance cover for her.

This is occurring present-tense this day. Just as the priests in Jesus' day, these religious men whom you look to? Just as then, knowing God's word, possessing religious demeanors and men's acceptance does not make them God-sent. This whore is the lover their soul cleaves to as they resist the Holy Spirit. Their being absent the witness and the power of the Holy Ghost reveals their strength is derived from *'another'*. The Great Whore provides for them through <u>your</u> soul being seduced, it is not God's provision. Your soul is being manipulated to reap your finances and accolades which make her amazing.

Yet in Revelation 18 we hear this redemptive word from Heaven to the believer,

> *"Come out of her, my people, that ye be not partakers of her sins, and that ye receive not of her plagues.*
> *For her sins have reached unto heaven, and God hath remembered her iniquities..."*

God is telling us to grasp, comprehend who it is we have been involved with, and abandon her en masse. As we locate her history, we will see her background as equally revolting. In the very last verse of Revelation 18, Babylon is located first in the Garden of Eden, and then outside the Garden at the second murder.

> *"...And in her was found the blood of prophets, and of saints, and of all that were slain upon the earth."*

She loves violence, she is a murderess. The first living soul's death by deception occurred when the woman was beguiled and made to forget God's word. Deceived, eating the forbidden fruit, she perished with God's son Adam (who was with her) consenting. Following that death, the physical murder of Abel locates Babylon, the Great Whore slaying Abel through Cain's offended soul, his emotions, his anger outside the Garden.

Babylon is a murderess and an experienced seductress. She excels in seducing souls, working on them from their physical birth, enticing them through their physical bloodstream which contains her access to their life, their soul.

It is the inhabitants of the earth who are '*dead drunk*' in her as she inflames their physical senses, manipulating their mind, will, and emotions. Scripturally we will view how Babylon works through every soul in this wilderness called earth.

Recall the '*whole world lies in wickedness*?' Babylon's scriptural realities can no longer just apply to a distant past civilization or to a particular religious group. Neither do they apply to some impersonal future event that does not involve us.

We will actually locate Babylon, the Great Whore in the bloodstream of our precious little flesh and blood carnal soul. This same flesh and blood soul is where Churchianity's

ministers are 'one' with the Great Whore. They relish her pleasing them as they bow a knee to her. She rewards them with her kingdom as they receive her 'comforting' them in their adulterous soul (their mind, will, and emotions). Obtaining accolades from her supporters, and their support, her ministers are among the precious stones that bedeck this Whore as they share her glory.
Rude, crude, socially unacceptable?
Consider King Herod, while speaking from his union with the Great Whore he was eaten up with worms. In his very bloodstream where her wickedness was relished, is where the reaping took place.
Too radical?
If so, then we are of the opinion my Father can be mocked...
King Herod? His sin was *imputed, retained.*
Like it or not, accept it or not, the judgment of God is as you read this being imputed against those who resist the Holy Spirit, deny the Living Lord, and willfully rule as the apostate head of *'their'* church.
These are the damned.
The believers?
They are God's children, God's sheep, God's planting.
The true apostle, prophet, evangelist, pastor and teacher?
They are the waterboys, as migrant workers who are to be husbandmen fulfilling the will of God in and by the Holy Spirit in HIS vineyard. They do not OWN the vineyard. If one becomes convicted of this unrighteousness, the redemptive message is to remove yourself, repent and be converted. The evidence of YOU actually being converted is YOU walking in New Life, abiding in the tangible Holy Ghost.
Disagree?
Then you have just been located outside of Christ.
You have not taken up your cross, you have not been buried. You have not lost your *'old'* life and became as a child learning to walk in New Life through abiding in the Holy Ghost who is life. The Holy Spirit is the substance of a child of God's

existence. You cannot live the *'resurrected life'* in God's power, it is an impossibility to you. Any man who ministers should do so as an oracle of God serving God, not men. The words a servant of God speaks should be witnessed by the Holy Spirit, or they are not God's words.

"*Pastor, those jokes, the humor, the lightness?*"

That is the god of this world working through your soul. Your identity is found in the presentation of YOUR soul, with the god of this world physically working through the life or the soul of your flesh.

It is <u>not</u> the Holy Spirit, that warm feeling, that false *'charisma'* you sense is a foul messenger of the Great Whore pleasuring you in your flesh and blood soul.

Grace? The reality is this, there never has been grace for your sin, it has God's mercy and His patience. It has been my Heavenly Father suffering just as the prodigal's father suffered waiting for his son to come to his senses. God's patience with you is gone, it is removed with this understanding. This error is now willful sin, it is being retained present-tense to those unwilling to hear.

This is the word of my Father. God spoke it through His servant Paul in Galatians 1, I am however reiterating it afresh by the commandment of my Father.

Once we know to do good, and do not do it, it is a willful sin, and there is no more sacrifice for it.

Again this is God's word.

A very short space for repentance is allowed, then this sin is being irrevocably retained. God is finished with it, and if we are wise, we will abandon it post-haste. The time of my Father enduring the pain of those who despise His Son's cross has reached its end, just as in the days of Noah. God *was patient with Noah* as he built the ark. God was not being patient with sinners any longer.

My Father's heart was breaking as He so loved the world, but the evil in men had reached the tipping point.

   (For those pastors/leaders who declare God is long-

suffering and relish the thought they can continue in sin? As a son I loved and protected my elderly earthly father from those who desired to pain him. Before God, you really have no idea that you are dealing with the Lord of Hosts, a Son who loves His Father, do you?)

Church Reality

A disenfranchised youth pastor at a large church in North Seattle opened up that at a staff meeting a church elder had commented on the church financials and the need for church growth. The elder had stated, *'Every fish has a coin in its mouth'*. This elder was using a take-off on the scriptural incident when Jesus told Peter where to obtain the Temple tribute money. A *'pastor'* in a small town in deep East Texas who I met selling construction services told me he had just taken the church's leadership back over after a sabbatical. He stated upon his return church membership was down from when he had left. Moreover, when he had left there had been six million dollars in the church's bank account, plus stocks and other investments. Upon his return that account was now down to a little over three million dollars.

Do either of these assemblies bear any resemblance to the Kingdom of God?

Neither of these man churches reflect heart attitudes that can exist in the Body of Christ where Jesus is the head. Actually understanding this is heart-breaking, and difficult times lie directly ahead for those who love their own soul. This is the first of five books which will deal with issues God is warning us to understand, repent of, and make new paths for our feet.

This writing is blunt, direct and offensive to every flesh and blood never to be redeemed soul.

There are no punches pulled, these scriptural truths can be argued, debated, but in reality before the Living God? They will be undeniable.

This book is not written to obtain kudos, or a following, but to put you, the reader born of God's word and God's spirit face to

face with God who has done everything for us...
And gets what?
Professional whoremongers who market His Son, His word? Their supporters who LOVE the favor and acceptance of others? For those whom God has called, they are being called to sincere repentance. This is a message of redemption. This is an opportunity for them as John the Baptist stated, to *"flee the wrath to come."*
To each and every person who intentionally, or even unintentionally is operating as the '*Head*' of a Babylonian church?
Pastor? Board member? God has this very special, very personal word, and it is... '*just for.. you*'. It is located in Daniel 5...

"MENE, MENE, TEKEL, UPHARSIN"

"Mene" means 'numbered'. God has numbered the days of your presumptuous reign and has brought it to a definitive end.
"Tekel" means 'weighed'.
Pastor? You have been personally weighed on the balances and before God? *You have not measured up.*
"Upharsin" means '*divided*'. The word to Belshazzar was that your kingdom has been divided and given to the Medes and Persians.
The word to the church leader is ... '*YOUR little kingdom, YOUR personal little rule is smashed*'.
Do we recall why these words were handwritten by God's messenger on Belshazzar's wall? Those sanctified, holy items that had been created and separated for God's personal use?
Belshazzar had taken them as his own and converted them to his own use.
These were a powerful holy God's vessels that had been consecrated for His personal use only. Can we understand this was highly offensive? Or do we regard the unseen God as impotent, sleeping, or without an identity...
Now being regarded as '*common*' by the man in charge, God's

personal items were used by Belshazzar in his kingdom for his personal pleasure as he saw fit.

Being dull, stupid, not taking to heart the things that happened to his father, not learning from history, this leader encountered the Lord of Hosts.

His knees knocked together as fear overcame him, his loins were loosed, and he soiled his garments.

He cleaned himself up, blessed Daniel and within 12 hours he was... dead. And in regards to his kingdom?

He was no longer large, nor was he in charge. That was *'his divine appointment...'*

To the self-called, man-approved, voted in deluded church leader you have an identical appointment with God. You wished to see Him, meet with Him? Again: *'You have no idea who it is you are dealing with'*.

To those who believe God has changed, and to those who have taken the things of God, His calling, His vessels (believers) and utilized them for your own benefit?

This book is specifically, personally written... *just for you.*

Again, as Belshazzar, you also have your very own personal divine appointment.

To those in ministry, every minister will be visited where they lie down. In your personal private space, there will be no rest, going to bed will be dreaded, as pain, torment and distress awaits. Where you have been comforted in the Great Whore, as King Herod, you will find the avenue of her access, is where you reap the fruits of this illicit union.

> *"Behold, all ye that kindle a fire, that compass yourselves about with sparks: walk in the light of your fire, and in the sparks that ye have kindled. This shall ye have of mine hand; ye shall lie down in sorrow."*

What I initially received was what occurred in Egypt on Passover night will pale in comparison to what the Lord is going to do. Rejecting the blood of the Lamb, turning your nose up to God resisting the Holy Spirit will result in grief and sorrow.

Disagree?
In the mid-1980's, I was driving through the Bothell Interchange on 405 in the Seattle area when the Lord showed me a cluster of grapes withering on the vine with this word:
> *"Ministries are going to wither as I withdraw my anointing from them."*

Within a short time the Bakker scandal was exposed, followed by others. The era of the TV Evangelist flush with cash, traveling by private jets was ending.

The sins that had occurred and covered were being brought to light. The words spoken in private, were being broadcast. The past... the history that could have been repented of and abandoned, covered by the blood of the Lamb? In their being exposed the tears flowed as high flying individuals realized their loss.

Repentance, or remorse?

That is not my call, nor yours, what is our call is our heart before God at this moment. What is happening now is intensely much more personal to the Lord Jesus Christ, with each and every single church leader being affected.

Babylon's 'Ministry'

The 5,000 who left? Not getting their *'bellies filled again'* by Jesus they departed. Now that Jesus has been crucified, they have returned using their Christ-less Churchianity as a path to get their bellies filled, and their dead souls satisfied.

It is called, *'Entering the Ministry'* selling their own little personal version of the *'Great Commission'* given to eleven men. *Wrong?* Where were the 5,000 when Jesus was meeting with the eleven giving them their commission?

The 70 disciples who choked on Jesus' words have likewise returned to get their slice of the pie, the *'gifts and offerings'*. They obtain their income presenting THEIR doctrines apart from the Holy Spirit. They will claim they are of God, they may even claim to have been visited by God, but their messages are apart from the witness of the Holy Spirit. Churches have hired Korah's peers, and those with Balaam's doctrines. These ministers are educated in seminaries, and they KNOW how to set *their church* up '*scripturally*', absent God's Holy Spirit, God Himself.

Those who present themselves as God's ministers are under God's direct judgement, this first book is a direct admonition and a clear warning.

In Jeremiah 23, God tells us if the prophets had sat in His counsel, and heard His word, they would have turned the people from the evil of their doing. Not sitting in God's counsel, they have delivered their personal messages structured for their hearer's ears.

They have defiled God's heritage.

That is the heartbreaker.

The message I get is one I deliver as directed. I am past being concerned about offending any. Yet before God, this message is tempered, its abruptness and direct manner is softened as much as allowable as not to detract from the message. I am instructed not to hold back. Judge the author, he really does not care.

As with any true believer, God the Holy Spirit is my life, my time, my all. Redeemed, just as you I am bought with a price. You, as I owe no man more than what we owe God our Father. There is nothing greater we can offer our Father than becoming a living sacrifice in obedience to God. For those with ears to hear?

God is going to bless those born of Him tremendously as they come to understand, and recognize the tangible Holy Spirit on God's word as their ONLY life. They will increase in Him, and He will increase in them as they regard His presence, His understanding, His kingdom as the greatest treasure. God will confirm His word by the witness of two or three.

Consider Job was warned in dreams which he disregarded. We need to be wise, and understand exactly who it is we are dealing with.

To those who disregard these warnings? I have about as much

concern for them, as God does, chaff is chaff. We will see that God had the trash taken out in the Old Testament, and no mourning by daddy Aaron was allowed, no paternal sadness was accepted.

In Malachi chapter two, likewise we see God dealing with those '*ministers*' whose offerings were full of excrement. God told those rebellious priests He was going to give them a facial with the excrement they had offered Him, and then throw them on the excrement pile.

This is God, this is God's word.

If one does not approve of these tempered words from my Father, I invite you to view His direct unfiltered words to the disobedient, rebellious, lovers of their own souls. You do know what excrement is, amen? The Malachi priests did also, they received a face full.

When we offer back to God that same corrupt, polluted soul Jesus went to the criminal's cross for? We crucify our Lord afresh, making Cain, Korah, and the Malachi priests look like fresh faced altar boys.

God sees the religious self-righteous ministers in the same way He saw the Malachi priests, IF you are wise, you will make a 180 very quickly...

Why this book?

Recall the parable of the man who planted a vineyard, hedged it, let it out to husbandmen? Remember when he sent servants to obtain a benefit? Do we remember when he finally sent His son?

The parable's ending here is different. A lot different. The Son? He IS returning, His fan is in His hand, the wheat He is gathering and the chaff?

It is headed for the fire, not a '*type of fire*', nor a '*metaphorical fire*'. But instead a fire that burns with the intense heat of my Father who is called a consuming fire.... Just an fyi...

This book addresses an intense anger in the heart of God toward carnal fools who are '*standing in God's stead*' for their own benefit.

There is anger, an intense heat that has built, if there is anything at all in this book that appears harsh, it does not compare to what is coming to these wicked husbandmen. Instead of hearing of the lie of God's grace for man's ignorance, we are actually looking at the rebellious having their sin retained as God's patience comes to an end. That is correct.
There are some who believe that retaining sin is error.
They say that God is forgiving, loving, and kind..
We quote *'God so loved the world that He gave His only begotten Son'*, amen? And we stop, because we have just heard all our precious little flesh and blood soul cares to hear. If we read one more verse we get clarity.

> *"He that believeth on the Son hath everlasting life: and he that believeth not (will not trust their life to) the Son shall not see life; but the wrath of God abideth on him."*

Rejecting Jesus the Word of God made flesh occurs when a man puts his back to God who gave His best. When God honors *their* decision, and they incur the results?
That is their sin being imputed.

> *If we choose to continue to grieve the Holy Spirit and drive Him from His purchased possession, should not God honor our decision?*

There are ministers who teach that sin being imputed is wrong as they mark those who do not support their ministry, or those who disagree with them. These are hypocrites, double tongued serpents and God's description of chaff.
Have we forgotten that man who had taken his father's wife in 1 Corinthians? Or Simon who thought the gift of God could be purchased? Were they graciously accepted by God as errant children? Or were dealt with for their error?
Have we forgotten that lovely *'early church'* couple, Ananias and Sapphira?
They committed something to God and then prudently held back a portion. This same error occurs as believers commit their all to God and then later decide it is too hard, and hold back their total commitment. They have a reserve, a back-up

plan in case God fails them...
How did that work out for Ananias, or Sapphira?
Do we serve a different God, or have we been seduced into confusing God's mercy, God's patience with God's grace?
It was Satan who filled Ananias and Sapphira's heart, he is a liar and the father of lies. It was Satan who involved Peter in savoring the things of men.
One of the above had a correctible heart.
The others?
They chose to follow Satan savoring the things of men instead of the Holy Spirit having faith in God who had supplied all their need.
God has NOT changed, but His patience has been preached as His grace.
That is the epitome of foolishness.
Back to the wicked husbandmen, not being God's children, not being of His Son, their sin is being imputed, and the patience they spurned? It becomes the source of their weeping. As with Esau the offer of repentance is off the table as they cannot understand flesh and blood has no part in the Kingdom of God. And again, before God, this message is greatly tempered...
This may be new information, but all five of the true ministry gifts found in Ephesians 4:11? The true apostle, prophet, evangelist, pastor, and teacher? These are actual servants loving not their lives to the death.
These were never prima-donna men reveling in their ministerial image cultivating the approval of men. That would have been... ungodly.
The true men of God, God's servants?
They have been crucified with Christ, buried with Him, baptized INTO Him, and raised IN HIM delivering the words given them in and by the tangible Holy Ghost, God Himself. The true gifts are operated BY God, the spirit of God, for the purpose of God obtaining HIS inheritance in us. These true ministry gifts reflect the heart of the Living God, and from God's heart they speak as the oracles of the Living God.

In Christ, there is black and white, there is yes and no. The promises of God IN Christ are yes and amen, not maybe.
Am I denying grace?
Absolutely not.
There is no denying God's grace.
However, Satan through his false apostles redefining God's grace that allows man to proceed a self-pleasing life apart from God?
Absolutely, I am 100% denying that willful disobedience and misapplication of God's word.
In short, this writing is about preserving God's people. If you are in leadership and unrepentant? If you present yourself as sent by God and you are not?
Your sin is retained, right at this very moment.
God's word.
You are on your way out. God is going to pluck you from where you have planted yourself, leaving you exposed to wither without the redemption you have rejected.
YOU... are part of God's trash day...
Those who God has ordained and sent?
They will not speak of themselves, or from themselves seeking their personal benefit.
They will not use the snake's gift of a charming personality to develop relationships with a few to make other church-goers envious.
Do we even understand that?
Pastor, apostle, when you address your 'yes men' from your place of power to make the other believers envious? You believe it is innocent? That is the work of Satan manipulating God's children through you his child.
Check on prices for a millstone to hang around your neck, it is a better deal than standing guilty of this before God.
There is an anger before God that you will experience. Personally in your precious flesh and blood soul, and it is not a 'genetic issue'.
If you doubt that, reread Peter about those who suffer in

the flesh cease from sin. That might tear down a Satanic stronghold in your fortified city.

These God given gifts were not given to men so they could enrich themselves, validate their self-worth, stoke their reputation, or lord over those whom Jesus Christ purchased to Himself.

If Jesus Christ is not the head of the *'leader'* in the local assembly, and the anointing and presence of God the Holy Spirit is not present in or on the *'leader's'* life? He is not God's servant.

In self-called ministers of Satan serving another, how in God's name can any child born of God under this so-called *'leadership'* increase to the stature of the fullness of Christ?

They can not.

THE MORE THINGS CHANGE...
the More They Remain the Same

The local church has become a business, often a multi-million-dollar business.
Those that are successful have '*business models*' that are repeated many times over as '*sister*' harlot churches become '*fun places*' for '*messed up people*' to be told they are '*okay*'. Their '*sanctuaries*' are entertainment centers replete with live music worship teams and large video displays.
The larger churches have CEO's posing as genuine pastors with business managers carrying the moniker of Assistant Pastor. They are degreed businessmen, asset managers with professional pastoral demeanors...
As a contractor I had one customer who introduced himself as one of the assistant pastors of a local 'successful' church. But then, he stated his job description was actually handling the church financials as he had graduated college with a degree in business. He was a business manager with the demeanor of a pastor.
There is an entire industry supporting the '*Professional Minister*' supplying them with sermons and study outlines. In 2018, this industry was estimated to be between $135 billion to $1.2 trillion in an UNTAXED industry.
Did we really believe this was God and HIS Word?
Recall the old song lyrics, '*money for nothing and the chicks are free*'? Easier than becoming a rock star, is becoming a pastor. The majority of those attracted to ministry struggle with porn and 4 out of 10 have been sexually involved with someone other than their spouse, SINCE they entered their

ministry. The spirit that has seduced them desires to expand its conquest to their subjects in their kingdom. Receiving their words, is receiving the spirit on their words in your own home. In your following them, your struggles are exacerbated, no deliverance is found.

> *(Husband, do you attend this debacle because your wife requires it of you? Now you understand why fishing, or time in a deer stand is more peaceful. Jesus is NOT the head of that business, and never was. This is not a reason to abandon your relationship with God, it is a call to GET WITH GOD, in His word, in yielding to the Holy Spirit from YOUR heart).*

Search online for "How to Grow <u>Your</u> Church" and you will find resources on how to keep the churchgoer, the financial contributor engaged by speaking to their interests. The believer is '*The Mark*' who is being sold a bill of goods. This '*sale*' is made with all the right words and genuine concern expressed for their attendance, financial gifts, and offerings to 'God'.

There should be '*Oscar*' for successful ministers as they '*sell*' their souls to obtain your support. Likewise, when we see the pastor's (CEO) family members, and '*friends*' being '*ordained*' to serve, keep in mind financial disbursements and decision-making regarding the 'corporate' direction must be tightly controlled.

Political in-fighting which is present in corporate environments must be kept under wraps and out of view.

A quick search of '*Ministry Jobs*' online reveals salaried job openings for Pastors, Christian Asset Managers, service planners and other ministry positions. As is true in any corporation, asset management and financial control are paramount to business growth, along with a good public image.

Do we feel '*blessed yet*'?

Too extreme?

Is God in charge?

No?

You are witnessing the amazing beauty of the *'Great Whore'*.

She IS amazing, amen? This is that glorious woman and her harlot daughters God calls Babylon being played out right before our very eyes, present-tense and in real time. Fact. Consider this...

Is it just a 'coincidence' nightly prayer meetings that continue until God moves deeply upon men have vanished?

Seriously, that woman in Revelation17 who dazzled the apostle John has no interest in humbling herself. She proclaims she is a queen, not a widow as she disavows having any authority over her.

Her intoxication is her union with the dead souls of believers as she garners God's children in HER houses pleasuring their uncrucified, unburied souls convincing them they are... saved. Does that sound wrong?

Have we forgotten that per the Holy Spirit in Colossians we are dead? Or is that just a *'metaphorical'* reference because the life we really love is in our flesh? The beast who the Great Whore receives her place, her authority to operate from? As she does not acknowledge his rule, God has put it in his heart to consume her.

The beast is going to consume her starting with her ruling elders, her pastors. When you see her pastors put out, pursued and punished by this beast, these words will ring in your ears.

You will be told the *'church'* is being persecuted, when in fact it is the judgement of God. When the beast has finished with them, her soul-pleasing supporters will be his next target. How is this going to happen? It is not rocket science and nothing will happen that God does not reveal to His servants, amen?

The warning to the believer is to *'come out of her'* in Revelation 17.

Not being condemned, the child of God is being told to *'depart her'*.

This is a message of redemption warning us of her judgement. This is the same message Jesus gave His disciples.

Jesus told His hearers to leave when Jerusalem was being surrounded, did He not?

The *'Great Whore's'* rule is through her cooperative self-willed, self-called man ordained *'ministers'* of righteousness with whom she shares her glory. It is her *'man approved'* leaders and their choices she reflects her glory through. It is her worship teams, and her elders (associates) approved by her *'person of the hour'* who share in her leadership positions.

In keeping with industry growth, the Babylonian Gospel message must be palatable to avoid disenfranchising existing and potential members. Corporate funding must be easy, so giving can be done impulsively online, or via text from your phone, and support. Your participation, your involvement is linked for your soul's convenience with *'Ministries'* on the web page header.

Welcome to Babylon's 21rst century commercialized faux Body of Christ. We are taught by her to love our local church, adore our pastor(s) where greed, idolatry, hatred, covetousness, humor, and man-pleasing can be covered with a gregarious personality, a prayer, and a sincere religious presentation.

We would not want to pass up the great smile, and the sincere warmth of her church greeters... or would we?

Those who serve her, are instructed it is *'their ministry'* to keep her schedule. If you are in this capacity serving as a *'greeter'* or another *'ministry'* it is between you and the Lord as to how you continue.

Study out the word 'leader(s)' and see how many times in God's word this was used as a positive reference. These words are not a message of condemnation, but of redemption. Serving the Lord from the heart is our being yielded to the Holy Spirit, and leaning all we are on Him in obedience. If we are man-pleasers, that is in direct opposition to God which is about as clear as it can be put.

Belonging to a *'local'* church is oft considered a covenant relationship. Your attendance, your support is depended on as you have attained the rank of being a valued 'core group' supporter! If you vacillate, or are unable to keep your contribution, a call from a church *'elder'* may be forthcoming.

One brother I know experienced a work issue, a financial downturn which not only affected his career, but his marriage. He was a long-time church member, part of that esteemed core group in the local 'body'.

Hurting, visiting his pastor, the first words out of the Babylonian Whore's lover revealed her concern for this child of God.

"I did not see your tithes check in the offering box."

The brother wisely put the church keys on the desk, put his back to the Babylonian pastor, his place of business, the church building and walked away.

These are businesses focused on mammon and power, not at all to be confused with the body of Christ.

Just as with a prostitute, this *'Cultural Woman'* conveys openness and concern for *'what you came for'* as you purchase her *'love'*, her services with your tithes and offerings. Special warmth and personal intimacy is extended to her leader's personal followers. In this she *'services them'* as she spiritually, physically pleasures them in their very souls.

Disbelieve? Pay her more, and watch the extras that begin to come your way.

Nasty?

Can we grasp why God compares her sins to Sodom's?

Don't Pay the Whore

Withhold from her your soulish and financial support? Do not pay her, and watch as her sweet *'covenant love'* turns to hate. Instead of the ministry of grace, her ministry will turn to an acrimonious relationship.

Not supporting her, her ministry will fault the believer for not being appreciative. The whore's tears of false humility will flow as her servants, her claw like fingers reach for your wallet claiming she is doing a work for God.

Taking the name of God in vain, she will endeavor to assign the responsibility of failing God, God's ministry to the ones who have ceased paying her. Guilt is her tool, yet in Isaiah 9 we find this amazing truth.
> "For unto us a child is born, unto us a son is given: and
> the government shall be upon his shoulder..."

The truth?
Jesus Christ is the Head of the Body of Christ, and He has sufficiently broad shoulders for His church, amen? If you had followed Jesus into the cornfields that Sabbath day eating corn, what would be the greatest lesson you would have learned?
That the Son of Man is Lord of the Sabbath?
Or would you watch, and hear your Master as He destroyed any reverence or respect you would have of these religious hypocrites?
Would you ever see them again as being of God because of their position?
From then on, would you give them respect as even being of God? In following Christ, any credibility you had given them before God would be destroyed.
Are you hearing the voice of the spirit and the bride?
Just as those who followed Christ left the temple's religious leaders, we can likewise watch our precious leader's reactions as they bleed congregants. As people departed to follow Jesus, the Great Whore's ministers, or priests turned from attempts to seduce, strong-arming, to being acrimonious, then to hate and then actual murder.
Finances, glory, and the seduction of souls are the purpose of the Great Whore's *'ministries'*. No challenge to her authority over the souls of men she has snared will be entertained, it is HER rule as she sits as a ruling Queen.
Her acceptance, her music, her faux love, her sincerity accepted by your soul ARE her professional services being rendered in exchange for your support.
Feel loved?
At one point the Apostle Paul personally worked to deliver

God's word taking no funds from those he ministered to. Why?
> *"What is my reward then? Verily that, when I preach the gospel, I may make the gospel of Christ without charge, that I abuse not my power in the gospel." 1 Corinthians 9*

Per God through Paul, true church elders who minister spirituals are worthy of receiving carnal things from those who received of their spiritual things. Note these men that were approved and set in by God. They were ordained of God, typically set in by the Holy Spirit and led by the same Holy Spirit. They were given a charge, and accountability was placed on them before God.

They were not voted in, or selected by the man in charge using his 'faux' group of 'yes men' elders declaring that God had chosen them.

Those that love the preeminence?

Not serving God, they cannot receive anything of God. What do they actually possess? It is the shared glory of their mother the Great Whore who exalts them and gives their followers that warm sense of being accepted as part of their special group.... *nice, right*?

Again, do not pay them, and it will become evident who they serve...

In the Old Testament Moses, as Samuel, took nothing whatsoever from the Israelites. This was in stark contrast with the wicked priests whose love and focus was the offerings and tithes.

But hey, it was God Moses and Samuel served...

Not paying them, never changed their calling!

These servants of God did not love their souls unto death.

Neither did they love this world, nor the things of this world.

They were looking for a city that had foundations, a city whose builder and maker was God. It was a city wherein dwelt righteousness, and nothing unclean could ever enter.

Wow, that IS a different perception, is it not?

Before we move on, let us note the smaller churches, the

siblings of the harlot daughters mentioned in Revelation 17. Receiving their power from the beast using a different corporate set-up does not make them godly.

Church leaders/rulers in these assemblies may call themselves pastors or *'board members'* possessing rulership in *'their'* churches as Kings over small kingdoms.

Board members who *'fire and hire'* are under the same judgement as a man who 'takes the House of God' as his personal kingdom. Those who bear the rule apart from being yielded to the Holy Spirit are the present-tense physical representatives of Babylon. They reflect their literal *'Head'*.

Consider sweet influential Jezebel, King Ahab's wife. Ahab may have been King, but Jezebel was running the show.

Christ is the head of His body and the head of every man. This same word of God tells us the husband is the head of his wife. But when a pastor's wife is unhappy, dissatisfied, or otherwise disenchanted, it is common for the Pastor to *'do whatever it takes to keep her happy'*. The desire of the woman to be seen as in authority, or privileged, has caused kingly *'Ahab'* pastors to anoint their wives as their associate or assistant pastor with *'perks'*.

Driving past a small-town church in Virginia there is parking set aside for the pastor, and another for the *'First Lady'*.

We ARE seeing true servant's hearts, amen?

Did Jesus go to Calvary so we could enter the Kingdom of God, or set up our own? The blatant lies, the believer's worship of *'royalty'* in ministry is in direct opposition to God. In cases such as these, it is not about God's will, the Kingdom of God, or the ministry of the Holy Spirit. It is all about *'Happy Wife, Happy Life'*. Adam himself in exiting the Garden might be inclined to offer a rebuttal, if at all possible. The question is, 'Would there be ears to hear'?

This book?

It is not a fun or happy message for the messed-up leader or your Jezebel; you absolutely are not okay.

The purpose of God's ministry through His servants is to

present the believers as the pure untainted Bride of Christ. Waiting for God to perform this contradicts the Apostle Paul's ministry, and the scripture where we read *'The bride has made herself ready'*.

The purpose of the Great Whore's ministry through her *'ministers of righteousness'* is to continue the intoxication of the believer through her fornication. Through her ministers, her servant/lovers she services souls through adultery as she pleases their dead souls with her false message of grace.

To those in *'ministry'*?

Being redundant, the Groom is visiting those who claim to represent Him to His body.

> *"Whose fan (winnowing fork) is in his hand, and he will thoroughly purge his floor, and gather his wheat into the garner, but he will burn up the chaff with unquenchable fire..."*

Take your pick of reading these words in either Matthew or Luke 3, the message is unchanged.

Some will say, *'The Master delays His coming'*. If we think for a moment we are exempt, Ezekiel 12:25-28 is present tense.

Accolades from church people, an accomplished church history, a position, our money, and our ease all have no value before the One, the Head of the Church, with whom we have our dealings.

> *"You see, we are not like the many hucksters who preach for personal profit. We preach the word of God with sincerity and with Christ's authority, knowing that God is watching us." 2 Corinthians 2:17 (NLT)*

THE STRUGGLE
The Problem, Clarified

To my family in Christ, this writer's intention is to make the truth of what occurred at Calvary intensely personal to the reader. The understanding is essential for us to encounter the literal power of God in our day-to-day living.

The cultural church with its *'man-pleasing, soul-pleasing'* teachings have misrepresented what actually occurred at Calvary. This life ex-changing event in the believer's reality has been portrayed as something if we believed it happened, no further participation is required. This results in the believer's path forward in Christ being obscured.

The path to victory, reigning in Christ is hidden as self-called ministers of Satan have headed up their personal churches for self-validation and an income. Their association with other *'like-minded'* leaders approving each other give them the appearance of possessing the approval of God. Nothing could be farther from the truth.

Calling themselves *"ministers of God"* they market their carnal powerless lifestyles. As the Pharisees presented themselves in the time of Jesus' ministry as acting on God's behalf, their counterparts today present their man-taught knowledge and purchased degrees, ordinations as them being *'spiritual'* and God approved.

Their authority?

It is you, the believing church-goer that gives it to them.

It is in our *'buying'* their being ordained, approved and qualified by men as being of God that we validate them. The underlying message of the church leadership?

You must accept their man-pleasing ordination as being of God, or be viewed by the '*group*' as a church-hater, heretical, or being labeled as divisive.

As we join a group, or are accepted into a group our soul will typically align our-selves with the group. Our acceptance is based on agreeing with the other sheep, following their approved leader. To separate our-self will cost our soul some if not all its relationships.

We would not want that, would we?

As enemies of the cross, these self-called ministers have not preached the message of the cross as they of necessity must personally sidestep the cross of Christ in order to receive your soul's approval and support.

Feel... blessed?

Not serving God, they absolutely do <u>not</u> possess His authority. Only those whom God has proven and sent can walk in His authority.

Those whom God has sent?

In truly serving God, His servants do not seek their own glory, they do not build their '*own house of worship*', nor do they have '*their own followers*'.

However, the '*self-called*' as Balaam, as Korah serve another god. In not being proven by God, unsent by God, they cannot exhibit God's word in power.

Instead, you, the church-goer are the measure of their success. You and the number of other like-minded core church members, attendees, and the size of their budget determine their success.

They are erring just as Peter did in savoring the things that be of men. The identity of Satan being attached to them as it was to Peter is not at all a stretch. Why? They are in direct opposition to God and His Kingdom.

It is offensive and we are going to see how Babylon and her ministers, her ministry team are intertwined both spiritually, *and physically*. Those that remain in pleasing themselves in this capacity after understanding who they serve? These are the uncorrectable self-important bastards God is finished with. In their eyes, they are actually just doing their job as they regurgitate the views and men's traditions/theologies purchased at seminary. Just as with the Pharisees, their traditions/theologies and the religious charade of false humility has made the word of God of no effect in the Body of Christ, my family.

Their presentation that declares God's grace covers a life lived satisfying one's own desires is a lie. That lie results from them personally, intimately serving *another* god, which results in their need to validate their own lie. Getting you to follow them, is obtaining a group, a support team that reinforces the lie, strengthening them in their error.

Crazy? With 57% of senior pastors, 60% of youth pastors struggling with or addicted to porn, they cannot present a life of overcoming in Christ. Four out of ten have committed adultery AFTER they entered their ministry. These miscreants are ALREADY described as literal beasts by God in His word.

In not serving God they are the god of this world's tools to manipulate your soul, your mind, your will, and your emotions. These professionals prostitute themselves in ministry as righteous with *'your betterment'* as their professed focus. The more adept they are at convincing you as being *'okay'* in your self-pleasing, typically the more success they have... with other soul-centered people committed to their *'work for God'*.

God? He is not at all impressed.

Believing vs. Faith

Sitting in his living room, one feckless 'minister' told my wife and I, *'Just believe, there is nothing more for you to do'*.

The error? That is like the Israelites coming out of Egypt being told the wilderness is the Promised Land. This blatant lie is being presented with Babylon's religious authority and the whore's son in his sincerity teaching her lies as biblical doctrine.

Family of God, we have some decisions to make.

When we accept that mental acceptance is our faith in God, we have forfeited our future of victory in Christ based on the personality and lies of our *'minister'*. We are being deceived just as when the serpent beguiled the woman. She actually was made to forget God's word.

Do we recall God's word that without faith it is impossible to please God? When we come to God, we must first believe that He is, and that HE REWARDS the one that diligently seeks Him. When we actually encounter God and His holiness there is a godly fear present. In contrast, there is no fear of God in cultural religion, as God is... absent.

You just *'feel good'* after the whore has serviced... you.

Feeling good is also tied in with you being personally accepted socially as part of her *'serviced troop'*...

When we find our identity in *'our'* church and accept corporate mental ascent/belief is the same as our personal faith, we are now cruising that *'broad path'* that leads to destruction with the many. To believe that we have done all and are passively waiting on God to finish everything contradicts this personal admonition in Hebrews 4,

> *"Let us therefore fear, lest, a promise being left us of*
> *entering into his rest, any of you should seem to come*
> *short of it. For unto us was the gospel preached, as well*
> *as unto them: but the word preached did not profit*
> *them, not being mixed with faith in them that heard it."*

Should that raise an eyebrow?

There is this inference that not entering God's rest is the result of our personally possessing an evil heart of unbelief. Wow...

Dying in the wilderness in unbelief after having been delivered and having a nice funeral is not to be confused with entering God's rest. That would be the same as the Israelites evil heart of unbelief basing their *'life'* on their carnal soul being satisfied. When physical dying is seen as *'life's end'*, we have no clue as to what real life actually is. The Israelites in becoming personally uncomfortable turned their thankful heart into a complaining heart. Taking heed to their stomach, their life in the flesh, they forgot the lamb slain at Passover, the death of the first-born in Egypt. They did not recall their deliverance, the Red Sea being parted, and their enemies destruction. Being self-absorbed, self-focused, a heart of thankfulness could not be present.

Regarding their situations they ceased relating to their deliverer and the visible '*cloud of His presence*'.

In being led by God, in our truly following the Lord, nothing, nothing can come into our lives apart from God allowing it. If this is true, then just as with Moses, Joseph, Job, Daniel and others, we see that EVERY situation we encounter following after the Lord is not...coincidental.

In everything we can give thanks to the Lord understanding there is something we are to learn. Let us look at the Israelites a bit closer. When Jesus came to save those who were lost, He was sent first to the lost sheep of Israel. These were covenant children through circumcision, the inheritors of the promise. These were not lost heathen, they were of the very lineage, the physical seed of Abraham.

Yet for some reason which was beyond them, they had lost any rule over their nation for years. And they had also lost any authority with God.

They as their fathers looked for a man to deliver them, not changing their heart to God.

Repentance was systematically replaced with resenting those that God had put over them.

> *(Likewise today, there are two kingdoms, two cities, one present and one to come. We do not 'vote' the New Jerusalem into replacing the current city of Babylon over the earth. Does Daniel 4:17 apply to 'your citizenry'?*
>
> *Being self-righteous in politics replaces righteousness with God. You will not have both. Not being raised up in Christ savoring the things that be of men define your source being the same as Peter's).*

It would take severe suffering to get the Israelites to turn to

God. But their temporary penitent heart would again depart once their flesh and blood souls were satisfied...

Their first temple being destroyed, these heirs of promise were repeatedly afflicted and dispersed. The temple was then rebuilt, but nothing changed in the Israelites hearts. so again, they were *'put under the authority of another'*.

Are we hearing what the Holy Spirit is telling us?

In pleasing your-self, you will NEVER walk in the life, the liberty, the power of God as you are serving another. In pleasing yourself, you remain a servant to sin. Keep in mind, it is called the *'body of sin'*, not the *'body of sins'* for a reason. The axe was supposed to have been laid at the root, amen? Believing your flesh and blood soul is saved will keep you focused on the fruit, contending with entities that manifest as you seek to save what cannot be saved. But... for those crucified with Christ, buried with Him, it is all about our Father.

If we are *'In Christ'* it is because we share His testimony.

> *"And he that sent me is with me: the Father hath not left me alone; for I do always those things that please him."*

Not pleasing God, we will always be under the authority of the *'one'* we please. There has been patience for our self-indulgent living, until this truth is understood.

That patience dissipates when we understand what took place at Calvary. What occurred there was that in Christ we actually died and were buried! Sin is deceptive.

You will feel and believe you are in charge. This lie is common and accepted by man as he lives his life with his plans. This does not exclude cultural Christians.

Our example?

The Israelites under Roman rule could live as though they were in charge, as long as they followed the Roman's rules for their self-governing. They could have their own religion, their own religious structure, under Roman authority. The Temple of God was even allowed to be called the Temple of God and used as long as they... complied. Do we have ears?

Do we ever contemplate what happened in our baptism? Or

do we identify the issues in our life as metaphoric mountains, and wonder why our miniscule faith cannot budge a dirt clod, much less move a mountain. It is because our metaphoric *'mountains'* that remain are the result of our disobedience.
They will remain until repentance occurs. *(This will be gone into more detail in a later chapter).*
The Israelites? The *'mountain'* they needed removed was the Roman occupation.
But instead of repenting, and pleasing God from their heart they would find fault with their brethren, devour widow's houses and hate the Romans. Loving the preeminence, loving the ability to keep people in line by threatening to boot them from the Temple, they enjoyed their rule the Romans allowed them to have...
Serving sin is like that.
Again, you will feel in charge, as you enjoy pleasing your-self being a *comfortable* slave to the sin you *'hate'*.
Your *'mountains'* remain until the day you die.
These Jews, these covenant children of Abraham?
In the middle of their being self-absorbed, in the midst of their enjoying their rule under the Romans they hated, along comes Jesus the very Son of God.
This man who made Himself of no reputation and became as a servant came walking in the liberty and power of the Holy Spirit!
Wow, again, are we hearing what the Lord is telling us?
If so, let us keep our ears open. Jesus then *tells these flesh and blood children of Abraham* they are lost, they are dead.
Those religious people were told their Abrahamic circumcised covenant flesh and blood could not, would not inherit the Kingdom of God. <u>Ouch.</u>
Their entire life, their heritage, their validation as Jews was based in being in Abraham's lineage. If that was removed, what would be their distinction?
Now?
Their justification in being Abraham's seed after the flesh

was being removed by Jesus, the Living Word walking in the authority of God. This was extremely offensive to these sons of Abraham. These men's lives were wrapped up in the promises to Abraham's Levitical seed that benefited their bellies and their rule in the Temple.

But in serving themselves, as Eli's sons they made a mockery of being God's servants. In knowing the word, they manipulated God's people being proficient at pointing out issues, and glorifying themselves in false humility...

In their knowledge, in their appearing to seek God daily, they were unholy, self-righteous, and uncorrectable.

They resisted the Holy Spirit in their religious order, in their *traditions, what we call theology* they did not recognize Christ and rejected the promised seed of Abraham (Galatians 3:16). And amazingly, just as the Israelites, today we are hearing the Holy Spirit tell us,

> *"Flesh and blood will not inherit the Kingdom of God,*
> *neither will corruption inherit incorruption."*

Have we been told our precious beloved identity in our flesh, our carnal soul is saved? That message is no different than the Pharisee's believing their Abrahamic flesh and blood was saved. Per our Lord, if we seek to save it, we lose it... forever. God's word.

Our belief based in Churchianity has taught us that our identity in our soul, our flesh and blood life is saved.

That stronghold is being torn down as that teaching removes our cross and our burial with Christ. There is no power to live a resurrected life without a death occurring, amen?

This will be offensive to those who insist their carnal soul is their saved... soul. We are called as children of God, as those born NOT of the flesh, not born of the will of man, but of God. Being born-again of God's word and the spirit we are to walk in the Holy Spirit.

The sword of God's word divides our dead soul-life from the spirit of Christ we have received so we can choose life in Christ. Willfully not walking in the spirit, is our choosing another kingdom.

Walking in the flesh is our actually choosing another '*city*' with the administration of that '*city*' being principalities, powers and spiritual wickedness having power over us. True.

Jesus went to Calvary and now the ruler of that Kingdom, and his fallen angels are subject to those who in their reality live in Christ. They are from above, not beneath, and they are citizens of a Heavenly City concerned about God's things, not man's.

Stubbornness

Just as the Israelites suffered in bondage, under the rule of others, they claimed correctly they were the Chosen People. They were the children of the Abrahamic covenant. This was true even as they looked for a Messiah to someday come and deliver them. Yet they refused to understand individually their hearts were naked and open to God 24/7. Taking God's word in their heart, simply loving their neighbor as themselves would have melted God's heart. They were ALL His covenant children, amen?

It sounds simple, and it actually is. When we have understand that everything before God is exposed, there are no secret sins. When in our difficulty, in our shame we come before Him acknowledging He knows, it is then we find in Him an ever present help in our time of need.

Our difficulty will be when we refuse to let go self-pleasing, and become angry when we think our self-control needs to be removed by God. Our offering up our bodies as a living sacrifice is what we do, and the enablement occurs as we abide in the Holy Ghost's presence, God Himself.

That is our part, this is where deliverance occurs.

Cross-less Churchianity

In not seeing ourselves as crucified with Christ we have no need to consume God's word, nor abide in the Holy Spirit's actual presence. We see our death on Jesus' cross as '*symbolic*' without actually seeing our soul as having been poured out at Calvary in Christ. Our life in the flesh, remains our '*life*'. Having been taught that our flesh and blood soul is saved, we cannot accept our little precious flesh and blood soul is lost, or truly dead.

> *But this truth remains, our flesh and blood carnal soul*
> *is in direct hostility to God.*

Is our carnal soul our mind, our will, and our emotions? Or is our soul just more symbolism, a metaphor disassociated from our power of choice?
Truth?
Our carnal mind is at enmity with God even if we call ourself a believer, fact. Resisting the Holy Spirit in following *'our'* churches religious service order, we do not recognize Christ as the Head of the Body, His church. As we adore our pastor and our church home, we actually reject Christ even as we gather to *"worship"* Him.
Disagree?
When, if ever was the last time *'your'* church assembled, and waited on God to reveal His plan for the service?
When was the last time you humbled yourselves, did a FULL stop and did not move apart from being led by the tangible presence of the Holy Spirit?
When?
Before we read on, let us review that last paragraph. If we did not wait on God, the Holy Spirit, we acknowledge our order, our church, our time, our schedule, our life, religiously. We expect God our Father to follow, or move within our schedule. That is simply ... *moronic.*
In not following the Holy Spirit, we have followed another spirit from within our 'soul' that demanded we please our... self, our plans, our traditions, our order. We say we *'believe God raised up Christ'* but this Christ we believe in is incapable of being in charge, so we are...
Can we not understand this is a *'wrong spirit'*?
Again, the stupidity of this is unfathomable. It brings to mind the Psalmist saying,

> *"Do not I hate them, O LORD, that hate thee? and am*

> not I grieved with those that rise up against thee?
> I hate them with perfect hatred: I count them mine enemies."

In following the god of this world we relegate God to the same place the Israelites held their idols. The idols were incapable of hearing, talking right? The idol being blind and dumb, the religious order, the sacrifices and worship? It was at the Israelite's discretion and timing.

What is the difference between Churchianity and idol worship?

Do we say, au contraire, our God is alive!

If so, why then can He not take over the service, why then is He not waited on?

If you wait on Him, as Cain, if He does not respond as you wish, what will you do? You will depart His presence and build your own organization.

You may call it doing a work *'for God'* as He obviously is not... the head. Now we understand Jeremiah 5 when God stated the Israelites assembled as troops in the whorehouses.

Keep the schedule, march one troop out, get ready for the next troop. Let us keep the servicing of the troops *'decent and in order'*. We can say Jeremiah is referring to idols, and their temples, but in our not waiting on the Holy Spirit there is NO difference, WHATSOEVER.

My Father is fed up with this, just an FYI. How can God lead us except we humble our-selves and follow Him?

> How could He ever even be our Shepherd?

If we do not follow Him, we are lost as we knowingly, now willingly follow another as we follow a man. In not yielding to the Holy Spirit, we find it much easier to follow that wonderful man we identify with.

We call him OUR pastor, that nice beloved approving shepherd *we paid for*.... Nice.

Moses was not like this at all.

Moses had a heart after God, he for one was not content with *'getting by'* without God...

"And He (God) said, "My Presence will go with you, and I will give you rest." Then he (Moses) said to Him, "If Your Presence does not go with us, do not bring us up from here." Exodus 33

I asked one self-glorified '*pastor*' outside Colorado Springs, why not wait on the Lord, just shut down your service order and wait on God? He replied,
'*The pressure to get things going is too great*'.
That is a '*wow*' statement.
Does that sound like he was being led by the Holy Spirit? It absolutely does not, amen? Yet if you were to meet him, you would be convinced his love for God was paramount. Not so...
He has another paramour directing his steps through him as he responds to her pressure. Not understanding faith in God, not seriously believing in the resurrection he does not relate to the Head of the Church. Instead, he must '*run this business*' he calls his church.
Because, if he truly believed Jesus was risen from the dead, he could trust Him.
In not understanding Christ whatsoever, he rejects Christ in resisting the Holy Spirit.
How?
It is in and through the Holy Spirit that Jesus manifests. As Adam, this pastor is willingly receiving another's word and loves the foul religious spirit on that word that pleasures his soul. His cover? He believes he is excused responding to '*pressure*'. In this he is following another spirit believing God does not see him as he sells himself as a God-fearing and God-loving man. The opposite being true, it is just a sell job targeting his '*group...*'
Responding to pressure this Coloradan pastor as others hooks up physically in his bloodstream with his mother the Great Whore. He cooperates with the pressure from her, so her servicing the saints can get underway. This begins in his soul as she pleasures him in his soul, religiously.
Nasty? Before God, this is spiritual adultery, from within his

physical bloodstream. Disagree? It will be explained, clearly. God, my Father is finished with this...

In our being born of God, of God's will, of God's word and God's spirit, in following a man believers are kept clueless. They are not taught how to abide in Christ, or walk in the Holy Spirit. This is only possible through their accepting they died in Christ at Calvary, and through acknowledging being the recipient of the gift of righteousness. It is through consuming God's word for life, and dropping all else that we can move forward remaining in the awareness, the presence of life, the Holy Spirit.

We have our example. Jesus left His home, His mother Mary, His brothers, sisters and departed LED by the Holy Spirit into the wilderness. In the wilderness Jesus died to every, every flesh and blood relationship, desire, and whim. Jesus died to His own sinless flesh and blood soul also. Those who would follow Him, would do as He did, in being led by the Holy Spirit. He actually tells us this in Luke 14:26,27.

Let us hear Paul, the apostle who abandoned his past, totally to fulfill God's call IN THE HOLY SPIRIT. The Apostle Paul as Moses directed believers to,

> 'Be ye followers of me, even as I also am of Christ'. KJV

Correctly translated we read,

> 'Imitate me, just as I also imitate Christ'. NKJV

Paul is telling us to love the Lord as he loves the Lord, yield to the Holy Spirit as he does. He is telling us to keep our body under and serve God as a living sacrifice. That is mimicking Paul. However when we instead focus on our situations, our needs, the pressures of this wilderness life we call our home, as Eve we become distracted, forget God's word and are seduced. Relating to our situations, we cease relating to our deliverer and the fact that in baptism we told God we *'buried the old man'*. This is resisting the Holy Spirit refusing to pay the price to abide IN Him. This is our choosing not to follow Him.

Instead we follow Satan's messengers as they tell us God orders our self-willed steps because we are *'good men'*.

This is the path of loss and frustration. The truth is this.
In our time here, the believer's life ON this earth is to be an overcoming representation of the life of Christ from being raised in resurrected living!
Yet, just as with the Israelites... *for reasons beyond us*, we have no authority with God, and Satan tramples our homes with sickness and financial struggles...
Our being of the same mind, or soul as the Jews, our issue mirrors their dilemma.
The first-born deceased soul is the issue.
Really.
Receiving any religious spiel that placates our soul, shuts down the Holy Spirit drawing us to Him.
This denying the cross in our own life is also our rejecting Christ.
Why? Because our flesh and blood life or soul cannot, will not inherit eternal life. God cannot lie, amen?

> "In whom also ye are circumcised with the circumcision made without hands, in putting off the 'body of the sins' of the flesh by the circumcision of Christ:
> Buried with him in baptism, wherein also ye are risen with him through the faith of the operation of God, who hath raised him from the dead." Colossians 2

God sees the believer as circumcised.
If we look at this scripture, we see in this circumcision it is the '*body of sin*' that is '*cut-off*' from the believer's life in God's eyes. The body? OUR BODY???!

The 'Problem' Lifted Up...

Jesus told Nicodemus that as Moses lifted up the serpent in the wilderness, even so the Son of man must be lifted up. The Israelites had become weary in following the Lord and complained. They spoke against God and Moses which resulted in fiery serpents biting them, and those bitten were dying.
God had Moses make a serpent of brass, and put the problem on a pole. Those who were snakebit looked upon the brass serpent

and lived.

But what does a snake on a pole, and the Son of man lifted up on a tree have to do with each other?

The pole, the cross we get, but... the snake, and Jesus both being lifted up?

What is the correlation?

The serpent on the pole reflected the snakebit Israelites actual problem.

Being snakebit the dying Israelite saw the likeness of the dead serpent skewered to a pole... He saw the death of the serpent that bit him.

In seeing the problem, the snake as lifeless, its venom in their bloodstream was neutralized and the snakebit Israelite lived.

The actual lifeless body of Jesus lifted up skewered to a cross with its blood poured out for our *'snake-bit'* blood revealed our actual problem.

We see His body as the actual flesh and blood creature that was made sin for us nailed to a cross. Now we grasp that 'our body' with its venom filled blood is <u>dead</u>.

Or should we just say, life-less?

Different?

Can we begin to understand why the blood of every sacrifice was poured out? Forget the sanctimonious religious presentations of how clean your life-less body is, or how the grace of God covers any willful walking after the flesh. Instead, look at the *'body of sin'* as the problem that was nailed up, just for you.

God's word?

Sin in the flesh, was and is present-tense actually condemned.

The blood, or soul of Jesus was poured out, amen? That was the price paid for me, how about you?! Our first born soul is now exposed as criminal. It is adulterous, cancerous, full of sin, it cannot, nor will it ever be redeemed. Our flesh and blood soul has been Babylon's home, and her place of rest. Adam sold God out, Adam's dead soul became another's habitation.

Do we recall God asking, *'What is the place of MY rest....?'* In our rejecting this message, in resisting the tangible Holy Ghost... what is it IN US that would be hostile to God's presence???!!! What could it be IN US that would not desire God to have His place of... abiding? Could it be the snake-bit life of the flesh? What is this in a man that declares,

> "This is MY identity, MY world, and MY doing MY will is MY LIFE?"

Jesus stated *'The prince of this world comes and has nothing in me...'* In following Him, in being crucified with Him, being raised in Him, we are not to be self-pleasing man followers, we NEED the Holy Spirit as a drowning man needs air. So we see we are not to train our dead soul or placate our snake-bit soul in our blood, we are to count it as *'game over dead'*. This is NOT the soul or the creature that is saved.

Again, recall Jesus' blood was poured out in our place?

Was Jesus' blood caught in a goblet, taken to Jesus' tomb and then poured over Him? Silly, inane, right?

When we see our physical body as lifeless, crucified with Christ, it is then we understand the tangible Holy Spirit is OUR only life! It is only then the serpent's access that ruled our soul is shut down.

In seeing the body's snake-bit blood poured out we see our powerless life, or our soul (our mind, will, and emotions, our identity in this body) as dead, literally. Satan's access through OUR dead soul is removed as we count our body with its life as dead. How many loved ones will you bury before you realize their body with its affections and desires is the influence they are now free from? Looking at a cadaver in a casket is second only to holding the body of a deceased loved one in your arms. That body?

All its enjoyments, the fine dining, the clothes, the make-up or the tattoos. The sports, the thrills all end there. If that person lived after the flesh, following the god of this world fulfilling the desires of the flesh and their mind, in relating to them...

"Who was your relationship really with?"

The believer?

They are dead to the flesh and free from the *'body of sin'* to stand clean before God.

Yet, get this...

THAT describes where we are to be right now.

That is what we are to understand when we accept Jesus died in our place and we WERE BURIED WITH HIM! The ONLY life we can now truthfully possess before God is IN the tangible Holy Spirit, who is found residing on God's word!

To the debater, the person ruled by that religious spirit, let us turn to John 14. But before we go there, we recall that in John 15, Jesus told the disciples to abide in Him, amen?

> *"...And I will pray the Father, and he shall give you another Comforter, that he may abide with you for ever;*
>
> *Even the Spirit of truth; whom the world cannot receive, because it seeth him not, neither knoweth him: but ye know him; for he dwelleth with you, and shall be in you. I will not leave you comfortless: I will come to you."*

If we are to abide in Christ, we are to intentionally, on purpose, drop everything to remain in His presence. This *IS* abiding in Christ. This is being a disciple of Christ. This message was to those who had left all to follow Jesus. He was telling them He would not abandon them, and entrusting them to the Holy Spirit.

That was His part.

Their part?

It was to follow the tangible Holy Spirit, in this they would follow the risen Lord Jesus Christ, just as they had followed Him before.

To say the Holy Spirit cannot be seen, therefore we must follow a man is being of the world. Recall why they could NOT receive Him?

There is a price to be paid, a cost to be counted...

To believe this is too hard, is to deny the Holy Spirit who is our Comforter, and our enabler. It is through the Holy Spirit we mortify the deeds of the body, amen?

To the carnal believer, just because we are conscious, or breathing does not mean we are living...

Believing God's word, taking God's word over the mind, will, and emotions with the witness of God's Holy Spirit is life. This releases the power of God. The Holy Spirit on God's word is released into us when we take His literal presence on His word as our life. Taking the conscious presence of the Holy Spirit as life is living.

This is our participating in the circumcision of the spirit, dropping all to abide in Him.

This is our living a different life, a New Life in Christ through the actual abiding presence of the Holy Spirit.

This new life is also where God's power is realized through a totally different *'soul'* or life than what we have been taught. This is where struggles end. Because...

> *"I am crucified with Christ: nevertheless I live; yet not I, but Christ liveth in me: and the life which I now live in the flesh I live by the faith of the Son of God, who loved me, and gave himself for me."*

THE SEAT OF THE FLESH AND BLOOD... SOUL

This chapter addresses the first born soul, the flesh and blood lived life. In short, what WE call our life is actually what God calls our dead soul. Being born-again, we are to draw *'our life'* from a new source, but being *'church taught'*? We take up the traditions of men, their passed down theologies which negate the power of God. The result? Being taught but Satan's ministers of righteousness, we believe in the finished work of Calvary, but do not participate in its... power.

We begin where man became a *'Living Soul'*. In Genesis 2:7,
> "And the LORD God formed man of the dust of the ground, and breathed into his nostrils the breath of life; and man became a living soul."

This first living soul was created through the spirit of God entering the blood in the body of clay. Adam possessing the life of God as his identity resulted from God sending forth His spirit into Adam's blood, which flowed to every cell of his body This creature, this man is identified as a living soul, NOT to be confused with a life giving, or quickening spirit.

The glory of God in the earth was to manifest through Adam, through his living soul. The manner in which this was to occur, God explains in easy to understand language. God is spirit, and initially the soul of man was created by God to be His Temple as God was initially seated and at rest in Adam, pre-fall. How was this to take place? In Leviticus 17:11, God tells us precisely where the life, or the soul of man is located, and again, it is not... his body.

> "...for the life (soul) of the flesh (body) is in the blood..."

What may sound strange is this, the very soul of God was contained in His breath. The breath, the soul of God became the substance of the first living soul's life flowing through that body of clay, in its bloodstream. Abandoning carnal thinking, we must accept that the life, or soul not the blood, but it contains it.

The identity of the first living soul, is Adam.

Adam's body was merely the vessel that contained his soul. The body having been created from clay, from dirt, was not Adam's life or soul. Adam's body did not define Adam's life, it manifest his life, or again, his soul.

God the creator, the Living Word? It was His abiding spirit, His presence that made Adam a living soul. This was God's precious gift of His own self, His own soul to Adam. God Himself was the very substance of Adam's life.

Now we can understand that the life of God, the breath of life which had made Adam a living soul had existed before creation IN God. Adam was 'predestined' in God to be the first living soul. Pre-destined is a totally different subject that again has been carnally defined through man's reasonings and passed down as religious traditions. God sending His breath into man, identifies Adam's life as having existed eternally in God BEFORE being separated into the clay vessel, amen? We have heard that language before amen? Adam pre-existing in God was in the very same manner in which the woman had existed IN man, before being separated, or sent forth from him. Adam's life or soul was in the blood of the *'rib'* from which the woman was fashioned. In this same way, the soul of God was in the *'breath of life'* He had imparted into His son, Adam.

God having separated His life to Adam, the opportunity for wholeness, to become 'One' now existed for God, and man. We see the picture of the woman being separated from man containing the mystery of Adam's creation, Adam's substance, <u>AND</u> God's purpose in creating him.

Adam was created in the likeness and image of God to reflect the glory of God for whom he was created, just as the woman

was taken out of, and created for the man.
It was at this point that God... had rested. And now we hear God's word yet if we pay attention, something is missing.

> "And God blessed the seventh day, and sanctified it: because that in it he had rested from all his work which God created and made." Genesis 2:3

What is missing?

> "And the evening and the morning were the seventh day."

In chapter 5 of the Gospel of John we hear Jesus telling us something that initially sounds, wrong.

> "And therefore did the Jews persecute Jesus, and sought to slay him, because he had done these things on the sabbath day.
>
> But Jesus answered them, My Father worketh hitherto, and I work."

God the Father had been working, and Jesus was finishing His work. In John 4 at the well, we hear Jesus telling His disciples,

> "Jesus saith unto them, My meat is to do the will of him that sent me, and to finish his work."

With this understanding, we can look back to Genesis,

> "And the LORD said, My spirit shall not always strive with man, for that he also is flesh: yet his days shall be an hundred and twenty years."

Striving is in itself work, amen? God did something to offload extra work, He decreased man's life expectancy from around 900 years, to 120.

Now? Through His Son Jesus Christ, God has condemned sin in the flesh (Romans 8:3-4). Flesh and blood living? Before God it is our abiding in death.

What God reveals to us as life is His spirit, to be more concise His Holy Spirit. The presence of the Holy Spirit also contains the Father, and the Son. It is living in the Holy Spirit we encounter the Last Adam, Jesus who is to us who believe on Him, who choose to abide in Him a 'life giving' spirit.

> "And so it is written, The first man Adam was made

> *a living soul; the last Adam was made a quickening spirit."* 1 Corinthians 15

These are the two souls, just as Jesus told us. We see them in the first Adam and the Last Adam. There is the soul that we must lose for His sake, for us to find the soul that is eternally saved.

Confusing the two souls has been Satan's work through his diplomaed ministers of righteousness. That confusion? For those who will not stumble or faint, this confusion comes to its end.

The <u>Living</u> Soul

Adam in the Garden lived by every word that proceeded from the mouth of God. There was no idolatry, evil desire, fleshly lust, as God tempts no man with evil. The woman was presented to Adam pre-sin, pre-fall so she was not presented to satisfy a carnal desire. She was given as a *'completer'*, God returned to Adam what had been separated from him so he might be made *'whole'*. Her name was Adam per Genesis 5:2. Sharing the same soul, the same flesh and bone they walked in the Garden.

Keep in mind, Adam knew what it was like not to have a help-meet. Adam knew what it was like to be... apart, alone. Adam desired a help-meet, someone who could witness his life/soul and from a point of sharing it be qualified to acknowledge it. Sharing Adam's life would also be sharing in Adam fulfilling his Father's will manifesting God's glory through his rule in the earth.

Do we recall when God created man, He said *"Let US make man in OUR image and let THEM..."*? God? He is One, and Adam, *their* name is Adam. They also share the same identity. How? They share the same soul, flesh and bone. They are equal in substance, in their make-up in creation, their only difference? It is in their created order, and their created purpose. In Adam receiving the woman, Adam received back his own flesh and blood, nothing less than him-self. God is telling us something if we have ears to hear. Adam and his woman are the soul(s), the *'them'* who were (past-tense) to rule the earth, not just men as the alpha males ruling their women as part of their domain. Now we have a picture of man, the living soul, living by every word that proceeded from the mouth of God, amen? Adam, they are the *'them'* who live by the spirit of God residing in their blood, their bloodstream quickening their mortal bodies. We can hear identical language in Romans 8:11, amen?

Death Enters
In Genesis 3:11, God asked Adam,
    'Who told you that you were naked?'
When they ate the fruit of the tree,
    '...they saw they were naked'.
There was no one around that could verbalize anything to them. Their name, their identity was still *'Adam'*.
The voice they heard? Again, it was from the very same place where God had previously resided and communed from within them. That word that told them they were naked came from within them. It was from within their soul, their bloodstream and it was the words of the prince of the power of the air... Satan.
There is a truth here we need to grasp, and understand in its entirety.
Your flesh and blood soul needs a spirit on a word to experience what it regards as living.
Shocking?
Without a word to animate it, your life, your soul would be expressionless.
Every soul *'has a narrative'*, a relatable history it identifies with as its life.
Just as with Adam your first father, your soul by God's design is animated by a *'word'* you accept in your soul. Apart from a spirit on a word animating our carnal soul from within the blood, our flesh and blood soul is expression-less.
Your soul is your mind, your will, and your emotions.

Free Will

Your soul is capable of offering up itself to save your *'brothers in arms'* in the military. A soul may offer up it-self in exchange for its child. You can choose in your *'soul'* to deny your-self' or seek to save your-self. So we understand we accept the word that *'pleases our rationale'*, in believing that word, it is the spirit on that word that manifests through our body.

Each word is spirit animated.
Each word possesses the power of life, or death.

Adam the *'LIVING SOUL'* lived by every word that proceeded from the mouth of God.
Where have we heard that before?
So then, what is the source from which Adam and his descendants receive their thoughts, their intuitions without question? Let us listen to the Apostle Paul describe what took place before those faithful in Christ Jesus learned to follow the Holy Spirit.

"...you once walked according to the course of this world, according to the prince of the power of the air, the spirit who now works in the sons of disobedience, among whom also we all once conducted ourselves in the lusts of our flesh, fulfilling the desires of the flesh and of the mind." Ephesians 2 NKJV

Paul is describing Adam, his wife, and their flesh and blood descendants walking according to the *'course of THIS world'*. They take their thoughts and imaginations that appear to originate from within them, as though they were their very own. *Wow... we can relate, amen?*

The desires of their flesh, are now seen as their appetites, affections, and they identify their *'thoughts'* as their *'personalities'*. Satisfying their self-image, their mind now compares themselves to others, and they locate their place among men.

They take ownership of these thoughts, these judgments, as again, they originate from within themselves.

We now see the soul, the life of man IN HIS body has become the access point of Satan, and his fallen angels. As Adam cooperated with Satan, the natural man then carnally reflects what self-gratifying word he receives through his soul, the spirit on that word then animates his body.
Again, it really is just that simple.

Children of Wrath
The expressions of rage, lust, covetousness (idolatry), and hate which is murder all portray the spirit on the word that we (including believers) have received in our soul, or life.
Again, every word a man receives has a spirit, or an unseen influence on it. Every consideration of the fallen soul has for its center, its-self. It is *WITH* this focus that every thought is derived from the same source.
Recall that question God asked Adam?
    'Who told you that you were naked'?
Adam unknowingly was now relating to the prince of the power of the air from within his mind, his soul.
Do we *'think'* this is maybe a bit extreme, or that it goes just a bit too far?
Where does greed, lust, anger in our-selves stem from? Where does the inflaming of the *'soul'* by fallen angels manifest?
Does one's bloodstream factor into any of the following tangible emotions?
Was the bad mood manifest in a *'dark'* countenance?
Was our face *'flushed'* with the heat of anger?
Was one *'consumed'* with jealousy?
What word did we *'act on'* IN our mind?
Was the person *'bound'* in hate or lust driven to commit acts against another?
Was it *'blood lust'*?
Does blood then factor into our *'emotions'*?
Or do we wish to just identify these manifestations as someone's personality, their lifestyle or their addictions?
Are we going to call someone with serious *'problems'* as

suffering from mental illnesses?
Or maybe, sister, it is just... how you were raised.
In reality, we are seeing the '*dead soul...*' as the believer has not been taught a different route by those who '*claim*' to represent the Lord Jesus in and through faith in His word... through abiding in Him, remaining in the presence of the Holy Spirit.
Our body?
A puppet?
We are seeing man's soul, or his life is located in the blood that flows to every cell of the body. The body then simply portrays the soul being its puppet.
It really is that simple.
The perception of the carnal man is this: He identifies his body with its sensory organs, its inputs as his identity, as his life. The natural man being dead then sees a puppet as his life and his identity. Any cell or portion of the body where the blood does not flow, that portion of the body, the puppet, becomes unusable and dies. The carnal believer shares the same view as the natural man...
So we understand that the soul, the identity, the life of man is in his blood. Now we also grasp the importance that our Heavenly Father placed on the blood, AND the soul of man. As we look back at Adam, we see that God never identifies him as '*spirit, soul, and body*'.
In Genesis, Adam is never identified by God as a living 'body'.
God never even said Adam is spirit.
Adam is identified pre-sin only as a living soul, and post-sin he is identified by God as dust, or dirt. Recall, the blood of the sacrifices? Do we remember that the blood of Jesus as the sacrifices blood was poured out on the ground? Why? Per God's word His soul was "*poured out unto death.*"
Now we see why our Father, God sent His only begotten Son to Calvary for me, and you.
Do we still _think_ God loves our flesh and blood soul? Do we _think_ God is endeared to our carnal life lived in adultery after the flesh?

What is it that God desires in us?

Adam's soul was to be where God accessed the world by His word through Adam, and God's Kingdom would have been established in the earth.

Heaven and Earth were to have been joined in Adam.

Instead, another Kingdom has been established in the earth, USING the very same access that God was to have worked through, Adam's soul.

The Kingdom of Darkness now thrives through *every single fallen flesh and blood soul of man*. Hold this next thought close, as we move to understanding this first soul is not redeemable; Keep in mind that as you love the Lord from a pure heart, the blood of the Lamb cleanses you from all sin, and all unrighteousness as you walk in the light.

This is not a message of condemnation, but light on a path that may have been obscured.

For this reason, those who believe on the One who sent Jesus, and TAKE HIS WORD for their life, can pass from death to life.

> "*Verily, verily, I say unto you, He that heareth my word, and believeth on him that sent me, hath everlasting life, and shall not come into condemnation; but is passed from death unto life." John 5*

Jesus did not say if we did not believe on Him we were '*going to die*'. He said that in believing on the Father who sent Him we passed from '*being dead*' to life.

Passed from... death?

That would be not regarding our life in the flesh, as our life. We live by every word that proceeds from the mouth of God... amen?

If we believe we are to find a balance, if we believer there is grace to keep our security in this world, and then somehow sidestep in to Heaven, keep in mind two situations.

The first is the rich young ruler who withheld faith in God, keeping his confidence in his wealth.

The second, Ananias and Sapphira who tried to keep their trust in finances hidden as they professed faith in God.

Now tell me about God's grace for that willful sin, please.
Trusting the god of this world is abandoning God and returning to your adultery, committing fornication.
If this has not seemed nasty enough, let us see who it is that is at work, and what her work entails. Let us look at the antitype of Jerusalem which is above.

Babylon: The Great Whore

> *".... Come hither; I will shew unto thee the judgment of the great whore that sitteth upon (at rest) many waters..."*
> *With whom the kings of the earth have committed fornication, and the inhabitants of the earth have been made drunk with the wine of her fornication..."*
> Revelation 17

The identification of the Great Whore is an expression of disgust and filth. Yet this is God's identification of a practiced seductress and murderess.

This *'woman'* shares an identity with the serpent who enticed Adam. Adam died as he believed her. He then grasped at equality with God, endeavoring to become as a god with equal authority. This resulted in him exercising his faith believing in her lie. Adam accepted another's word, and his faith in that word resulted in his eating the forbidden fruit.

Adam's unprotected wife in being deceived also died. In their dying, in becoming lifeless the first thing they noticed was their unprotected bodies, their exposure, their nakedness.

The spirit on the word Adam received entered his soul, impacting the life of the flesh in and through the bloodstream. In then accessed every cell of his body making him aware of it and its surroundings. Immediately Adam was intoxicated, drunk on the body's mental, and sensory perceptions. Any spiritual sight or insight is gone, he is blind. Adam is overwhelmed as a man severely poisoned with alcohol, his focus is now a drunken *'tunnel vision'* of his physical senses. He is aware only of his body, and a thought process that alarms

him.
Previously Adam had enjoyed the fruit of the garden, but the awareness of his body had never been demanding. His senses had never occupied an administrative rule.
But now?
From within his soul, he had thoughts, urgent thoughts. The voice, the thought he now heard was the serpent delivering 'God's word' that he was going to die. This fear enslaved him to seek to save his soul, to cover his nakedness, to hide among the foliage as he was being told that physically he was going to die. The truth?

>*Adam was already dead.*

This is Adam inebriated, drunk with the wine of Babylon's fornication as she finds a place of rest in the temple initially created for God. Do we recall,

> *"...the great whore that sitteth upon many waters..."*

This is her being at rest. In Revelation 17, verse 15 tells us the waters she is sitting upon are the peoples of the earth. This Whore is sitting at rest in what had been God's place of rest, Adam's soul.

> *"... and the inhabitants of the earth have been made*
> *drunk with the wine of her fornication."*

The inhabitants of the earth, the earth dwellers, are those who find their life, their soul being fulfilled here.
We are not excluded.
Abiding in her, finding our life in her is in opposition to finding our life in Christ. Recall the Lord's prayer, in John 17 that those that are Christ's are IN the world, but they are not 'of it'. Finding your 'life in this world' is being at enmity with God.
Every soul that has been born, and lived any amount of years has had the 'Great Whore' as their life with one exception, Jesus Christ. Living in and after the flesh is abiding in the false vine, abiding in death. Living pleasing their selves, they are drunk with the wine, or spirit of her being joined to them. The church that declares the flesh and blood soul can be saved is her harlot daughter. Absent a true abiding love for God, absent His

approval, the fallen man's seminary degreed religious soul is the Great Whore's access.

This foul administration of principalities and powers has used God's word to manipulate and seduce believers. She has headed up her churches by her disciples, her *'ministers of righteousness'*. Do we recall Jesus telling the religious leaders in His time here,

"Ye are of your father the devil, and the lusts of your father ye will do. He was a murderer from the beginning, and abode not in the truth, because there is no truth in him. When he speaketh a lie, he speaketh of his own: for he is a liar, and the father of it." John 8

Every minister needs to be tried to determine if they are God-sent, or not. Man sent, self-sent ministers are in abundance and as hirelings minister for money. Those that God sends speak God's word with God's Holy Spirit bearing witness. The others? The church of Ephesus tried those that declared they were God sent and found them to be liars, Revelation 2.

The dead soul of man is the market, it is the Great Whore's *'church/business'* building program's source of income and... validity. As Balaam taught Balak how to get the covenant children of God to violate the covenant and incur judgement, her ministers preach and teach that God's grace covers carnal living. Welcome to participating and fornicating with the 21rst century Whore...

For The Love of God

This understanding flies in the face of the belief that man, as woman was created to enjoy their-selves. The lie they have swallowed has been that their bodies were given to them for their own personal pleasure. Self-rule, self-pleasing is exposed as their unknowingly sharing the glory of the Great Whore. Abstract?

Does Romans 3:23 come to mind?

You and I are to reflect the brightness of God's glory, and be the expression of His person in the earth, amen? Is this not what the Last Adam did?

These understandings are as Hebrews 4:12.
> *"For the word of God is quick, and powerful, and sharper than any twoedged sword, piercing even to the dividing asunder of soul and spirit, and of the joints and marrow, and is a discerner of the thoughts and intents of the heart."*

This scripture exposes the Living Word that divides between the first born soul, its death and the spirit that animates it. It also lays the groundwork for the Holy Spirit to produce sons and daughters of the Most High. This will occur as they abandon self-serving, to serving God through paying the price to remain in His presence. To deny Christ, is to choose self-pleasing, over and above the presence of the Holy Spirit as it would involve... suffering. The first born soul does NOT want to be denied. And now? Now we know the repulsive nasty truth, the strength, the source behind our soul resisting the Holy Spirit...

Babylon's Stones
> *"...And the woman was arrayed in purple and scarlet colour, and decked with gold and precious stones..."*

The Great Whore amazed the Apostle John, her beauty seemed to be, overwhelming. She is a antitype of the New Jerusalem, as Satan has desired to be as God. The stones that bedeck her, are the false apostles, prophets, evangelists, pastors and teachers. They also make up her harlot daughters, churches headed up by her revered ministers. They have Satan's religious respectable man-approved puppet as their head along with their finely honed service planning.

> *It is another spirit over these assemblies,*
> *not Jesus Christ...*

Satan's ministers in their religious local houses/assemblies have not entered life, and in their ignorance constrain those who would. This occurs as they manifest Babylon's glory and her religious authority.

This reinforces Jesus' words that WE need to be careful how

WE hear.

Again, if our *'beloved pastor'* does not minister under the anointing of the Holy Spirit, it is another spirit we are hearing from. Go ahead, you can love him, support him, he is counting on it.

But it is not God, nor is it God's house.

Is Jesus Christ his head? Is Christ the head of the church, and does the Holy Spirit set the service order?

If not, then it is a religious order set up just as those who worship dumb and deaf idols. And the worship service may resemble the prophets of Baal in the fervor of their dancing and waving banners. It is exciting, amen? They are relishing the witness of the Great Whore's approval of their soul based displays in their... bloodstream.

Again, let us read and understand Hebrews 4:12...

Disagree? I understand, Pastor Ahab it is hard to tell your wife Jezebel that her fleshly displays have nothing to do with God. Especially when the women who support *your* church regard her as their role model.

We DO need to understand why Vashti was replaced, and King David's wife Michal was displaced and excluded.

Back to our precious *'service order'*.

Newsflash:

Jesus is alive and well.

But if the assembly leaders do not really believe in the resurrection, then their 'Jesus' cannot hear them. Their 'Jesus' does not have a voice, and a service order must be created and followed as their 'Jesus' is incapable of being the Head of this church.

It is another Christ...

I have witnessed an assembly who believed in and served a resurrected Lord Jesus. In this house, Jesus was acknowledged as the Head of the church, and those saints assembled went to prayer. The apostle/pastor went before God and waited.

They waited... and waited, they quietly worshiped. Then when the Holy Spirit began to move, the power of God filled that house. That place became an extension of Jerusalem which is above.

For those with their own house, with a different gospel, a different lord? Maybe their *'ministry'* believes as one seminary registrar believed. He declared that God knew the school's order, and the Holy Spirit would follow them.

Those he discipled became twice the child of hell that he was, God's word. It was the wrong god, and the question is, '*Was his demise from a heart attack related to a heart problem with God*'?

Or was it just the result of poor diet... or maybe, a genetic defect?

Ignorance can be offset by knowledge, amen?

But *stupid remains forever...*

Were the snakes that bit the Israelites the result of their murmuring? Or were they just in the wrong place, at the wrong time? Per Korah's teaching, they were all holy, and if they were holy God would never allow this, right?

As a sincere believer, nothing, NOTHING can enter your time here without God allowing it, and I do mean nothing. We need to be sensitive to God's Holy Spirit, we do need to take heed how we hear.

Hmmm... Per Proverbs 26,

> "*...the curse causeless shall not come.*
> *A whip for the horse, a bridle for the ass, and a rod for*
> *the fool's back.*"

Can we be warned and learn? This IS written for our admonition. Fact.

Could the snakes have been present because of the words of the murmurer's mouth?

Could the heart attack have manifested a *'heart problem'* with God?

Too many questions?

God tells us that it is from the abundance of man's heart that he speaks.

The tongue contains the power of life and death, each word has a strength to it. There are no innocent words. Jesus told us to let our speech be yea or nay, as anything more comes from the evil one.

This reveals that every word the soul, or our life in this body accepts or receives, the entity or spirit on that word then has a source... of expression through us.

That is worthy of grasping and understanding as there are only two kingdoms. That being true, there can only be two sources we draw from.

Born into sin, we have taken our thoughts, our intellect, our emotions, as our identity. Our flesh and blood soul or life, what we regarded as living even as a believer has actually been living as a child... of the god of this world.

This explains the manifestations that accompany the thoughts of man.

Concluding...

The *'body of this death'* refers to the believer's unburied life as he either refuses to count it dead, or in ignorance tries to be obedient to the Lord in his own strength. Not knowing how to mortify it, bury it, it is in bouts of addiction, anger, uncontrollable urges that this *'body of death'* manifests its rule over the child that is born of God. This occurs as he has not known how to walk in the Holy Spirit on God's word.

Now let us take a look at how we take on, or find our New Life, the New Creature IN CHRIST.

Let us look at the very soul of God.

OBTAINING GOD'S SOUL
(personally...)

Before we continue, I am reminded to address a couple of things. One thing is this, my Father is finished with the cultural contemporary church leadership.
I say this again, as the title of this book is very clear.
This chapter, as others contains a demeanor that is not flattering to Babylon's church ministry. This is a call to exit Babylon and *'get right'* before God in order to exit a place of severe judgement.
As stated elsewhere this is a redemptive message to flee the wrath to come. Repentance before the living God is the word for today. Each understanding presented in this writing brings accountability. There is a charge to each reader to be responsible before God for what we know. There is an accountability that follows our hearing God's word, amen?

God's Flesh and Blood
The scripture we are going to review is absolutely an eye opener, and it is amazing when understood. Yet when taken in its context, it will stagger the carnal mind. To those mentored or discipled by men, this word is just as perplexing today, as it was to those who initially heard Jesus.
Why?
Because this word that Jesus spoke to the his followers initially? To this day it still sounds as extreme, strange, and macabre as when Jesus first spoke it. Today, Satan's ministers of righteousness in their man taught self-righteous ignorance declare this word of God to be hypothetical, figurative, or a metaphor.

However, Jesus' meant exactly what He said. We realize this when we hear the last five words.

> *"Then Jesus said unto them, Verily, verily, I say unto you, Except ye eat the flesh of the Son of man, and drink his blood, <u>ye have no life in you</u>..."* John 6

This statement tells each of us, just as Jesus told the seventy disciples, and the twelve, there is something here we must grasp to possess life. There are *"no if's, ands, buts or maybe's"*. Jesus did not offer a path of greasy grace, it is a very direct *'do or do not'*. Hearing this word, the seventy disciples then left murmuring among themselves. Jesus then asked the remaining twelve if they were going to walk away. When their answer was no, Jesus FURTHER challenged them!

Looking at this scripture, Jesus' definitive conclusive word to you and to me is this;

> 'Except you eat my flesh, and drink my blood you have no life in you'.

Do we think just because we are conscious of our body or breathing, we are alive? Or that we possess life? That is our living life as our dead first father Adam. The dead soul is oblivious to God's tangible Holy Spirit as life's responsibilities, and pressures define its life. In pleasing their church, in not comprehending spirituals, Satan's ministers will frame these words in an acceptable manner so that the souls in *'their church'* can accept them. But...do Jesus' words sound figurative?

Or was Jesus just presenting a hypothetical statement? Do Jesus' words in this context pass the smell test for a metaphor? Would it stumble us also to understand Jesus meant exactly what He said?

Because Jesus did not stop there. No, from there Jesus then declared personally He ate His Father's flesh, and drank His Father's blood when He told us that He, likewise, lived by the Father. That was when the seventy disciples choked, became offended, and departed.

And note... Jesus never, ever chased anyone who departed.

Never did my Lord even negotiate offering an easier path, ever. Let us also keep in mind, when Jesus spoke this hard saying, the Pharisees, the scribes were not present. The religious had not left their places of comfort, of knowledge, already possessing the support of the people. Being full, their need for God's Holy Spirit that King David had was and remains today, absent. However, the religious spirit that had ruled the temple through them? That same religious spirit would soon twist Jesus' message accessing the *'believer's' carnal soul'* with its new soul pleasing message inclusive of the hiss, *'Thou shall not surely die...'*.

Just as God's word through Moses and the prophets had been twisted, the word of God delivered in and through God's only begotten Son would soon be twisted.

This is evidenced today in Churchianity as the five thousand have returned entering the ministry to get their bellies filled. The seventy likewise have returned to relish the glory, the accolades and reverence of men. Ordained by men they occupy places in churches and men's hearts sharing the religious glory of their mother, Babylon. Having already stumbled at eating Jesus' flesh and drinking His blood, they have not choked on Satan's smooth practiced people pleasing doctrines, they have relished them. Possessing no life in Christ, they present their seminary imparted religious airs and demeanors seducing men's souls. They study history, God's word and men's traditions they call theology to present their spiel. They then present their cross-less message to others even as they religiously represent... Satan.

These are Satan's lifeless ministers of righteousness, 2 Corinthians 11:14,15. I seriously doubt that any of them intentionally went to seminary to become Satan's ministers. But just as Peter was concerned for the things of men, he unknowingly was being used by Satan. When Peter was confronted and dealt with by Jesus. Peter's heart was one of love for God and His Son, he received correction. The reader in ministry has that same opportunity. We can pretend to understand '*eating His flesh and drinking His blood*' pastor, and no one will be the wiser, amen? In your pretense you may act knowledgeable as if you actually understood this scripture by erroneously calling it the '*blood of the covenant*', amen? Yet the same darkness that cloaked the Pharisees is your obscene darkness. The absence of true brokenness before God reveals your carnal religious mind. As you choke on this portion of scripture you join your peers who walked away unable to eat His flesh and drink His blood. You, as they, are dead men.

Those are Jesus' words to you; *Unadulterated and untwisted.*

The reality of relishing *your* ministry is your personally enjoying a wrong spirit working in your physical bloodstream. Gather your books, communicate with your peers, and support each other. All this does is reveal your heart that has chosen the god of this world and his future. *Fact.*

The defense of your position, your credentials, your heart is of the same spirit the religious rulers entertained. This enabled them to murder Jesus, the apostles and be religiously justified. Yet if the spirit you yield to had known God's wisdom, it never would have crucified the Lord of Glory through its religious leaders back then, amen? Not consuming God's word for life, those religious miscreants studied it. Resisting the Holy Spirit, they as today presented men's reasonings which today are referred to as theology. In this men's reasonings have become their '*divine inspiration*'. And still, this question remains.

What will we do with Jesus' words? What will we do with this scripture??!!

I have discussed this scripture and others with pastors, sitting with them in their living rooms, standing with them in their parking lots, and have heard their answers with all the religious confidence of men protecting their position and place. To a man, it was a quick answer with an assertion of spiritual authority as they related that it was the '*Blood of the Covenant*', or a metaphor in receiving Christ.

Retired ministers, retired missionaries, senior pastors, new pastors, and youth pastors have followed the same path. These

men paid for their credentials, and now they study God's word to preach, teach, and deliver their presentations.
<u>Not one has ever</u> *told me they studied, and waited on God to know how to walk with Him in the Holy Spirit.*
Not even one....
My Father sees them as disgusting.
These are the temple prostitutes who serve another god as they sell themselves. Their selling their sincerity occurs as they are being pleasured in their soul, in their bloodstream writhing in union with their mother, the Great Whore.
It is her unclean spirit that soothes their dead souls along with those who receive them and their words. She is sharing her glory with them as they market God's Son.
As related previously, Malachi delivered God's word addressing their peers, those ministers who delivered the same filth in his day;

> *"I will ... splatter your faces with the manure from your festival sacrifices, and I will throw you on the manure pile." Malachi 2 NIV*

The priests as the pastors today have offered up their words, not speaking as an oracle of God.
In Malachi they offered up the sacrifices full of excrement, the feces in them. This is identical to your pastor delivering his theology as he pretends to speak in God's place.

Eating Flesh and Drinking Blood

So, again, as Jesus lived by His Father, so those that ate His flesh and drank His blood would live by Him. This could not be a reference to communion, as Jesus never broke bread, or offered a cup declaring it was His Father's flesh and blood.
Do we just read over that fact, ignore it and move on?
As we partake in communion in remembrance of our Lord, we partake of His body broken for us, and the blood of the New Covenant. We do not say *'except we partake of communion we have no life in us'*, as that would be... inaccurate. Participating in communion does not factor in to what Jesus is telling you,

and me. The truth is...

If we religiously regard our body as our life, eating Jesus' flesh and drinking His blood is abstract, crazy and heretical. Yet this scripture in context contains an amazing truth to those who actually love our Heavenly Father, and our saviour Jesus. This scripture will confirm what we are being told by the Holy Spirit. Jesus does not say that our not eating His flesh and drinking His blood would make it difficult for us to possess life, no. Instead, Jesus says apart from our doing this, exactly this, we possess NO life.

> "...Whoso eateth my flesh, and drinketh my blood, hath eternal life; and I will raise him up at the last day.
>
> For my flesh is meat indeed, and my blood is drink indeed.
> He that eateth my flesh, and drinketh my blood, dwelleth in me, and I in him.
> As the living Father hath sent me, and I live by the Father: so he that eateth me, even he shall live by me."
> *John 6*

What then is Jesus' flesh?
What then is Jesus' blood?
Additionally, if Jesus lived by the Father, how did Jesus consume His Father's flesh and drink HIS blood?
Maybe we grasp a little better why the seventy departed....
When we desire to understand this hard word, the question we must ask is this:
What does God's word tell us?
The Holy Spirit reveals that Jesus gave 'keys' to understanding His parables to His disciples. For example, in the parable of the sower, the '*key*' was '*the seed is the word of God*'. That enabled that parable to be understood by the disciples. In this '*hard saying,*' what are the '*keys?*'

Jesus' Flesh
First key: Jesus is the "*Word of God Made Flesh*" in John 1:14,

amen? So now we have the *'key'* that reveals *'eating His flesh'* would be consuming His word for LIFE.

Grab this; In our eating God's word, consuming the word with the need for life, God's Holy Spirit is essential. Being poor in spirit is NEEDING God's Holy Spirit as your life, without which you remain in death.

Consuming God's word is not *'soul reading'* it to obtain information to teach others, to impress our *'fellowship'*, or to improve *'our'* ministry. This type of reading is revolting to the Holy Spirit as it is self-glorying, self-promoting, NEVER taking my Heavenly Father's heart into the equation.

Reading the word of God for life is reading it with the NEED of understanding our Father, His concerns, His desire for His place in us. We read His word as if it were to us only. If His word is to every individual, it benefits me nothing if I do not consume it personally.

This is not complicated.

As we consume His word, we desire His will be performed first in us, and then through us. We read God's word consuming it as God's spirit literally rests upon it breaking it down for our life. The revelation of God's word by the Holy Spirit becomes the Rock, the foundation of our personally identifying with God our Father, who is our life. His righteousness becomes ours by faith in WHAT He has done, not by our church affiliation, our religious peers or our religious history.

Our life is found in His spirit on His word sanctifying us as we take HIS WORD back to Him. Why is this critical? Because again, God only receives back to Himself what has proceeded forth FROM Him.

Did Adam receive back anything less than himself for a help-meet? He did not and just a heads up... Neither will Jesus, the Last Adam.

Jesus' Blood

Second Key: Do we recall Leviticus 17:11 telling us the life or soul of the flesh is in the blood?

Could this understanding from the *'Old Testament'* also apply here in John 6?

Or would this Leviticus reference only apply to the flesh and blood offerings we see pre-Calvary as substitutionary, symbolic sacrifices...?

If we see this reference to drinking blood as referring only to the sacrifice's blood, then this scripture is abhorrent, repugnant, and our consensus is Jesus' words must be rejected, amen? But for those *'born not of blood, nor of the will of the flesh, nor of the will of man, but of God,'* we will understand what our Father is telling us.

> *"For the life (or soul) of the flesh is in the blood."*
> *Leviticus 17:11*

Could the life or soul of God be contained in the substance that gives life to this *'flesh'*, the word of God? Could this *'substance of things hoped for'*, this *'evidence of things not seen'* be the blood, the tangible Holy Spirit? Remember, Jesus told the disciples the world would not receive the Holy Spirit because they could not *'see Him'*.

The *'key'* to identifying the blood we are to drink is found when we understand that the flesh is the word of God. Let us hear Jesus as He tells us,

> *"It is the spirit that quickeneth; the (carnal) flesh profiteth nothing: the words that I speak unto you, they are spirit, and they are life."*

It is the blood that animates the flesh, the body, amen? So then it is the Holy Spirit that quickens or makes the New Creature, the word of God in us alive with the carnal flesh profiting nothing.

It is the Holy Spirit on the words that Jesus is speaking that gives those words, or His flesh life.

Do we need to meditate that a few minutes, digest that?

We need to grasp, comprehend this spiritually;

> *'The blood contains the life (soul) of the flesh'.*

Or...

> *'It is the Holy Spirit (the blood) that quickens, or*

> *contains the life of the word of God (the flesh)'.*

If the word of God is the *'flesh we are to consume'*; then it is the the Holy Spirit that *'quickens that flesh'*. The literal blood we must drink then is the Holy Spirit.

The Holy Spirit on the Word of God we consume becomes our NEW identity.

This IS THE NEW MAN, the New Creature who finds His life IN CHRIST! The authority of God resides in the New Creature. This is the son of God!

The New Creature has a different family...

This New Creature is a NEW creature, not a flesh and blood diplomaed, ordained by men minister who has not the faith in God to overcome in his own life. The old creature will struggle with strife, sickness, financial issues because that creature, that beast has its life UNDER the rule of the elements of this world.

The New Creature is born of God's word and finds his life is the very presence of God, the Holy Spirit. His meat is doing the will of his Father. His word? In Christ it shakes the foundations of creation... THAT is the son of God! His identity is not what his physical parent's birthed.

He is not from below, He is from above, and He is not an *'inhabitant of the earth'*. His home is at the right hand of God IN Christ. This is the New Man.

Now we understand,

> *"Except ye eat the flesh of the Son of man, and drink his blood, ye have no life in you."*

No more is it a mystery, nor is it hypothetical, theoretical, or merely a metaphor. Eating His flesh is consuming the word of God for life. Abiding in the tangible presence of the Holy Spirit is drinking His blood. The Holy Spirit on the word of God is now seen as our possessing life, just as Jesus now lives. The New Creature's consciousness is now seen as the tangible Holy Spirit, not the dead man's awareness of the body's physical senses.

God Receives... God?
Really? Let us remember Adam. When God presented Adam's wife to him, Adam received nothing less than his own self which had issued forth FROM him! Adam received back his own flesh and blood back from God. Their name was Adam. The woman was not called Eve until after the fall, and then only in a retroactive sense of her identity. Originally, her identity was her husband's identity.
God has sent His Son the Last Adam, the Living Word of God made flesh. God has sent His Holy Spirit to teach, to make alive, to quicken His word in us.
God received back what had proceeded forth from Him, NOTHING less.
God will receive NOTHING less than Himself in us.
God will receive ONLY His flesh and blood back to Himself.
Did not Jesus confront Saul of Tarsus with,

"I am Jesus whom thou persecutest.."

Those who loved not their lives/souls unto the death, had returned the life they received back to God. Jesus identified with them *as Him*! He saw them as His flesh and blood, word and spirit family. Is that not an awesome understanding?!!!!
In our coming before God;
> *We bring His word that Christ is made unto us wisdom.*
> *We bring His word that Christ is made unto us righteousness.*
> *We bring His word that Christ is made unto us justification.*
> *We bring His word that Christ is made unto us redemption.*
> *It is impossible for God to lie, we thank God the blood of His Son continually cleanses us, and we stand before Him holy!*

That is HIS word. We who are born again, are born of the incorruptible word of God, and God has sent forth the spirit of His Son into our hearts whereby we call Him our Father!

God will only receive that which is born of Him with His spirit on it... ONLY!

God will not receive another's word with a different spirit on it, pastor.

That would be a fallen spirit, a creature that finds its expression pleasuring your soul, your mind with its self-promoting will, with your emotions tied in with the god of this world. It is nasty, and already condemned. It has seduced you, and is endeavoring to make its condemnation... yours.

The cross is your opportunity for life as detailed in the prior chapter.

Disagree?

That is being in opposition to your own self, as Paul wrote to Timothy.

Can we now understand why our beloved church leadership relies on their charisma and their presentations that connect with you in the struggles of your... soul? If you love it, and *'feel better'* without the power to overcome, it is the god of this world being intoxicated in your soul...

We must grasp this.

If your pastor does not minister in the power of God's spirit, on God's word, he is offering a corrupt load of his own feces, and God has rejected both it and him. Quite frankly, this word is tempered.

God is finished with these idiots, and if this describes you in '*your*' ministry?

I cordially invite you to walk away, become the rare individual that actually submits to God, learns to remain in His presence as King David and walk with God.

If you wish to be offended, be offended. Sweet words are yours from the liar who wishes to comfort your soul, that same soul you told God you buried.

This is an eternal choice, and my Father will NOT accept a balance of self-pleasing, as you try to straddle a fence. As believers, we have been culpable. Why?

Because we have supported this religious spirit with our

approval....

Abiding in the tangible Holy Spirit is now seen as the strait gate that leads to a very narrow path. The gate is now exposed, there remains no excuse not to take it, unless we prefer the old man we told God we buried. In drawing back we choose the pleasuring of our adult dead soul, with all its affections and approvals.

The cross? We can take it up, or walk away. In reading this, our choice before God is being made clear to us. God already knows. Abstract? Radical? I understand....

Moving on.

Another fact? It is the person, the tangible presence of the Holy Spirit that contains the very Godhead, the life, the very soul of God. Let us look at excerpts from John 14,

"And I will pray the Father, and he shall give you another Comforter, that he may abide with you forever;

Even the Spirit of truth; whom the world cannot receive, because it seeth him not, neither knoweth him: but ye know him; for he dwelleth with you, and shall be in you.

I will not leave you comfortless: I will come to you."
"...At that day ye shall know that I am in my Father, and ye in me, and I in you."

Do we see the Father, the Son who is the Living Word of God, AND the Holy Spirit being sent to the disciple that has left all to follow Christ? Is not our Lord present to lead us if we follow the tangible Holy Ghost? In resisting the Holy Ghost, we also now understand we personally turn from following the Lord Jesus Christ.... If we count the cost, and abide IN HIM, we partake of so much more! We now see the indwelling Godhead promised to the disciple cleaned by the word of God, John 15:3.

We see that just as with our Lord, it is the Holy Spirit that quickens, or makes us live. Jesus could do nothing of Himself, His words were not His own, even His will was to do His Father's will.

This is the very soul, the eternal soul of God. The Word and the Spirit that proceeded from God is the Flesh and Blood Soul of God that God receives back to Himself when we choose living by His Holy Spirit on His word.
Again, this is literally God receiving back to Himself... Himself.
We see God's word being God's flesh.
We see God's Holy Spirit that is the blood animating the word.
We see it is the Holy Spirit that is the FIRE of God on the living sacrifice.
It is through the fire of the Holy Spirit that the body becomes the temple of God holy and acceptable to God. Do we see God accepting the dead flesh and blood soul anywhere in this? We now see the very path to life, living by the Holy Spirit on the Word of God as our New Man, our identity.
Now we see what we buried in baptism as the old man, that lifeless man hanging on the tree. Recognizing in that mangled body there is no life is the same as the Israelites looking on the image of the dead serpent on the pole and being healed. The serpent seen as dead can no longer have power, its venom is neutralized. In seeing our body as dead, we now view it as God sees it and live a New Life through His Son in and by the Holy Spirit. Through His grace, we are delivered from the kingdom of darkness and translated into the Kingdom of God's dear Son. In listening to a true servant of God, we will be challenged to follow God, the Holy Spirit, never a man. Paul used a Greek word meaning mimic, when we read of him telling us to follow him as he follows Christ. We are to *'mimic'* his love for God, his heart of being a servant.

Privacy: Making This Personal, Intimate
In Matthew 6, Jesus relates that in whatever we do we should do it as unto the Lord, privately. Taking God's word back to God in private, in faith, is actual faith in God. Recall, God receives God? It is personally acknowledging that God is... *'as he that cometh to God must believe that he is, and that he is a rewarder of them that diligently seek him'*. This is personally

accepting God's reality, coming into His presence as Abel. Abel brought an acceptable sacrifice. Coming before God initially may be difficult, because where we think we are in God, may be radically different than where we actually are. If we sense frustration and anger when what we bring before God is not accepted, that is our being influenced by the same spirit Cain yielded to.

We do not need to yield to anger... we need to change the offering.

This is the same thing God told Cain. Changing our offering is our changing our heart, and our words to God. We go before God in faith taking His word back to Him, discovering what He witnesses with His Presence, the tangible Holy Ghost. This is what it takes to follow the Lord. In learning this, while spending time with the Lord, in His presence, I sensed His presence lift. I cried out, '*Why are you leaving me?!*' The response, '*I am not leaving you, I am leading you, do what it takes to follow me...*' I did, I changed my heart, I prayed for others. I prayed for the body of Christ, I thanked Him He is made wisdom unto me... I found where His presence was and I learned to follow Him. This is our seeking the Lord while He may be found.

When we come before God believing that we are righteous and holy because we have been a '*child of God*' for thirty years?

Even the sinless Son of God Jesus did not '*play that card*'. Instead, He was heard in that He feared the One able to save Him from death. We see that there is no basis to stand before God on our pride and service. If we have not walked in the Holy Spirit for those thirty years, and then attempt to stand before God in self-righteousness? God will say He does not know us. Fact. However, God will meet that same believer on the basis of faith in God cleansing Him from all sin and unrighteousness through Jesus at Calvary. As God's child we can thank Him for this. If that is what the Holy Spirit is witnessing by His tangible presence, this is where we start.

This is our bringing the acceptable sacrifice before God which

He accepts.

God ONLY accepts His word declared by us, back to Him in faith. God witnesses His word He is speaking to us by His Holy Spirit on that word.

Again, God accepts, God, amen? We can religiously contend with that truth, or understand God only accepts what came forth from Him. Can we understand what our parents produced, that product of flesh and blood was the child of wrath? God sees it as dead at Calvary, and then accepts it as being a living sacrifice. Jesus showed us what a living sacrifice looks like, amen? Jesus lived by consuming God's flesh and blood, which was God's word quickened by the Holy Spirit. The result? Jesus always had the presence of His Father as He did only those things that pleased Him.

Different? Strange? Jesus is the first-born among many brethren, amen? If He is our brother we will serve the same Father. We will live the very same way He lived here. We now see our Lord as our example. Jesus from John's baptism was filled with the Holy Spirit and THEN followed the tangible Holy Spirit dying in the wilderness to what Mary had birthed.

A New Soul was being prepared to be manifested, the very Son of God at One with God His Father's soul. We are seeing the Last Adam...

The life of the New Creature is the very word of God, with the Holy Spirit being the blood that gives life to God's word. Fulfilling the will of God sustains this New Creature.

> "Jesus saith unto them, My meat is to do the will of him that sent me, and to finish his work." John 4

We now understand the *'meat that ye know not of'* that Jesus partook of at the well in Samaria! That 'meat' sustained Him. This is our Lord living by our Father, just as those that eat His flesh, and drink His blood will LIVE by Him.

We now see that extreme, defines our walking with God. This is our loving the Lord thy God with all our heart, and with all our soul, and with all our mind, and with all our strength that we consume His word and abide in the awareness of His

Holy Spirit. His word is our flesh, His tangible Holy Spirit is the blood we drink in as He breaks down God's word for living. This is the New Creature, this is finding our 'soul' in Christ. This is the Kingdom of God first having its rule in us, and then as we follow the Lord Jesus Christ through the tangible Holy Spirit... it will be God's Kingdom through us to His glory.
The fire of the Holy Spirit on God's word is our life, it is the zeal of God that consumes the living sacrifice..

The Holy Spirit reveals our identity as a living stone, which is also our location in the very City of God..

BORN AGAIN, AND UNCONVERTED

For ye are dead..." Colossians 3

Dead? Seriously? This scripture taken in its context only reinforces that God is telling us we are... dead. Not dead in sin, but dead in the sense that our life in Him is not to be confused with this body's breath and heartbeat that we possibly identify as our life.

The *'life in the flesh'* is exactly what God is saying is dead, that identity, that 'who you are' in the flesh... that is the *'you that is dead'*.

That is not a metaphoric death....

The truth?

We have been born again of God who is spirit. In being born of God, per God we are dead, buried with Christ and our life can now only be found in the tangible awareness of the Holy Spirit. That may sound wrong, radical, and off base because we have based our life on men's theologies and their eloquent presentations of God's word. All this being done apart from the presence and power of God, Himself. Our entire understanding has been based on pastors, teachers, men that possibly our family respected, so we likewise *'fell in line'* trusting them. But for the most part, these *'spiritual leaders'* are those we paid to teach us, what they likewise paid men they respected to teach... them.

Man pleasing man, obtaining man's stamp of approval with the earned degrees and certificates, but absent God's approval entirely. How else could they ask or expect YOU to accept THEM? The tuition, the diplomas, the courses? It was all done so they could stand before you, and obtain YOUR approval, your validating them as special. They wanted to be looked up to, seen as spiritual and they paid the price in money, internships, getting the needed job history so that you could not deny their credentials. Not sent by God, unconverted, these are Satan's ministers of righteousness Paul warned us about.

And yes pastor, board member, and church member, I am talking about that person, that *'entity'* you adore, respect, valuing its acceptance and approval. This is blatant idolatry, the covering for this error is removed, repentance is an option, or not. As with Balaam, Korah, it will be hard to turn around as Satan's hooks are set deep in that precious identity he has given you...

For the believer, the result?

> *Everything you and I have been taught in the church apart from the Holy Spirit is a twist of the truth or an outright lie.*
>
> *Everything you and I have been taught in the church about living satisfying the flesh, or after the flesh is a lie.*

This can be an exceptionally hard lesson to even begin to learn. A young man of 25 years old was sitting by the cadaver of his wife who had died in a car accident in Central Oregon. He related the following...

> *He was sitting in the mortuary next to the gurney she was on, a sheet covering her to her neck. His tears were streaming down his face onto the concrete floor, and he was bawling his eyes out.*
>
> *The Lord spoke to him and said:*
>
>> *"As long as you are behaving like this, do not expect anything from me."*
>
> *At first, he thought,*
>
>> *"How cold!!!"*
>
> *But as he sat there, within a few seconds he realized God was still on the throne. God was not in shock, and God was still God. As he calmed himself and remained there, he accepted she was not there.*

For three days, he went in and sat by her body, once in the morning, and once at night.
He got an education.
He could have squeezed her hand but there would have been no response. He could have stroked her hair, but again, there would be no response. He realized the many hours she had spent on her hair, make-up, it all ended... right here.
He began to see that on that gurney was everything that had ever given her a problem in her serving the Lord, the pride, the ego, and her perception of herself based on her appearance.
He understood that anybody could say anything to that cadaver and there would be no hurt or offense.
Someone could slap it or spit on it and she would not be offended.
She was dead to her flesh.
He began to understand that 'the life of the flesh' was the issue.
                    His education continued..
His wife was not there, she was free from her 'robe of flesh'.
His next question was, where was she?
She obviously was gone, but now, present tense, where was she at!!??
Was she free retaining her power of choice?
Or was she in a place where she had no choice?
On the last day, the morning of her internment, he had seen her. Her body was in the 'slumber room', a small room off the chapel where the family would have privacy with the deceased's body in the casket. It was here they would say their final goodbyes before the internment.
And he was here, he was asking, begging, pleading for God to restore her.
Sensing his powerlessness with God, he began trying to

'push all the buttons' with God he could think of trying to provoke a response, any response. There was none. He then looked up and there she was, in her favorite pink fuzzy top with the black slacks, standing there about 5 feet away.

She told him she was not coming back, but that she loved him with the love of God. Their marriage had been until death parted them, and he was free to provide the best home he could for himself and for their infant son.

Then she was gone.

There had been no negotiation, no further conversation.

Where was she now?

She was dead to her flesh.

She was in the presence of God.

He returned to the chapel, and to the family and friends that were mourning.

Feeling detached, he could say nothing. It would have been offensive to those present.

Unknowingly, as a believer being unconverted, he still had to grieve. He still must walk through this loss and learn what death to 'this body with its life' was. The knowledge, the education he had received was not the same as his knowing how to 'walk it out'.

But this experience of sitting beside her cadaver had changed him.

He now experientially understood what the scripture meant when it referenced the believer as being '*dead*' or in '*being dead to the flesh*', the '*body of sin*' but '*alive to God*'.

But to actually live a life of freedom WITH God?

To actually walk through life with its experiences, its realities moment-to-moment while living in the presence of God as 'one dead' to the flesh, but alive to God in the spirit?

That remained a mystery.

<u>Can we relate?</u>

(*The scriptures are clear it is the 'how-to' that has been the issue...*) This knowledge and how to apply it, the understanding on how to actually walk it out before God... That would take a few years...

Failures

The marriage had been rough, with plenty of blame to go around. The brunt of the blame rested on him. He had been a failure as the head of his home. Instead of dealing gently with her, taking her before the Lord, pain had shaped his responses. Pain had been met with pain, heartache was met with heartache, until separations had become his way of escaping the pain.

The reconciliations became increasingly short lived.

A miscarriage had occurred early in their marriage. Later the death of an infant son, a business failure, bankruptcy, and house fire all within a year added stress that pushed them both to their limits.

People began to call him Job.

Their last short lived reconciliation had resulted in a pregnancy. Agreeing to separate for a year, he took her by the arm, knelt down at a sofa and released her to the Lord. He released all his rights to her as his wife to God, and asked God to bless her with His best. As he departed, an abyss of darkness had overwhelmed him. He knew this abyss, but did not understand it was the final separation, the end to the relationship he was experiencing.

Then another son was born, six weeks later the car accident occurred resulting in her funeral.

A year later, attempts to move on and restart his life had met with failure upon failure. Regardless of his best efforts, his failures had kept piling up.

Everyone he developed a relationship with for support, was somehow removed.

He and his son moved back in with his parents. A short time later, he was told his dad had a heart condition and may not be around very long.

Unable to take anymore grief, devastated, he asked his parents to look after his son. He threw a suitcase into an old van, and hit the road with no destination in mind. He wandered aimlessly through different states sleeping in that old van with no destination in mind. One day, he realized he was near his in-laws.

At the funeral his heart broken father-in-law had held him personally responsible for his daughter's death. The father in pain, in his grief had told him if he saw him again, that he would shoot him.

The young man was ready to face whatever awaited.

Driving up to their house, they met him on the porch. As they kept looking over his shoulder at the old van, he realized they were looking for their grandchild. Realizing the child was not present, they opened their home to him. He realized they would endure his presence for a chance to know their grandchild, this was not going to be a warm environment.

It was then, it was there that he began seeking the Lord. In this environment, the only relationship he would develop would be with His Father.

Why this story? Why this record of tragedies, human errors, failures and pain?

The End of All Flesh

In Genesis 6, God told Noah,

> "...the end of all flesh is come before me..."

That is ancient history, amen?

But in Romans 8, we hear Paul speaking by the Holy Spirit,

> "God sending his own Son in the likeness of sinful flesh, and for sin, condemned sin in the flesh..."

Call it *'missing the mark'* or call it *'the struggles of the flesh'* but in both cases sin in the flesh has been judged, already. The end of all flesh has again come before God, in the person of Jesus' lifeless body on Calvary. All flesh has been judged, the end of all flesh is revealed.

Recall Adam was made a *living soul*, but the Last Adam is a *life-giving spirit*?

The flesh and blood we are now born of is God's word and God's spirit. Make no mistake, possessing your identity as this body with its life, you <u>are</u> dead. The verses that state '*Let the dead bury the dead*' and '*she that lives in pleasure is dead while she lives*' now make perfect sense, amen?

In Genesis 4, a full two chapters *before* God told Noah the '*end of all flesh is come before me*', men had begun to call on God. Their calling '*on the name of the Lord*' did not work out too good for them, right? What could have been missing?

Enoch '*got it*', Noah '*got it*' but those on the '*broad path*'? They missed it...

God had so loved the world that it broke His heart He had made man. He strove with men, but they grieved His Holy Spirit to the point His long-suffering found its limit. Making the Holy Spirit '*suffer*' with us while we profess '*We are under grace*' is likewise unwise.

It makes you wonder what messages were being preached during the days of Noah.

Noah was a preacher of righteousness, the others? Maybe their messages were of grace, or possibly that the '*coming flood*' God's messengers spoke of was a metaphor. Could that be the reason God's word was not taken seriously.

God watched over His word, He performed His word, and cleansed the old world of all flesh, with the exception of the righteous.

Back to that young man.

He had come to the point where he needed God. Not the point to where he wanted a better life, he really needed... a life.

So, looking for life, back to church he went... He was ready to '*tough it out*', ignore the discrepancies and make any changes necessary.

He began attending church. Being desperate for life he committed himself to being there before the doors opened, and being the last person to leave. But in attending, he could

not find God's peace as he attended each and every meeting. Grieving, he asked the Lord why he could not go to church.
The answer was immediate, among the two reasons given was,
> '... you are going to please man, you cannot please men and please me'.

After that he remained at their home as they both worked during the day.

He then began consuming the word of God.

Consuming the word of God was something his *'self'* resisted, and fought against. He had to make his *'self'* read God's word out loud in order to even focus.

The Holy Spirit then began to bring understanding to God's word.

As he read, he also recalled that lifeless body in the mortuary having no desire, of her being in the presence of God not being capable of being hurt, or offended. The understanding how to be *'dead'* to his self and live before God could hold the key to get past the hurts, the failures that had brought him to this point. He saw that lifeless body on the gurney as his late wife's *'self'*. He meditated how to actually live before God, and be dead to his own body with its life, his own living *'self'*.

He began seeking God, as a reality. He recalled how in a worship service he had been in the presence of the Lord, the Holy Spirit and a bill had come to his mind. Immediately, he was out of the Lord's presence. Refocusing on the Lord, the presence of the Holy Ghost was again... experienced. He understood he needed to love the Lord with ALL his heart, with ALL his soul, that included loving the Lord with ALL his mind. He focused his mind on God's word, retaining scriptures in memory to repeat and meditate on when he was not actually reading. He endeavored to remain in the tangible presence of the Holy Spirit. Thoughts of failures, memories of mistakes made, images of his past would flood his mind. His heart broke, but taking God's word he began to go before the Lord adamantly, verbally declaring God's word was true. With strong crying, before God he declared that *"Your word is true,*

I HAVE been cleansed from ALL sin and ALL unrighteousness."
He fought, he struggled, taking any understanding of God's word back to God, loud at times, insistent, and not backing down. Praying, weeping when the Holy Spirit broke him, at other times bold as a lion, declaring the impossibility of God ever lying, His word was forever settled in heaven. That Jesus righteousness was made unto him HIS righteousness...!
He read of Jesus not doing the things that pleased His *'self'* even though His *'self'* was sinless. Jesus did only those things that pleased His Father...
This was how Jesus had the tangible presence of His Father in the Holy Spirit.
That truth impacted Him.
He realized his *'self'* was literally his body possessing its own desires, for the mere fact it had.... life. Being cleansed of all past sin, it still was not to be his point of relating to as his life. Like any creature, in possessing life it possessed an appetite, and the fundamental essentials that any creature possessed.
All because it possessed breath.
This flesh and blood creature he lived in, was <u>not</u> born of God.
It was then the Lord began to deal with him to do everything he could to remain in the tangible presence of the Holy Ghost, pleasing the Lord, not his... *self.*
His first-born soul was being counted dead.
Everything that had occurred... had reduced him to Christ.
Christ, the anointing on God's word was to become his only life.

Raised In Churchianity
He had been born again at 6 years old in a powerful manner where as a child he KNEW his desperate need for the Lord. He had encountered a frightening dark abyss, and knew that it was separation from God. At that point he had accepted the Lord Jesus as his personal savior. He had always accepted the teaching that in accepting Jesus, he had been converted.
Raised in church, he endeavored to live for the Lord, but

was powerless in himself to live godly. He experienced the presence of God, the Holy Spirit powerfully at different times. But looking to church, looking to the ministry, he had never been taught the need to *'abide in the Holy Spirit'* as the *'abiding in Christ'* that Jesus commanded His disciples. (John 14:16-18, John 15) He had never been shown the power of living in the Holy Spirit from his youth, hence his life was... vacuous. It was unfulfilled, powerless, with an unending history of failures.

He then tried everything looking for fulfillment, and it was not to be found.

<u>Can we relate</u>?

He had never been taught he must be converted, or why he needed to be converted, much less *'how to be... converted'*.

Why would the scriptures tell us to repent and be converted if our conversion had taken place when we repented and believed?

Maybe better questions are:

> *When the minister is powerless or in bondage, what can he teach you?*
>
> *What can a man who is NOT walking in the power of God teach you?*

To be as he is?

Nice, right?

Is that why we hear, *'No one is perfect'*?

Is it because our beloved pastor has issues he cannot overcome?

The truth remains true, regardless of our soul's desires for social acceptance and positive interactions.

> *Your soul is the body with its life, its 'self' you are to count dead....*

Do we believe a man-called minister in financial bondage, or addicted to pornography can give us the keys to live victorious IN Christ? *Really..?*

What 'conversion' took place in HIS life?

Instead, we are taught by him and his peers we are converted when we are born again, when in reality we ARE born again of

God, but not as yet converted.

When WE purchase an item it is to convert it to OUR use, amen? That would mean it belongs to us for our personal use, not for another. Right?

> If we purchased a house and we were not given possession, what would OUR response be?

Now we see we are purchased by God for His use... solely, amen?

We may have been redeemed from the god of this world, but what has changed?

We might even say *'We belong to the Lord'* as we live lives pleasing ourselves, obtaining our validation from *'our church'*, from men we esteem as religious, or spiritual, or those who esteem us as valuable, but none from our Lord resulting from our abiding in Him.

In this we remain willful babes in Christ, milk drinkers who need constant affirmation from those we look to for *'making us feel'* approved and accepted.

Let us look at our High Priest, our forerunner, our example, the One who Hebrews declares the author, the source of salvation to *those individuals who... obey <u>Him</u>*.

Is this beginning to sound, personal?

Jesus, The Convert

When sinless Jesus was baptized, it was NOT for sin, nor repentance of sin.

Religiously, and scripturally we are told, *'It was to fulfil righteousness'*.

Fulfilling righteousness, was fulfilling God's promises, the prophecies of a Messiah, and of a New Generation, a New Race, a People that would be created (Psalms 102). This would include God the Father changing Jesus' source for His living, His life.

> "Then cometh Jesus from Galilee to Jordan unto John, to be baptized of him.
> But John forbad him, saying, I have need to be baptized

> *of thee, and comest thou to me?*
> *And Jesus answering said unto him, Suffer it to be so now: for thus it becometh us to fulfil all righteousness. Then he suffered him.*
> *And Jesus, when he was baptized, went up straightway out of the water: and, lo, the heavens were opened unto him, and he saw the Spirit of God descending like a dove, and lighting upon him:*
> *And lo a voice from heaven, saying, This is my beloved Son, in whom I am well pleased."* Matthew 3

This baptism?
Again, it is Jesus fulfilling all righteousness, fulfilling a promise, bringing to fruition the prophesies of a Saviour.
In this case, we hear the prophetic voice revealed in Hebrews 10.

> "*For it is not possible that the blood of bulls and of goats should take away sins.*
> *Wherefore when he cometh into the world, he saith, Sacrifice and offering thou wouldest not, but a body hast thou prepared me:*
> *In burnt offerings and sacrifices for sin thou hast had no pleasure.*
> *Then said I, Lo, I come (in the volume of the book it is written of me,) to do thy will, O God.*"

Fulfilling His calling as God's Lamb, Jesus was baptized and a different life, a totally different life lay ahead for this 'convert'. The *'body prepared Him'* was a flesh and blood body in the likeness of sinful flesh, to be offered up as both a living sacrifice, and God's spotless Lamb.
From this baptism, Jesus placed His entire future IN the leading of the Holy Spirit, in following the Holy Spirit ONLY.
Into the wilderness Jesus went, following the Holy Spirit. It was in the wilderness He fulfilled or *'walked out'* Luke 14:26-28.

> "*If any man come to me, and hate not his father, and mother, and wife, and children, and brethren, and*

> *sisters, yea, and his own life also, he cannot be my disciple. And whosoever doth not bear his cross, and come after me, cannot be my disciple.*
> *For which of you, intending to build a tower, sitteth not down first, and counteth the cost, whether he have sufficient to finish it?"*

Speaking to those who had followed after Him, He continued not only His teaching, but His personal testimony,

> *"So likewise, whosoever he be of you that forsaketh not all that he hath, he cannot be my disciple."*

In the wilderness, that body with its life prepared for our Lord? Jesus the Creator of heaven and earth died to it.
He died to its affections, familial relations, and His own soul? Everything related to flesh and blood living was counted dead in the sense of it demanding its approval or preservation. Food, drink, the comfort of home and family were all abandoned as the Holy Spirit became His Comforter. Jesus was converted to fulfill the will and calling of God, He became the very temple of God the Father through the Holy Spirit.
Jesus, the son of Mary had *'reckoned His body dead'* from His baptism. When Jesus called His disciples to follow Him, those that heeded the call LIKEWISE left all behind. Jesus requires those that follow Him, to walk His path, otherwise they are NOT following… Him, amen?
That path?
It was the death to His body with its life and its affections Jesus experienced BEFORE Calvary. The death?
It was to the flesh and blood natural man born of God and Mary who He buried in baptism.
Our baptism, as His, is *for us* to as Jesus fulfill all righteousness. Recall He is our *'forerunner'*?
In Hebrews 2, through our participating in Jesus' death we are delivered from *ALL* bondage resulting from the *'fear of death'*. A dead man does not fear death! If we have believed God offered Jesus up for our sin, and raised Jesus from the dead, we have passed from death to life! We have received power to

become a son of God, per the apostle John.
But the path, to follow the Lord? It remains the same.
> *"He that loveth his life shall lose it; and he that hateth his life in this world shall keep it unto life eternal.*
> *If any man serve me, let him follow me; and where I am, there shall also my servant be..." John 12*

Recall that Jesus was heard in that He feared? But what would Jesus possibly have had to fear? Do you recall Romans 8, there is a verse that sounds very close to what God told the first Adam.
> *"For if you live according to the flesh you will die; but if by the Spirit you put to death the deeds of the body, you will live."*

That was written to believers, would it also apply to Jesus Christ? If Jesus had lived after the flesh, even sinless He could not have inherited the Kingdom of God, much less walked in the power of God. *It is not about being sinless*, it is about loving God and being converted to HIS use, for HIS Kingdom, amen? Flesh and blood, even sinless will not inherit the Kingdom of God. Jesus became our High Priest in that He encountered EVERYTHING we would encounter and overcame without sin. Again,
> *"...And being made perfect, he became the author of eternal salvation unto all them that obey him..."*
> *Hebrews 5*

Can we grasp this? Jesus became the author, the source of salvation to those that obey Him!
Not those who as in the days of Noah just call on the name of the Lord.
Not those who state they believe and assume they are saved by their *'knowledge'*.
In order to be where our Lord is at present-tense, we must personally follow Him.
Is that not obedience?
Jesus took this same route, and followed the Holy Spirit. It is God's Holy Spirit that enabled Him, and will enable those of us

who choose to trust God.

Jesus was not given a pass on taking up His cross, neither will the believer be given one. This would be inclusive of the fact that Jesus learned obedience by the things He endured. In his strong crying, prayers, and supplications, He yielded Himself unto the One who was able to save Him from death.

Why would Jesus need to be saved from death?!

Because I needed that deliverance...

Do you, or did you need deliverance also?

Again, *it is that personal.*

There could be no compromise, there could be no pleasing of Himself, only the pleasing of God through the tangible Holy Spirit. The Holy Spirit is the enabler, the One who empowers the believer to mortify the flesh. Likewise, Jesus relied on Him as the One able to enable Him, save Him from death, and raise Him up restoring His soul. From this strong crying, this bringing His flesh and blood soul to the grave, it was then in following the Holy Spirit just as we must that Jesus would exit the wilderness in the power of the Holy Spirit.

As stated, it is no different for us.

This is NOT accomplished by pleasing man, getting a degree, and then foolishly presenting your plan, your spiel as God's word. That is the voice of the damned. Disagree?

Maybe if I told you that you were chaff, not containing the seed, the power of life, would that help?

Debate it, argue it, and realize the strength of your argument is... deceased flesh and blood carnal reasoning. That is being as the Pharisees and scribes who crucified the Lord of Glory.

God's word...

Except we become converted from living after the flesh paying the price to live in the tangible Holy Ghost we cannot enter the Kingdom, the rule of Heaven.

The promises of God are to HIS children.

His children are those who walk not after the flesh, even in it being blood washed and forgiven. Instead they live by His Holy Spirit on His word. It is in becoming as a child, a child of God we participate in a realm that is not carnal flesh and blood.

This is extremely frustrating for the unconverted soul. Strong crying, strong praying occurs just as with our Lord is part of our learning to follow the unseen yet tangible Holy Spirit. In not giving up, the child of God will overcome as he learns to lay down all the Holy Spirit will not witness with His presence, His approval.

Short and simple, this is our faith in God that results in our being converted... Converted from walking after this *'body of sin'* into the liberty of walking as a *'son of God...'* Romans 8:1-2, and 14

Redundancy...

Acknowledging our need for a Savior, we declare that our life lived in the flesh, even forgiven flesh cannot satisfy God's holiness. As flesh and blood will not inherit the Kingdom of God, we bury the first-born natural man, and in our fulfilling righteousness as Jesus we commit to a New Life following the Holy Spirit.

> *"Therefore we are buried with him by baptism into death: that like as Christ was raised up from the dead by the glory of the Father, even so we also should walk in newness of life."* Romans 6

It is only in striving to remain in the tangible presence of God the Holy Spirit, that we are circumcised, cleaned up and converted.

This is the suffering with Christ to reign with Him.

This is the *'circumcision of the spirit'*.

Or... you can take man's traditions', their theologies that negate the power of God... does that sound familiar?

This fact remains, if we deny Him, He will deny us. God's word. As a disciple, we are to literally follow the person Jesus in and by the Holy Spirit.

The conversion for Jesus was not easy, just as it is through much tribulation we likewise enter the Kingdom of God.

Converting: Becoming as a Child?

In Matthew 18,
> "And Jesus called a little child unto him, and set him in
> the midst of them,
> And said, Verily I say unto you, Except ye be converted,
> and become as little children, ye shall not enter into the
> kingdom of heaven."

If we live by every word that proceeds from God's mouth, then what is our Lord telling us individually and personally?

What does becoming as a child have to do with you or me entering the Kingdom of Heaven?
> *What history does a child have?*
> *What experience does a child have?*

None to base their life on, right?

If we are a respected, mature established adult we may respond as Nicodemus. To become as a child would initially reflect vulnerability, a lack of understanding, and we definitely would not be someone to be... followed.

Do we recall Nicodemus' response to Jesus when he was told he must be born again, Nicodemus initial response was both carnal and ludicrous.

In our response to becoming as a child, we may echo Nicodemus' mentality;
> 'Gosh, how do I as an adult become as a child when I
> have completed my studies, and possess a degree in
> theology?'

Nicodemus, a better response might be,
> "Lord, I believe you, you are the Living Word and I
> thank you that through you I will understand how to be
> converted."

To be converted is to absolutely make a change, not hypothetical, not theoretical, not even in going to church religiously.

Remember that cadaver?

Remember that in being dead to her flesh she was in the presence of God?

Can we understand why those living after the flesh that will be

discarded are referred to in scripture as being already dead?
Too many questions?
Before God, the gospel of Jesus Christ is FOR the dead, that those who are dead may hear the voice of the Son of God and LIVE!!! Amen?
Wrong?
That would involve our being converted from following after the flesh to be raised up and seated at God's right hand from walking in, living in God's presence through abiding in His Holy Spirit. That will involve our becoming as a child and learning to follow the Holy Ghost, hence...
Our need to be crucified with Christ, buried with Him, and be converted. It cannot be put any simpler.
Still disagree?
Then why in God's name did the disciples FOLLOW the Lord for 3 ½ years BEFORE being told they were clean (born of water?) through the word they received?
Are we so blind, so self-centered from following the God of this world that we cannot grasp this simple concept? If so, it is because our *'righteousness'* precludes God's righteousness.
If the self-righteous *'Churchian'* in their knowledge, as the Pharisees believe they ALREADY have life they will denounce Jesus Christ personally THROUGH their resisting, rejecting the Holy Spirit.
That would be them abiding in the *'false vine'* that the Great Whore offers.
That false vine is believing your flesh and blood carnal soul is saved.
I AM tempering this pastor, your inability to understand God's word is based in your dead soul, your very own personal intimate fallen beast that validates your flesh and blood soul with its master.
Again... again recall the first Adam was made a living soul, and the Last Adam is a life giving spirit. Hold that truth, retain it, and secure it meditating it in your conscious thought-life.

Churchianity's Religious Lifestyle

That is where we hear the Great Whore's ministers preaching Romans 7 as OUR testimony on this earth.

We hear that Romans 7, is a description of our earthly life, because the one preaching and teaching that lie is dead in sin. Being carnally minded he is not only in bondage, but hostile to God and His Holy Spirit.

Again, what can he teach you?

To struggle as he does?

Why would anyone desire to live a life of frustration and defeat and then tell others that is God's plan for an abundant life?!!

My God, can we grasp this???!!!

What is the difference between Romans 7 the *'body of this death'* and the liberty of Romans 8?

Could this *'body of this death'* also be the *'body of sin'* Jesus died in the likeness of?

MAYBE??!!

It is right here in front of us...!!!!!

> *"There is therefore now no condemnation to them which are in Christ Jesus, who walk not after the flesh, but after the Spirit.*
> *For the law of the Spirit of life in Christ Jesus hath made me free from the law of sin and death."*

It took this young man coming to the end of his strength to encounter God's power.

It will not be any different for any disciple of Christ.

The path of the cross became his pathway to deliverance from a life of addiction, failure. His Romans 7 experience transitioned to a life walking with the Living God through abiding in Christ through the Holy Ghost!

Strongholds

Being taught by your seminary, having Satan's ministers of righteousness that you looked up to?

> *(Before God, I am being direct, the offer to get offended is being presented. The Holy Spirit will not always strive*

with the self-righteous children of another, no joke. My heart is breaking for my Father as His heart consumes me. The price He paid to have sons in the image of His Son was total. The cost was immense. He deserves sons who love HIM, who value HIS presence more than ANYTHING else.)

Do you for one minute believe obtaining man's approval replaces submitting to the Holy Spirit, bringing every thought into captivity and abiding in Him? Absent God's power, what authority has been bestowed on you and by whom? Jesus called the religious leaders who bestowed their approval on their disciples, fools. The accolades of men, their support? Those fools had already received their reward. Your graduation certificate or degree reveals you pleased man, that is your reward, <u>*enjoy*</u>...

Now you know the '*why*' you have NO power with God whatsoever.

In this, you should readily understand you have become twice the child of hell of those that taught you.

As the title of this book is clear, having taken God's vessels and used them for your personal gratification, your immediate future is extremely dim.

Absent God's spirit, absent His approval, absent His power, you are the chaff waiting the fire.... This is why, this is the reason why YOUR grief will match the limit of your stubbornness and obstinacy, this IS God's personal word, to you... My Father is NOT mocked, you DO know the rest of that scripture.

There is a fire burning in the heart of God, it is a consuming fire. If the reader possesses an ounce of wisdom, they will begin to live in God's Holy Spirit recognizing Him as their life.

Your soul? In its breathing, experiencing physical sensations, or watching shows are you enjoying those emotions??? Your enjoying your physical body calling that life, is actually your abiding... in death. You '*are an unconverted soul*'.

The Word, AND the Spirit

A young man in his mid-twenties was sitting by the cadaver of his wife who had been killed in a car accident in Central Oregon...

He got an education. He needed a life change. He learned a New Life, a New Creature was before him, but it would never be in the strength of his cadaver he had buried at HIS baptism. That old man which he had called his life was now considered dead. He had New Life he found living by God's Holy Spirit, on God's word. This is where we meet God, this is where the power of God manifests to deliver you...

> "...Then the angel that talked with me answered and said unto me, Knowest thou not what these be? And I said, No, my lord.
> Then he answered and spake unto me, saying, This is the WORD of the LORD unto Zerubbabel, saying, Not by might, nor by power, but BY MY SPIRIT, saith the LORD of hosts."

Romans 7? It becomes old news, ancient history as the *'body of sin'* is no longer the *'mountain of disobedience'* you wrestle with... why?

As the Apostle Paul tells us,

> "They that are Christ's have crucified the flesh with the affections and lusts."

CHOOSING GOD
Or Willfully Not...

At the small assembly in East Texas, the pastor stated, *'We are just flesh, aren't we? God gave us this body to enjoy!'*
The body the pastor referred to was the flesh and blood physical body. Yet in Adam dying to God, this physical body became his everything. His eyes opened, his awareness has changed, and now?
No longer does Adam or his descendants live by God's word. Adam is now a different creature, a dead man living by the knowledge of Good and Evil as it relates to his dead soul, i.e.., the life based in, and of the flesh. This is what we as his children call living. Life is based on how we feel, how we think, and if we enjoy our life. Our fulfillment is based on how well we are doing in relating to others, and comparatively how we are doing in our sphere we call business and family. God is an addition to our world, and we incorporate Him into our realm as needed, especially to obtain acceptance and validation from others.
As a sincere believer, in this *'living'* our prayers in desperation go unanswered, and we fall back relying on man's theologies to explain away illnesses, death, and *'why bad things happen to us'* when we know, or we believe in our hearts that we are *'such good people'*. Individuals who live with their *'life'* in this world being the gauge for their wellbeing reveal their soul as dead.
But in support of these dead souls, Adam's children now have teachings in their churches with men approved, man ordained ministers that teach enjoying their dead souls is real living.

Is that not cool, or what?

Churches and their pastors reinforce Satan's words that the flesh and blood soul is not really dead, but saved. If you follow their spiel you can live after your flesh freely. Additionally, if you contribute more, their god is going to bless you with more, and you can live as a god truly enjoying life with more... money!

Now those who identify as believers enjoying *'life'* no longer hear of their cross. Instead they have live music identified as worship teams, and casually dressed smooth-talking seminary degreed approved of men *'ministers'*. These professionals, the absolute best money can buy, deliver convincingly that smooth sweet hiss, *'Thou shall not surely die...!'*

One beloved pastor declared God's word is wrong. God was asking *waaay* too much when He told us to;

> *'...present our bodies a living sacrifice, holy, acceptable unto God, which is our reasonable service...'*

Our ministers?

They have a much better message than God, they have a better idea.

Presenting the god of this world's faux grace they declare that God telling us to be perfect, to walk holy is just asking too much of anyone. Their god's expressed love for your soul is all inclusive.

Just one issue, it is the wrong soul, it is the wrong god. It is a different Christ, it is a different gospel, with a totally different... eternity.

Yup, I checked.

Welcome to Dead Adam's World

These ministerial fellas remind me of that awesome guy Korah, and his doomed followers. Remember Korah, that *'everyone in Israel is holy'* guy? He was popular, and supporting him were 250, that is *two hundred and fifty* princes of renown, the popular men! These were those that knew him, from among the people, his very own prestigious and popular worship team.

They all could not be wrong, could they?

How can YOU disagree with... an entire movement???

Could disagreeing with the masses possibly be... loving the Lord more than your own life?

Everybody that was anybody loved Korah, amen?

That is true, until you consider Joshua, Caleb, and Moses who were not drawn away. These were those that risked being stoned, being the servants of God.

The others?

If you did not love Korah, that was being unrighteous, unholy, and not part of the 'IN' group, who would want that?!

My goodness, that man, Satan's *'minister of holiness'* had it going on!

Just one wee little issue. Just a small problem....

The problem, it was not God.

Nope... again, I checked. Here is the issue, those people that loved Korah, and his message that everyone is holy? In the Israelites loving Korah's message, in loving that Old Testament Babylonian message of grace they were following the wrong god. If we recall an earlier section in this book, we remember Adam eating the fruit of the Knowledge of Good and Evil. In that sin he began to live by a different word and in receiving that word, he received another spirit.

If we can hear it, that was adultery before God then, JUST as it is NOW...

If we think that was waaaay back then, and ancient history, God has a bit of news for you, it is...disturbing news. God had told Adam in Genesis 2:12,

> "but of the tree of the knowledge of good and evil you shall not eat, for in the day that you eat of it you shall surely die." NKJV

God does not change, right? If so, is it possible He gave us an identical very clear warning in the New Testament? God through His servant the Apostle Paul in Romans 8:13,

> "...For if you live according to the flesh you will die...."

NKJV

Note the similarity in the wording, there is a warning with a direct consequence attached, not future, not someday, but death occurs as the willful sin is committed.

Let's back up in Romans 8:1-2,

> "There is therefore now no condemnation to them which are in Christ Jesus, who walk not after the flesh, but after the Spirit.
> For the law of the Spirit of life in Christ Jesus hath made me free from the law of sin and death."

Now let's look at verse 3,

> "For what the law could not do, in that it was weak through the flesh, God sending his own Son in the likeness of sinful flesh, and for sin, condemned sin in the flesh..."

Note in verse one there is no condemnation to those in Christ identified as walking in the spirit. Paul was writing to those *'called to be saints'*, amen? Those called to be saints are being exhorted to walk in the Holy Spirit. They, as Adam, are hearing a warning. They, as us are being told, *'if they walk after the flesh they <u>will</u> die'*. Reading in Romans 8 just a little bit more we find this.

> "But ye are not in the flesh, but in the Spirit, if so be that the Spirit of God dwell in you. Now if any man have not the Spirit of Christ, he is none of his.
> And if Christ be in you, the body is dead because of sin; but the Spirit is life because of righteousness."

Here we are presented a direct contrast to being *'in the flesh'* versus *'being in the spirit'*. If we abide in Him, we are not in the flesh as we are walking following the tangible Holy Spirit and we have His indwelling presence.

We see our flesh as dead.

It is called the *'body of sin'* and we do not value its reputation, its glory, or men's approval.

In contrast we seek God's approval only as witnessed by His Holy Spirit.

That is how *'Jesus did it'*.
We identify with Jesus in His criminal's death, the crucifixion. We then count our body as dead through the Holy Spirit now being OUR LIFE!!
Correct? God's word that no flesh will glory in His presence now begins to make sense. We cannot abide in His presence and live pleasing our mind, will, and emotions, our soul. They are contrary to the Holy Ghost, that explains His absence, amen?
That is why we MUST pay the Great Whore for her message of grace that placates our... soul. If we believe our flesh and blood soul is saved, in our NOT paying the price to walk in the Holy Spirit, we choose the spirit of this world on the words that please our... selves.
We are at this moment warned just as Adam was warned.
We are told,
> *"...for if you live according to the flesh you will die...."*

Where in this do we see grace to willfully live apart from the tangible Holy Spirit, which is being in Christ? That reminds us of Galatians, the only epistle <u>NOT</u> written to those *'In Christ'* as these believers had actually fallen from grace.
How had they fallen?
They had fallen from grace when they had gone back into trying to please God in dead Adam, in his dirt bound living.
God's grace is... amazing. But we see God's grace being taught in error when man is excused to continue living a *'self-pleasing'* Christian religious life in the *'body of sin'*. The Apostle Paul in Romans three was accused of preaching grace for willful sin.
> *"And why not say, 'Let us do evil that good may come?'*
> *as we are slanderously reported and as some affirm that*
> *we say. Their condemnation is just."*

The Apostle Paul shut that down, and then declared his accuser's condemnation, or damnation as deserved. For those today that preach God's grace covers willful sin? As their brother Balaam, their future is anything but bright.
Jesus came in the *'likeness'* of sinful flesh and through Him God

condemned those who wilfully live after their flesh.
This identification belongs to Adam and his offspring, his flesh and blood descendants are those who living after the god of this world as they please their mind, will, and emotions.
Those who do so in church, even religiously, have ALREADY been condemned. Seriously...
Death has *already* entered through one man, Adam. Adam had died in wilfully receiving, and living by another's word.
There is a distinction to be made here.
Adam did not '*die to God*' and then in receiving another's word begin to '*live after the flesh*'.
Adam in receiving another word, another spirit did not resist it. Adam did not cry out to God. Adam began focusing on what was good, or evil in regards to his self. It was in this '*living for his self*' Adam died to God.
Why would this distinction be important?
There is a simple reason for us to live in the tangible Holy Spirit on God's revealed word... a very simple truth.
> *Our reality is God's spirit on His word we receive in our spirit...*

or..
> *Our reality is our body and mind being satisfied by the god of this world.*

This results from our choosing a word that pleases our soul.
> *We will choose one spirit or the other.*

We are at the present moment relating to what we perceive as our life, our reality based on a word we have received, whether it be God's word, or another's word, fact
What? Can we look at that again?
> *We are at the present moment relating to what we perceive as our life, our reality based on a word we have received, whether it be God's word, or another's word, fact.*

Our father Adam accepted another's word, and the spirit on that word. The result, he died.
When we believe God, we reverse this scenario in accepting

God's word. We then live by God's spirit on His word, and die to the god of this world.

We cannot die to ourselves and THEN live towards God. It is in choosing the tangible Holy Ghost on God's word for our reality, for our life that we die to the god of this world.

Adam died to God. In the same way he died, we die to the god of this world by exchanging the words we receive, our source for living from our mind, will, and emotions to the Holy Spirit's revealing God's word, personally to us...

This is an exchange that takes place when we *'believe'* in, or on the Lord Jesus Christ who took our place on Calvary. It includes our burying that *'old man'* in baptism to *"...put on the new man, which after God is created in righteousness and true holiness."*

It is in being *'in Christ'* that we are a New Creature, it is ONLY through abiding in Him that old things pass away, as we live a New Life IN the Holy Spirit. (Romans 8:13) We now see it is through Christ, through living in the Holy Spirit that God's grace abounds. This is not relying on our works, our social religious associations with others, but our Father, God Himself in and by the Holy Ghost.

That is real faith... in God.

This real faith is evidenced in the saints of old.

> *"But to him that worketh not, but believeth on him that justifieth the ungodly, his faith is counted for righteousness.*
>
> *Even as David also describeth the blessedness of the man, unto whom God imputeth righteousness without works,*
>
> *Saying, Blessed are they whose iniquities are forgiven, and whose sins are covered.*
>
> *Blessed is the man to whom the Lord will not impute sin."* Romans 4

That was always confusing to me, how do I *'not work'*? How do I enter the *'Rest'* God promises in Hebrews 3, and 4? It is through doing all I do as unto the Lord abiding, remaining in the conscious awareness of His presence.

That is being In Christ.
> *(That makes that religious spirit in you want to debate, right? You know better, amen? Powerless, impotent, self-righteous, you have your knowledge. That spirit wants to destroy you, repent and obtain deliverance. Wait on God, offer the acceptable sacrifice and be delivered.)*

As willful sin in the flesh is now seen as condemned, we with a heart after God *have a different* covenant. As we walk in the light of God's word as revealed by the Holy Spirit, any error that we would make is not imputed to us, that is the Gospel!

There is NO condemnation to those in Christ Jesus, who before God walk relating to Him in the Holy Spirit. However, if we sin willfully after receiving knowledge of the truth, this is not faith, it is not trust in God and there remains no more sacrifice for our sin.

For those who have been born again, filled with the Holy Spirit, and choose to not walk in the spirit, with this knowledge they are fallen from grace.

It is in self-pleasing that we put our back to the cross, returning to the tree of the Knowledge of Good and Evil and are now *'self-determining'* what is best for us. This results from our *'receiving another's word'* that please our self. This *self-comforting* excuses us before God, as the god of this world serves us an *'acceptable'* lie, just as he did Adam.

We who value our covenant with God can turn our hearts to God, turn from our own ways, and seek HIS will, HIS purpose, choosing to abide in Him.

At this point we are totally forgiven, as all we have ever done is attributed to our walking in the flesh, and that price was paid at Calvary!!!

Endeavoring, dropping all our carnal concerns that hinder us from abiding in the Holy Spirit is being IN Christ, and there is no condemnation!!!

This abiding comes at a cost, the cross where the body born of the will of man is counted dead, having no more effect on the

child born of God.
Plain Spoken Jesus In John 12,
> *"He that loveth his life shall lose it; and he that hateth his life in this world shall keep it unto life eternal."*

This is clear, so let us read a bit farther.
> *"Now is the judgment of this world: now shall the prince of this world be cast out."*

God judged the first world by the faith of one man, Noah. The prince of this world was shut down in the flood as his access point through every living soul perished. These were the *'children of wrath'* of Noah's generation. The only souls that remained were on the ark. This is a clue as to *'how'* the prince of this world shall be *'cast out'*.

Do we recall the *'last enemy that will be destroyed?'*

Amazing... amen? Possessing eternal life is walking in the Holy Spirit, in faith towards God.

When the *'believer'* no longer walks according to his mind, will, or emotions but lives by every word that proceedeth from God's mouth, the enemy's access point to that *'believer'* is shut down.

That believer is *'dead'*.

They are buried with Christ, risen and seated at the right hand of God...!

Note the wording, *"... now shall the prince of this world be cast out."*

The word *'shall'* is not to be confused with *'is'*. Satan's authority with us is as it was with Adam.

Satan HAD to enlist Adam's cooperation in order to destroy his life, and occupy Adam's inheritance.

In order for Satan to work in the *'believer's'* life and destroy in the believer's home the believer MUST cooperate with him. Satan has no power when the *'believer'* is walking in the tangible Holy Ghost, not after his mind, will, emotions, the seeing of the eyes, the hearing of the ears.

When the *'believer'* is a dead man, he is present with the Lord enjoying God's presence in the Holy Spirit...

That is the result of faith in God, His word, not a mental decision based on a soul pleasing option.

God judged the old world by the faith of Noah. Noah revealed that real faith in the unseen God, real-time trust in Him had value. Remember in Genesis 6 God told Noah *"...the end of all flesh is come before me"?'*

God has present-tense judged this world by the faith of one man again, His Son, Jesus Christ. Jesus revealed and does reveal that real faith in the unseen God, real-time trust in Him has value. The condemnation of walking after the flesh is now revealed from Noah to Jesus Christ. Again, through Jesus Christ those who trust in Him will no longer live after their dead, carnal, flesh and blood soul. It is blatant stupidity to think wilfully living after the flesh in any manner correlates to pleasing God.

It was through trusting in the One able to save Him from death, that Jesus was raised from the dead and lives forevermore.

Taking God's Holy Spirit on God's revealed word as life, the path is revealed for us to walk with God pleasing Him. Just as Noah's family was saved. Those born of God through Jesus Christ are preserved with Him, through abiding IN Him.

How?

A Simple U-Turn?

When Adam sinned, Adam died. His body's breath, appetite, sensations became his.... death. Alienated from God, Adam *'lived'* in death believing his physical existence was life.

The way into the heart of God, is our doing a literal *'U-Turn'*.

We take that journey back to God, we deny the lie that our body is our life and *take God's word as our reality.*

We actually in reality count our *'body of sin'* as dead, crucified with Christ. Bringing every word, every thought in to obedience is our shutting down Satan's access. This occurs as we consume God's word, learn to abide in Christ remaining in the Holy Spirit through personal faith in God.

This is when we begin to truly live. That is not too hard to grasp, amen?

For dead Adam to live, Adam would have to die to every word that was not from His Father manifesting through his dead soul.

We as his flesh and blood offspring would need to do the same....

Those who are crucified with Christ see their bodies as dead, physically. Their ONLY life is in Christ, abiding in the Holy Spirit the tangible presence of God. This is walking in the spirit. This is abiding in Christ. Recall that word to the eleven disciples to abide in Him?

That word was *not spoken to the five thousand, the seventy, nor the twelve*, but to those eleven men who had left all. They had been cleaned through the word that Jesus spoke, and these eleven would soon receive the Holy Spirit in greater capacity. Their life was Christ.

This world IS judged.

Sin in the flesh IS condemned.

Life IS FOUND in the tangible Holy Spirit.

Following Satan's ministers of righteousness will result in pleasing one's self through possessing a carnal mind that is alien to the Holy Spirit and hostile to God. The comfort and enjoyment of belonging to your ministry's group is your (adulterous soul's) reward.

God? He is unmoved. Recall He destroyed the world once being grieved at His heart?

The Prophet EVERYONE Loved....

Do we remember the prophet, that
man that everyone loved?

We do recall him, we may even know and fellowship him. He was the false prophet. He speaks the words of the god of this world as though they were of God. His *'godly'* presentations carry the spirit that soothes your emotions, your mind, convincing you that your dead soul really is a good person. The message of the cross is Jesus died so you do not have to. People flock to hear him, with multiple shows being performed on Sunday all in the name of God.

This is Babylon, she is drunk on the blood, the souls of the saints, and if they do not depart her they will share in her judgement.

The man of God, the true prophet, or priest? God's men? The love for them was typically not much at all. Actually the prophets God sent were not popular at all... until they were dead.

Then? After they were dead, usually for years, these holy men of God were then revered.

If a man of God desired accolades, it could not be in THIS life! Talk about delayed gratification!

When did God ever call a man to tell everybody they were doing good? The men whom God called typically were rejected, scorned, made fun of and killed. We are not limiting these men to the Old Testament, we are also looking at those the Lord Jesus sent.

These men? Sometimes, they were really strange, one dressed differently and lived on bugs and wild honey. Our Lord was called a glutton and a 'winebibber'. Others were 'smart-mouthed,' even a bit... lippy. Possibly seen as sarcastic, or caustic, like Micaiah.

Micaiah

All the false prophets, this awesome and appreciated covenant group of followers had prophesied King Ahab's great success against Ramothgilead. Like Korah, Ahab had an awesome support group. They were covenant supporters, to them?

King Ahab could do no wrong...

King Ahab had a great home with a killer wife! She fulfilled his desires, no matter the cost... to someone else.

But King Jehoshaphat wanted another opinion.

So, the prophet Micaiah was sent for.

Micaiah had not been involved up to this point, nor was he hard to find. Micaiah was in prison. We need to understand this man of God had this stigma of being a *'con,'* judging him after the flesh was a no-brainer.

So this prisoner Micaiah was brought before King Ahab and King Jehosaphat.

He chimed in with the false prophets and told the King, (slightly paraphrased), *'Go ahead, you got this big guy!'*

King Ahab caught the message, and the tone. King Ahab told King Jehoshaphat, *'See what I told you, this guy will not prophesy anything good to me'.*

When King Ahab asked for the truth, he got it. It was not good news, it was disturbing to this self-ruled man. Micaiah related,

> *"I saw all Israel scattered upon the hills, as sheep that have not a shepherd: and the LORD said, These have no master..."*

This was not what King Ahab wanted to hear. Micaiah told King Ahab if he went to war, King Ahab was a dead man.

King Ahab had Micaiah thrown back in prison with orders to feed him with the bread of affliction until he returned. Even that did not stop Micaiah. In parting he told King Ahab,

> *'If you come back, I did not hear from the Lord'.*

Talk about doubling down! He was just a tad bit lippy, but then again, Micaiah knew who he was hearing, he knew God's word was sure.

Prison was preferred over being a king/pastor/teacher/man pleaser. Micaiah goes down in history as an awesome man of God!!!! The word of God could not, would not be broken.

Being a man of God, Micaiah was looking to God for His honor, His reward. Man's approval, even a king's approval was not desired.

Today?

We have multiple men who tell us how great we ALL are doing. The question for us is whether we are as Ahab, do we seek out those who tell us what we desire to hear? If so, we can share his end also. God was gracious to Ahab, extremely gracious to a man who tops the list of wicked kings.

Understand that the false prophets spoke words that bore

witness *to the spirit Ahab followed.*
Unknown to Ahab, this spirit had Ahab's destruction and the destruction of his followers in mind.
This spirit is the same spirit that works through the self-called pastor and his ministry team pleasing your first-born never to be redeemed flesh and blood soul. Enjoying *'this spirit'* before God is adultery.
Babylon, the name itself means *'confusion'*. Can we grasp that God's grace is being confused with God's patience by the pastoral Ahab?
Unknowing, as Ahab the path he is on is destruction.
Should we heed the spirit of God telling us to depart her so as to not partake of her plagues? But the issue that should concern us is this.
Per God's word, scripturally at some point God will honor our choice, and respect our evil heart's decision in choosing to follow man, not our Heavenly Father, personally.
King Ahab's sorrowfulness moved God at one point, King Hezekiah's sorrowing also moved God, but Esau?
No such... grace.
Trading your future for a bowl of beans, is like... just stupid.
Why was Esau unable to find a place of repentance?
Esau is a *'type'* of the first-born undisciplined soul. This soul will trade an eternity with God, for a life of self-gratification.
The spirit that worked through Esau also works through the *'body of sin'* is that *'Whore'* that intoxicated your *'feelings'* in the bloodstream. It will convince you that you can satisfy your flesh and still inherit.
It is a liar. Believing it, it being as dense, obtuse and stupid, as Esau. But I suppose, the *'flavor'* is to die for, amen?
Hard to hear?
Jesus' dead body being hoisted on the tree exposes the actual issue. The body of Christ with its blood drained out reveals both the problem, and the solution.
We are to find our life in the Holy Ghost or knowingly now choose death, living after our precious dead soul. Fact.

Despising your inheritance, is glorifying yourself to be a minister instead of learning to abide in Christ. It has been said that walking in the Holy Spirit is like being pregnant, you either are, or you are not. There is no balance you can achieve with God having one foot in the world, and one in Christ.

Before God, this is the message of the cross, take it up, or leave it.

That in itself determines the *"grace of God"* on your next few days....

In Noah's day, Adam's descendants resisted God's striving with them. Their choice to live as if there was no pending judgement was ultimately honored by God.

Marrying, giving in marriage, planting, building was taking place until the flood took them all away.

They had their 'Mene, Mene, Tekel, Upharsin' moment, amen? Likewise, we can live out the days of our flesh, and spend our time pleasing the creature we told God we buried in baptism. We can enjoy this body as if it is our life. We can attend funerals for others and look away, maintaining our blindness to our dead soul's future. We can value this body which in function is as the chaff or husk that is discarded. In so doing we despise the cross and crucify the Son of God afresh living as if His death was unnecessary for us.

This is our despising the grace of God, but then again, if this is the message we hear and the message we love? It is because it resonates with our self-pleasing ways.

The next word we will hear has quite a different message.

> *"...He that is unjust, let him be unjust still: and he which is filthy, let him be filthy still: and he that is righteous, let him be righteous still: and he that is holy, let him be holy still." Revelation 22*

As Esau, we may think our decisions are reversible, we can cross back over THAT bridge when we get to it. We may believe we can repent... later. The only problem is this; God is telling us THERE IS NO BRIDGE to cross back over, just a fearful looking forward to God's righteous judgement. This judgement results from our following a man who tells us what we want to hear, just as Ahab listened to the false prophets.

Our following these false prophets who tell us it is okay to live in and after the flesh, will in no way, change our future for the better.

Adam tried telling God that someone else had given him the forbidden fruit, that attempted distraction did not work. Believing we can stand before God and fault a smooth-talking pastor for our decision, is equally as foolish. We will not successfully patronize God.

The Joking Minister

> *"Behold, I am against them that prophesy false dreams, saith the LORD, and do tell them, and cause my people to err by their lies, and by their lightness; yet I sent them not, nor commanded them: therefore they shall not profit this people at all, saith the LORD." Jeremiah 23*

Unsent by God, the pastor whose humor and jokes make you laugh as you become comfortable? It is not the Holy Spirit, Jesus is not his lord. You are being set-up regardless of his Korah demeanor and acceptance by renowned men.

Joking was never part of Jesus ministry. Lightness in 1 Corinthians 1 is defined as *'levity, fickleness of mind'*. In Jeremiah it comes from the root word meaning *'frothy, reckless, and wanton'*.

Do either of these definitions fit the Holy Spirit?

Why would someone speaking as the oracle of God by the Holy Ghost even begin to entertain you?

The fruit of the spirit is (1) righteousness, (2) peace and (3) joy IN the Holy Ghost. There is an order to that beginning with right standing with God. Right standing with God results in peace with God, amen? The result is the joy of standing before God cleansed 100% of ALL sin, ALL unrighteousness, in his very presence. Psalms 16,

> *"Thou wilt shew me the path of life: In thy presence is fulness of joy..."*

This takes us back to abiding in the tangible Holy Spirit, the presence of God! Per Proverbs 24, the thought of foolishness is sin. I do understand, I was raised with joking, with acceptance being found in making others laugh.

I did not understand it was based in fear. Joking, *'cutting up'*, or *'breaking the ice'* was putting others at ease with me avoiding any confrontation.

Ministers who use *'lightness'*, which is humor (levity) operate opposing God's Holy Spirit.

The Holy Spirit was sent to convict the world of sin, righteousness and judgement.

Can we find lightness in Him?

The world? It is within the walls of the church, just as it was in the temple, John 7:7-8. In contrast to those who love the preeminence, the Apostle Paul told those at Corinth,

> *"For I determined not to know anything among you,*
> *save Jesus Christ, and him crucified.*
> *And I was with you in weakness, and in fear, and in*
> *much trembling.*
> *And my speech and my preaching was not with enticing*
> *words of man's wisdom, but in demonstration of the*
> *Spirit and of power:*
> *That your faith should not stand in the wisdom of men,*
> *but in the power of God."*

God's word is life. Death reigned from Adam to Moses, it was then that God delivered His word by which man could... 'live'. Jesus is the living word of God made flesh, He is made unto us right standing with God, and in this righteousness we find the path of life in the Holy Spirit.

Jesus is not a joke, those who abide in Him are focused on pleasing Him, not placating man.

If those who present themselves as *'ministers of God'* are pleasing men, making them comfortable through humor, they cannot be the servants of God.

We need to understand God's word as revealed by the Holy Ghost, we need desperately to realize who it is with whom we

have to do.
> "...but to this man will I look, even to him that is poor and of a contrite spirit, and trembleth at my word."
> Isaiah 66

The life we choose is our decision.

God is NO respecter of persons, as God does not respect one person above another. We can choose God, choose to abide in the tangible Holy Ghost, or not. Either way, our response to God can never be...

> *"I did not know."*

Instead it will be,

> *"I was too self-centered, too self-absorbed to humble myself and seek you. I had more important things to do than spending time with you."*

The truth is, we will stand before our Lord, and answer for our willful choice regarding choosing life, or not.

> *Will we desire that God at THAT moment disregard the decision we make at THIS moment?*

ORDAINED
By God? Or Man?

What are the qualifications needed to be a church *'Leader?'* What are the requirements to be a Pastor, Youth Pastor, or an assistant Pastor? A doctorate? A diploma or degree from a seminary or Bible school? Is there the need for experience and referrals? If so, from whom? What do all these have in common?

They are all earned from men whom the applicant respected, or valued their approval. Obtaining their recommendation, would also be obtaining the approval of those they could refer him to. This would increase his employability, qualifying his ability to serve those paying him. This is his start in building his... ministry.

Do we hear any warning bells?

No?

The fact is, God is not a part of this process.

Do we disagree?

I would disagree also, if I accepted the approval of men, over the approval of God. The difference between the two is going to be made abundantly clear. If God is not part of this process, how could we accept any resulting message from them, as from Jesus Christ?

In Galatians, the apostle Paul addresses those who preach another gospel and then he states this,

> *"For do I now persuade men, or God? or do I seek to please men? for if I yet pleased men, I should not be the servant of Christ."*

Jesus through His Apostle is plain spoken. Yet, ignoring what

God is telling us, ministers readily accept pleasing men is acceptable. They are wilfully oblivious to the fact that in pleasing men, they cannot be the servant of God. They create resumes boldly persuading men and their churches to hire them based on their giftings, and their education.
This has nothing to do with God as Jesus Christ becomes the faceless someone they learn to market.
If we have no issue with this, we do have an issue with God as we cannot have it both ways.
Religiously, hypocritically we can do scriptural gymnastics, and state we went to school to...
> "Study to shew thyself approved unto God, a workman that needeth not to be ashamed, rightly dividing the word of truth."

But then, we have to ignore the text that speaks of presenting ourselves approved to God being without shame before Him. *'Approved unto God'* cannot be apart from what we just heard Paul tell Timothy,
> "...For if we be dead with him, we shall also live with him:
> If we suffer, we shall also reign with him: if we deny him, he also will deny us..."

Paul is reminding Timothy, and us that we were crucified with Christ, buried with Him, as in being dead.
This death refers to the death of our first soul, our reckoning it dead. This must happen before we can abide in the tangible Holy Spirit on God's word IN US as our life. Tangible? Yes, the conscious awareness of God, His Holy Spirit in our living present-day, present-tense reality. This would involve our natural soul suffering as God will never join in the self-ruled, self-willed, soul-life.
In a small Colorado mountain town a young man related he had attended an *'Open House'* at a seminary. In that event he was told to *'follow the Holy Spirit'*.
Their worship team *'rocked out'* their music, the sell was on...
Upon leaving, they asked him if had any plans on attending the

seminary/bible college. He replied he did not sense the Holy Spirit leading him to attend.

Their response?

You are not supposed to be led by emotions, you are to walk by faith. In resisting the Holy Spirit, in being religious *they labeled God the Holy Spirit an emotion.*

The Holy Spirit to them was just a... *'feeling'* that was in their way of selling the school's curriculum.

This was the work of the enemy to destroy a child of God when the Holy Spirit instructed him to not subscribe to their program.

It is in this darkness as the Pharisees and the scribes we cannot recognize or even know God.

Our Adamic soul loves being pleasured. The god of this world is adept at pleasuring our soul with the message of there is no cost, (*other than paying its 'Great Whore'*) no suffering needed or implied. In following a fallen spirit on a religious word we then can focus on our ministry, not the Kingdom of God or His Christ.

We have *'bent a knee'* and swallowed a lie. As Adam, our life in this body is our glory, and our reward, so we rock on....

Not abiding in Christ, not suffering with Him, is our choosing to please what we told God, we had buried in baptism.

Once we know this, this is the equivalent to lying to the Holy Ghost...

This is denying Christ, and He likewise present-tense denies those liars who prefer their dead soul over Him. God witnesses His word, with His tangible Holy Spirit as the reality of the New Creature. As no flesh will glory in His presence this would involve our suffering just as He suffered. Letting this mind be in us which was in Christ means we receive no glory. The reality that no flesh can glory in His presence, reveals that apart from His tangible Holy Spirit, we relish living after our flesh. This is abiding in death.

It really is NOT that hard to put together, amen?

True repentance is paying the price to REMAIN in the presence of the Holy Spirit.

That is death to the natural man.

Try it, pay the price to abide in Him one hour. Take His word back to Him, privately. Thank Him that He is made unto you righteousness, believe that all manner of sin and unrighteousness is cleansed by what He did at Calvary. Thank HIM! Stay with Him, if His presence lifts, learn to follow Him, learn where His heart is...

This is the strait gate. Learn to follow Him in prayer, then never end the prayer. Stay with Him, learn to be led through following. Because, so very simply, how can we be led, if we do not follow?

Does Psalm 23 make sense now? He cannot be OUR shepherd, if we will not follow Him...

This is the suffering of dying to self, this is the narrow path to reigning as flesh and blood will not, and cannot inherit the Kingdom of God.

Our rejecting suffering is our attempt to offer back to God what was cursed on Calvary. As Cain, offering to God something from what God has cursed is not... intelligent.

We have all offered to God something God did not accept.

The question is, did we change what we were offering, or did we walk away from God's presence as Cain? Cain departed the presence of God, and built his walled city. Have we learned to live apart from the Holy Spirit calling it faith? That is our 'walled city'.

What we really need to change is our offering. We need to understand that our reputation, our identity, all we ever were in this body was crucified with Christ. The ONLY life we have is IN HIS PRESENCE.

If we reject this truth, when God's Holy Spirit does not accept our self-centered effort at prayer, we will walk away making religious excuses and quoting scriptures to placate our dead soul.

Cain? He now has us as his peers.

What is it we religiously *'think'* God should do when we offer back to Him, what put Jesus on Calvary in the first place, declaring we are relying on His grace?

The Local Church; God's View

Do we recall the Pharisees? The scribes? The very mention of these two religious stereotypes bring to mind hypocrisy and religious pride. Yet, these men knew God's word, inside and out.

Righteous in themselves, recognized righteous by their peers, being obedient to God's word outwardly they went to great lengths to *'walk the line'*. Being directly descended from Abraham, they prided themselves as being physically chosen of God.

They were powerless with God, and they accepted that *without questioning it......*

Wow... this does sounds familiar, right?

There was no question, because it was their power with men that was their *'meat'*, and their *bread and butter*. The people feared them for their ability to *'put them out'* of the temple.

These white washed sepulchers served their own selves. as they presented God's word to establish their *'ministry'*. This enabled them to be revered, respected by... man.

God's view is from a different perspective than man's self-centered view, always.

Jeremiah spoke of men such as these, but the reference God uses was lost, and will be lost on self-centered, self-justifying, and self-approving ministry *'types'*. These are men who believe God's word applies to someone else, not them. They study God's word to apply to others, but to them?

Their own heart is established in knowledge which is their great darkness.

God's word was lost on the Pharisees and scribes as they religiously burdened others and walked free, the god of this world satisfying their lost souls.

Today it is the same, but today the spirit that murdered our Lord sells its twisted version of Jesus to seduce them...

Jeremiah joins Isaiah and Ezekiel as God tells him He cannot find ONE man to stand before Him. To Ezekiel it was to find <u>one man</u> to stand in the gap. To Isaiah the challenge was to find <u>one man</u> that was not a hypocrite, and to Jeremiah, just find <u>one man</u> that seeks the truth.

In Jeremiah 5, it gets ugly, real ugly.

> *"Run ye to and fro through the streets of Jerusalem, and see now, and know, and seek in the broad places thereof, if ye can find a man, if there be any that executeth judgment, that seeketh the truth; and I will pardon it." (verse 1)*

This is where it sounds... bad.

> *"How shall I pardon thee for this? thy children have forsaken me, and sworn by them that are no gods: when I had fed them to the full, they then committed adultery, and assembled themselves by troops in the harlots' houses." (verse 7)*

It looks bad, real bad as it looks like they were all guilty of meeting up at a *'house of ill repute'*. But sexual immorality does not make sense as these people prided themselves on seeking God and delighting to know His ways...

> *"Yet they seek me daily, and delight to know my ways, as a nation that did righteousness, and forsook not the ordinance of their God: they ask of me the ordinances of justice; they take delight in approaching to God." Isaiah 58*

That sounds like the cultural church and its worship service, right? Offensive? God showed Jeremiah these hypocrites who made a pretense of loving Him as assembling in whorehouses. In Jeremiah it appears they may be assembling in houses of idolatry. Yet an idol is anything, anyone you would look to for satisfying your needs, or validating your worth. Whether they attended a synagogue, or a temple for idols, there was no distinction made by God.

In attending their assemblies they obtained approval one from another, yet none from... God.

Their houses of whoredom were their synagogues, their solemn assemblies.

Their whoredom?

In receiving accolades and approval from one another, they were committing adultery entertaining fallen spirits that pleasured them in their carnal, flesh and blood self-serving meetings.

Today this is the same whorehouse where believers are entertained by the god of this world in their soul-pleasing religion with their *'paid for'* ministers.

Extreme?

> *How can it be the house of God, when Jesus Christ is expected to play second or third fiddle to your beloved pastor?*

The price Jesus paid *was His own soul poured out.*

The price your pastor paid *was his tuition.*

Knowing God's word, does not make your church leader holy, or righteous, or even God sent, amen? He was hired. Or possibly he is the *'founding pastor'* that built his own house.

Wow, that explains a great deal, amen?!!!

Rude?

Ungodly, unrighteous, spiritually they are in bed writhing with their mother, Babylon.

Beyond disgusting, their sin as Sodoms has reached in to heaven, God's word. Maybe now we can better understand that whoremongers will not enter God's kingdom. They will continually be distressed.

Where there was faux victory, it is being removed.

Where there was patience, it is *'right now'* gone.

This is not funny, this is not a misprint.

Where they are blissfully united with the Great Whore manifesting her glory, is where the issues are beginning to manifest....

This all seems like gross error until we read Revelation 17 and get a clear picture.

> "And upon her forehead was a name written, MYSTERY,

BABYLON THE GREAT, THE MOTHER OF HARLOTS AND ABOMINATIONS OF THE EARTH. And I saw the woman drunken with the blood of the saints, and with the blood of the martyrs of Jesus: and when I saw her, I wondered with great admiration."

Martyrs? As stated prior, that word applies to those who are the witnesses of Christ, as well as those who have been slain for their testimony. She is drunk on them as they enjoy their flesh and blood first-born soul being pleasured in her little whorehouses, the local churches.

Jeremiah saw Babylon's daughters as the assemblies of men, assembling as troops, all arranged and partaking of the *'service order'* that gave them pleasure in living apart from the living God. It sounds like people attending an early service, followed by those who attend later services, as Jeremiah declared they...

"...assembled themselves by troops in the harlots' houses."

Absent the tangible Holy Spirit, actively resisting Him in their heart as they sought their own glory, God abolished the Israelites place sending them into Babylon telling them to just go ahead and plan on dying there.

God has not changed.

It is no different today as pastors perform their job serving their own careers, ordained by man, sent and approved by man. Not serving God they are absent His authority.

Their authority? It is given by those who pay these hirelings their wages. As your beloved pastor is not serving God, not representing God, those who follow him then seek their own ministry, their own place. They desire the microphone, to be as him, a self-validated, man-pleasing somebody. And if accepted, as Balaam they can partake of the King's 10%.

How many in your assembly have branched off, wanting to be the *'head of their own church'*? They were following the lead dog's example, amen? Their desire? It has nothing to do with Christ in you. Or you as God's child being transformed into the image of Christ by the Holy Spirit. Jeremiah?

You nailed it.

Whoremongers in whorehouses...
It is no more different today than Judas selling his Jesus...

Different, Peculiar

However, a servant of God, a disciple of Christ will follow their Lord. Jesus had told His disciples to take up their cross, and if they did not hate their life, their life in this world, they could not follow Him.

This is not the mainstream gospel message we hear, is it? Why? There is NO money in that message.

But to those that receive it? It contains the power of God... Jesus' message has not changed.

Again, God has not changed.

The *"believer"* has been marketed a *'soul-pleasing'* message and they have loved it, as they are now approved to live pleasing their-selves. In Jeremiah, God states the ministry rules by their own force, and the people love it...

So this next Sunday.... if you are so inclined, you can head out to your local church service and once more be *'serviced'* by the woman God hates. Her sins are as Sodom, as you go just keep that in mind....

If we disagree?

At what point does anyone stop, do a FULL stop, and request that everyone break their hearts, humble themselves and wait upon the Living unseen God?

At what point does the *'leader'* declare I am NOT the man in charge, sit down and break before God asking the risen Lord Jesus to have His way, by the Holy Spirit.

One Colorado *'pastor'* told me he could not, because the *'pressure to get things going was too great'*. If that sounds like god, it is because it is his god, the god of this world...

And it is a different spirit that is over that assembly, not the Holy Spirit of God....

As you attend your local assembly, remember to put in your illegitimate tithes and your love-offerings Sunday, the whore and her lover you adore that she is joined to are counting on it.

Judgement Has Begun at God's House

Why? Well, for all the reasons mentioned above, and more below. Judgement does not happen without God having allowed time for the ill-advised, the feeble-minded, and the downright rebellious to come to their senses.

Yet once the judgement is set in motion, and put into play, there is no recourse.

Once the flood began, once Sodom was being lit up, once the Romans surrounded Jerusalem, it was like Judas praying for the rope to break.

There was no stopping point, until the last pence was exacted. To Timothy at Thessalonica, Paul had spoken of the doomed, we will also see this in Isaiah, Jeremiah and Ezekiel. Today's unrepentant church pastors, leaders are just as doomed as the Temple leaders when judgement began at God's house back then.

We could just read over these prophets of God and look for something more pleasing, but that would evidence our willful stupidity, amen? Plain words? I cannot get any plainer, and my wording is actually tempered.

Using third-grade terms is on purpose, so the high-minded knowledgeable degreed schmart hypocrites have an elementary reason to critique this writing.

Before God, the Lord Jesus Christ is issuing the sternest, clearest, and most direct warning possible. Ignore it, and be as the chaff that is swept into the fire without remorse, grieving, or care.

Trash, is trash.

Just as gender-equality began in the church leader's home, spread to the church and became gender-confusion in the world; The spirit of the anti-Christ has its roots in the pulpit, the leadership of our local cultural church. The cultural church has replaced the temple as Satan's tool in the world...

Disagree, again?

In Israel, the Jewish Temple of God was the very source of the violence that filled the land.

> *"Then he said unto me, Hast thou seen this, O son of man? Is it a light thing to the house of Judah that they commit the abominations which they commit here (the inner court)? for they have filled the land with violence, and have returned to provoke me to anger: and, lo, they put the branch to their nose." Ezekiel 8*

In Isaiah 9, we hear the same message,

> *"Therefore the LORD will cut off from Israel head and tail, branch and rush, in one day.*
> *The ancient and honourable, he is the head; and the prophet that teacheth lies, he is the tail.   For the leaders of this people cause them to err; and they that are led of them are destroyed."*

Years prior during Eli's ministry, through Eli's sons Israel was taught to disrespect the offerings to God, with sexual immorality appearing, well... acceptable. Judgement followed, and the Ark of the Covenant, the presence of God was lost. Eli's neck was broken, Eli died. Eli's sons also died on that very same day.

Similarly, God's judgement in Ezekiel began at His house.

> *"Cause them that have charge over the city to draw near, even every man with his destroying weapon in his hand.*
> *And behold, six men came from the way of the higher gate, which lieth toward the north, and every man a slaughter weapon in his hand..." Ezekiel 9:1-2*

> *"...and begin at my sanctuary. Then they began at the ancient men which were before the house."*
> *Ezekiel 9:6*

To say the church, the present day business called the 'house of God' is excluded from this pattern, is willfully being part of the problem. This ignorance starts first in the educated knowledgeable pride filled stubborn heart, second it is excused in the home, and thirdly, it manifests in the assembly.

Walking Away
When the Holy Spirit is telling us, warning us to stop, but we will not? It is because ceasing the enjoyment of what we are doing is too high a price to pay. As Judas, someone has filled our heart. This is our enjoying adultery, our joining the whore in fornication with what we told God we buried in baptism. This occurs in our physical bloodstream as we crucify the Son of God afresh. The heart rapidly beating, the skin becoming flushed, and we thought it was just a pleasurable emotion? It is the spirit of this world infusing your bloodstream, and literal spiritual adultery is manifesting physically.
Not having crucified the flesh, not being buried with Christ, now we are not resisting the devil, but intertwined with him. To experience this, then identify the tangible Holy Spirit as an identical *'emotion'* is blasphemy of the Holy Spirit. It is *'dooming'* our own soul. Comparing the Holy Spirit to an unclean spirit pleasuring our soul is worse than committing spiritual adultery. The flesh and blood natural soul is the path for imputed sin, judgement to work death in our body. Having sown to the flesh in our bloodstream with her, corruption will be reaped in our bloodstream.
Recall King Herod?
Heretical?
Too much?
Is God mocked, as you have sown, shall you not also reap?
This is not a message of condemnation, it is a message to depart her, come out of her, pay your vows, bury that old man of sin, and be raised in Christ in the Holy Ghost. That is a message of redemption, ignore it and reap...
Bastards in the pulpit will pretend, or present they are led by God as they are absent the approval of God in their heart, and home. In loving the honor of men, they will present testimonies of *'miracles'*, healings to validate their ministry. Claiming to be humble participants, it is a sell job. Jesus is not buying it any more than He did with Korah. Being gifted as

Balaam, does not mean it is God the *'gifted'* man is serving.
> *"Thou hast ascended on high, thou hast led captivity captive: thou hast received gifts for men; yea, for the rebellious also, that the LORD God might dwell among them." Psalms 68:18*

False apostles, false prophets, false teachers are operating apart from being yielded to and walking in union with God, the Holy Spirit. They are not God's sons, as they take the approval of men, and those precious payments for services rendered as God's blessing. Jesus speaks plainly,
> *"Many will say to me in that day, Lord, Lord, have we not prophesied in thy name? and in thy name have cast out devils? and in thy name done many wonderful works? And then will I profess unto them, I never knew you: depart from me, ye that work iniquity." Matthew 7*

This was and is today the cultural church. Church leaders manipulate believers they regard as *'these people'*. I have met multiple pastors who label their church members as being without understanding. This attitude that the attendees are stupid is played out in the service order. Service planners intentionally *'play the believer'*.

They will orchestrate upbeat music and watch you dance, they will render somber, reflective music and watch you move to meditative worship.

You are being played.

It is in their service order where they set you up with a transition to worship as Babylonian's image of her *'man of god'* steps in.

This is the moment you have been *'prepped'* to *'receive'* him with his religious holy presentation as your pastor, your man of God, and follow him, or her.

It is a circus, a confidence game with a finely honed tool called music, or worship being utilized just as in the movies. Follow the plan, stay with your troop, remember, they have a schedule to keep. The clock is ticking, when does the next service, or the next *'act'* begin? It is all about manipulating the mind, will, and emotions, the soul of man.

This is Babylon.

This IS the god of this world.

These are not the sons of God, nor those who are in Christ. These are the 50% to 60% of pastors the Great Whore inflames with lust, as they accept her pleasuring them through pornography. They can call it a personal issue, and then express it as a common battle. As they justify their sin in the assembly, it gives that same evil spirit entrance to ensnare those in their assemblies, attacking their marriages.

It is not God's Holy Spirit telling your pastor he married the wrong woman.

It is Satan offering him an escape through pornography from being a castrated eunuch for his wife, his sweet appearing Jezebel. Ordained of men, men pleasing pastors follow another spirit in their bloodstream, in their dead soul as 40% of them acknowledge adultery SINCE they began doing their false god's work.

Paul in Galatians 5 exposes their godless ministerial hypocrisy...

> "And they that are Christ's have crucified the flesh with the affections and lusts.
> If we live in the Spirit, let us also walk in the Spirit."

Obviously, those who are not Christ's, have not crucified the flesh, nor are they seeking to abide in Christ. Yet before God, this sham of ministry of representing God is the real issue. It is through Satan's approved ministers of righteousness in God's house that evil spreads forth and pollutes the land, God's word. This is history repeating itself. When you love authority, you cannot abide the presence of the Holy Ghost, as He is not, nor will He ever be part of your support team.

You Cannot Make This Stuff Up

Attending a church in Seattle years back, a two-week nightly prayer meeting was held. At the end of two weeks, the Holy Spirit had begun to move. People walked in and immediately were in prayer, having learned to follow the Holy Spirit in prayer as He led.

I met with the recently 'voted in' pastor and related that the Holy Spirit had begun to move, why not continue these meetings and see what God will do. The answer was immediate, 'Yes, we will do this again sometime'.

The Holy Spirit was not subject to His control. Later, it was spoken by the administration that the Holy Spirit knew their schedule, and He would not interrupt it.

What will we do when it becomes obvious it is us, we are the leaders who actually reject God, and follow the god of this world? Will it be repentance? Or maybe just an intelligent discussion among our peers, the dead board members....?

> "Ye stiffnecked and uncircumcised in heart and ears, ye
> do always resist the Holy Ghost: as your fathers did, so
> do ye." Acts 7

There is NO difference between that mission-oriented godless Seattle assembly, and those who crucified Christ!!! None...

They are bastards, uncircumcised, meaning covenant breakers, stiffnecked, continuously resisting the Holy Spirit.

There is NO difference between that mission-oriented godless leadership of that Seattle assembly, and those who crucified Christ. Jesus is counted absent, as a man who took a long trip and the husbandmen have taken over as it were their own vineyard.

I was much younger, teaching an adult Sunday School class. In the front row were two pastors visiting from a sister church just above Seattle. As I opened my bible, the Lord spoke to me, clearly.

> "When they entered my heritage, they defiled my land,
> and made mine heritage an abomination."

I was at a loss, I knew it was the word of the Lord, and did not know how to proceed. I simply stated, there are two people here, I have a word from God for you, here it is. I read the scripture, stating you know who you are. Once completed, I returned to the Sunday School lesson. I did not understand what the Lord was telling me. *It was His word to me*, not them. My Father was preparing me to face this issue. It was a word to me that morning in Sunday School regarding those who had polluted God's heritage. Before God, there is a fire burning in me that will not be extinguished until His work is completed. I had known in my mid-twenties that God had a serious issue with those who stated He had sent them. I did not know how to... proceed. Heart breaking, constantly weeping, I was at a loss, and I struggled.

Today, many years later the message is clear, the message is direct, and it is being expressed as clearly as possible.

What this message is, in this book, in this chapter, is a message of judgement that will not be long delayed. The judgement of God beginning at His house with those who claim to be of Him is coming quickly. Before God, there is a consuming anger, a fire in the heart of God that breaks my heart. Not for the chaff, not for the trash... but for the words of His holiness.

Pastor, we are not looking at someone else, you are either a servant of Jesus Christ sent by Him, or you are not. You have been proven, crucified with Him, buried with Him, and raised walking in the tangible Holy Spirit or you are a self-deceived fool. Believing God's grace covers willfully walking after the flesh is you being an idiot, a fool.

Teaching false grace has put you in God's cross-hairs.

I will be direct, 'Mene, Mene, Tekel, Upharsin' is God's word to you personally. If repentance is not part of your immediate future, per Isaiah 50:11, you will lie down in sorrow, and these words will echo in your ears.

I would be more blunt, but the coarse language describing you in God's sight would take away from the point being made. References to the Malachi priests who had offered God the sacrifice full of excrement, is a parallel to what the minister apart from the Holy Spirit looks like to God. Their end was being thrown on the excrement pile, God's word, God's description. God is not clinically clean, germ free when it comes to Him taking out the trash. Consider Aaron's sons who offered strange fire, no mourning by daddy Aaron was allowed as nothing of value was lost.

A Call To Repentance

Do not think God dealing with you indicates His grace. It is His patience, His mercy. Do not believe for ONE second that you can turn your heart later. If God is dealing with you, it is from His heart of love. One who loves, is capable of being hurt deeply, amen? We understand God is long-suffering. Yet, if we loved God our Father, why would we ever want Him to suffer? With this understanding, only an evil heart would knowingly continue apart from God.

If we love God, as King David we will break before Him, and endeavor to please the One who gave His all for us, amen?

Recall, God so loved the world that He strove with man? But then, it so broke God's heart He had made man, and He washed the earth clean of all flesh with the exception of eight souls.

God dealing with their hearts, may have made them comfortable that God was still working with them… that was a fool's mentality. Before God, the foolishness of man operating in God's stead is done with. John the Baptist asked the Pharisees and scribes who had warned them to flee the wrath to come. Jesus plainly warned His disciples to flee the wrath that was coming. Those who heeded were not in Jerusalem when it fell.

Those who did not, participated in her judgement.

Babylon is judged.

The warning is posted.

The choice is ours to continue with her, continue to be joined to her in our own soul, or to take up our cross, abide in Christ, becoming a servant of God.

But that would be too hard a message for a self-willed god, or king to hearken to, amen? The fact that over 2,000 Jews were crucified on the sides of the road the captives walked out on will not register on us. *'We will not surely die…'* are the words we relish from the god of this world, just as they did.

The word of God to each pastor, each church leader, each board member, is to honor their vow before God, and before His people.

Confess your sin, your false doctrines, and make Jesus the Lord of your life in and through the Holy Spirit. Break before God, shut down your order, which is not yours at all, abandon her. As broad as your transgression, let your repentance equal it. Humble yourself before God, and everyone who has heard you and glorify God, just as Achan was requested to give God glory before Joshua.

Give God what you committed to Him, deny yourselves, pick up your cross, and actually follow through on what you told God when you were baptized.

Remember? You told God you were burying the *'old man'*.

You told God you buried the body of sin, and you committed to walking before God in newness of life.

Honor your vow, or not...
Either way, trash day is coming.

THE BEAST
and
The Child of God

As noted in previous chapters, we do not wrestle with flesh and blood, in our private walk before God or in our assemblies. Satan's ministers of righteousness masquerade as ministers of God, presenting themselves as *'God-sent'* necessitating the believer to learn to follow the unction of the Holy Spirit.

The apostle Paul tells us that Satan disguises himself as an angel of light and transforms his ministers into ministers of righteousness. The result is a magnificent religious display with the god of this world embellishing the Great Whore with his precious stones. These *'stones'* are her servants, her anti-types of the servants of God that bedeck her. They appear to be reigning with her in their prosperity, in their casual manner they appear to *'have it all'*.

This is the glory that amazed John when he saw the woman identified as the Great Whore.

When you attend their assembly, their services with their planning and choreography, as John you might be amazed, taken back thinking,

> *'How could this NOT be of God'?*

But absent the Headship of Jesus Christ manifest through his servant(s), it is not God's house. The dead flesh and blood soul of man is being manipulated through the god of this world.

It is NOT Jesus Christ, it is not the power of God released through God's ministers yielding to and following the Holy Spirit. Before this could ever occur in public ministry, it would of necessity have to have already occurred in their private ministry to the Lord Jesus Christ.

As stated, *we do not wrestle with flesh and blood, not in our private walk, nor in our assemblies.*

Being redundant, if your soul is placated in Babylon's religious facade, if you are at ease, at rest in her, you will partake of her judgment, God's word.

Jude describes those in clear language who operate apart from God, God's Holy Spirit building up themselves based on man's recognition.

> *"But these speak evil of whatever they do not know; and whatever they know naturally, like brute <u>beasts</u>, in these things they corrupt themselves. Woe to them! For they have gone in the way of Cain, have run greedily in the error of Balaam for profit, and perished in the rebellion of Korah." Jude (NKJV)*

Jude joins Peter in referencing the religious dead soul as comparative to a beast.

This is where conflict is born when our first-born flesh and blood soul encounters God's word delivered in the power of the Holy Spirit.

God's living word speaks life to the word and spirit we are born-again of, but death to the corruptible flesh and our first-born... identity.

Yet as we take in God's word, we can be as a child at a buffet. Passing the vegetables, and healthy foods we may go straight to the sweets. In hearing our soul-pleasing minister or in reading God's word we may focus on precious promises made to those who had left all, or endured hard trials.

> *We then appropriate those sweet promises for our-self.*

For example, we may claim God's word to Joshua regarding to *'be strong and of good courage for I am with you...'* as to us, personally. As we claim this *'promise'* we may forget Joshua was one of only two men (other than Moses) who stood with God enduring the hatred of millions of evil-hearted covenant children of Abraham. The evil-hearted *'chosen people'* preferred their sweets, and the abundant food of Egypt as they resisted God and His servants.

Those servants of God faced being stoned, but that escapes us as we savor the sweet words God spoke to them, as though they applied to us in our self-pleasing.

The truth is, walking with God can never be confused with living pleasing ourselves going along with the multitude. We are going to look at some scriptural truths.

In being born-again of God, our Godly birth is distinctly *different*, as in separate from our first born flesh and blood corrupt soul.

That first-born life, or soul is the corrupt soul we received from Adam. This life, this soul? Our first-born life with its world? Its identity?

>*It is already condemned.*

Do we recall God telling Noah,

>"The end of all flesh is come before me..."

In Hebrews we hear that God condemned the world through the faith of <u>one man</u>, Noah.

>"By faith Noah, being warned of God of things not seen
>as yet, moved with fear, prepared an ark to the saving of
>his house; by the which he condemned the world..."

Does this reference ring a bell?

In Hebrews 5, we read that Jesus was heard in that He feared the One able to save Him from death. Noah likewise was moved with fear, and saved from the death of those who... had no fear of God. They however were quite content calling on the name of the Lord. That did not work out too good for them... amen?

The apostle Paul writes in Romans 8 of another man,

>"God sending his own Son in the likeness of sinful flesh,
>and for sin, condemned sin in the flesh:

Not some flesh, not unredeemed flesh, but all sin in the flesh. In Colossians 3,

>"For ye are dead, and your life is hid with Christ in God."

Again, God identifies the first-created man as dirt, and returning to dirt. born as dead. Ishmael, Esau, the first-born flesh and blood soul is exposed as being dead.

The New Man, the New Race, the New Creation is not an old flesh and blood man that is revamped, cleaned up and acceptable to God. The New Man is found in Christ, walking in the tangible Holy Spirit who IS our life.

Jesus, *not* the second Adam, but the Last Adam was heard in that He feared the One who was able to save Him from death. That death would have been Him walking after the flesh, *even sinless flesh.* Flesh and blood, *even the very Son of God's sinless flesh* could not inherit the Kingdom of God. In our being blood washed, being forgiven all manner of sin, our first-born flesh and blood will not inherit incorruption.

In Christ, as with Noah the '*end of all flesh*' once again is come before God. The family of Noah found safety abiding with him, fulfilling his purpose in constructing an ark.

The body of Christ finds its life and safety abiding in Him through the tangible Holy Spirit, fulfilling His will.

As Noah's faith condemned the world, the faith of Jesus Christ has condemned sin in the flesh as we are shown *HOW* we are to walk with God.

The end of all flesh once again has come before God...
Debate it, argue it, but this fact is inescapable.

God sees the end of your flesh lived life at Calvary.
If we still relish the enjoyment of our flesh as our comfort, our validation, this does not bode well for us. Recall the Israelites who were delivered from Egypt, but carried the lust for Egypt in their evil hearts? Those writings are for our admonition....

Seeking to bargain for your soul, or finding a balance in your life between serving God and living YOUR life is the same as '*seeking to save it*'. These scriptural truths will fly in the face of Satan's '*church/business builder words*' that draw people.

Remember the rich young ruler, or the man that wanted to follow Jesus, but had to first go bury his father? They were not given religious soul pleasing words, were they?

Pastor, the cost to follow Jesus was not and never will be tuition and an internship. It was and remains to this day dying to your carnal soul, and learning to live from God's Holy Spirit on His revealed word, only, as in exclusively.

"He that findeth his life shall lose it: and he that loseth his life for my sake shall find it." Matthew 10
"Whosoever shall seek to save his life shall lose it; and whosoever shall lose his life shall preserve it." Luke 17

The word translated *'life'* here, is also translated *'soul'*. That is our little precious, loved, valued flesh and blood soul which demands the enjoyment of its time here in this wilderness. That should raise some questions when we see worship teams with *'saints'* rocking out. Maybe now we can understand Jesus asking if He would find faith when He returned. Because I guarantee you, Jesus did not *'miss it'*.

As flesh and blood will not inherit the Kingdom of God, *'feeling good'* following a live music session that incorporates Jesus' name is not an accurate measure of having worshiped God. God will not anoint, or witness flesh and blood with His approving presence.

In contrast, when the power of God is present there is a Godly fear present. All through the scripture, there is a breaking, a humbling of that soul in man that takes place from deep within him in God's presence. No flesh, sinless, forgiven or otherwise can ever glory in His presence.

This presents the carnal cultural Christian with a very real problem.

When we attempt to abide in, or stay in the presence of the Holy Spirit, we encounter imposing distractions and opposition. In allowing the distractions of life to divert our focus, we give our soul, our life in the body a higher priority than God Himself. To remain in the Holy Spirit requires an *'I will not be denied'* resolve. The kingdom of heaven suffereth violence, and the violent take it by force.

This force is our *taking* authority over our own soul, making it stand by our decision to please God, not it. This authority, this personal decision is to take our adult soul and humble it in obedience to the Holy Spirit as a child.

The Holy Spirit on God's word will step-by-step correct us, as we choose to follow Him. It is through our abiding in Him that He will clean us up, and a New Life will be revealed in His power.

Abstract? I understand. The war on your soul has been through both misdirection and providing mis-information. Those are common warfare techniques, amen?

We will see following the Holy Spirit as taking God's word in His spirit and ruling principalities and powers that war from *within our very own soul*. This is personally, intimately in obedience to God enduring the circumcision of Christ. This involves our choice to drop the things that do not please Him, that is suffering with Him. Self-pleasing ends, as abiding in the Holy Spirit, making Him our priority will incur our soul suffering. The way of the cross, is not the path of '*going along to get along*'.

We must choose trusting God in the issues we face from God's word He has revealed to us in private. It is in our private prayer we learn yielding to the Holy Spirit and being taught how to abide in Christ. But if we have not humbled our soul to spend time with God, in private, in His presence, we will reject suffering with Christ falling back into living in our strength.

This produces frustration in the child of God who desires to overcome, but has not developed strength in and through the Holy Spirit. It is through choosing to abide in the Holy Spirit we in His strength mortify the deeds of the flesh, not the will power of the soul.

As we abide in the Holy Spirit, everything we do is done as unto Him. This is shutting down our emotions, our thoughts, and actually serving the Lord from the heart in all we do.

> Recall, Jesus did not do the things that pleased His-self, but only those things that pleased His Father?

This suffering with Christ is dying to our own soul which also contains a real-time experiential promise. We will become aware of Christ in us as a distinctly different life than what our parents birthed.

This experience results when we overcome and remain in the tangible presence, the actual awareness of the Holy Spirit serving God, not our soul's interests.

This is an identity change that results from enduring the circumcision of the spirit. We have a part to play in this just as 99 year old Abram did. He had an identity change as the flesh that contacted the promised seed was cut off. Being a disciple who consumes the word of God, and becomes aware of the Holy Spirit is our being directed by Jesus to abide in Him.

In our being bought with a price, being led
by the Holy Spirit is not optional.

Per Romans 8 this is our becoming a son of God as we become a living sacrifice being led of the Holy Spirit. But as believers not reckoning our souls as crucified with Christ, buried with Him, what creature is it that remains?

We are going to look at references in scripture of men's flesh and blood souls that actually identify them as brute *'beasts'*.

There is Ishmael, a wild ass of a man (Genesis 16:12, multiple translations), and three other men referred to in Jude.

We are going to see the flesh and blood self-centered soul, the lost dead soul of Adam as a beast, with its identity becoming a child of wrath. Adam has died, a different creature was manifest than God's son living by every word that proceeded from God's mouth.

Just as the animals went from eating vegetation to biting and devouring one another, Adam diet has also changed.

The beast's kingdom is the flesh and blood soul pleasing kingdom.

Can we now understand why the sin offering under the Law was a beast? Offered as an atonement, as a proxy for man's sin, the life of its flesh or soul was drained, the head removed and burned. The innards would be removed and washed with water. The flesh and blood soul is not the living soul God had initially created...

Its reality, its realm is the Kingdom of Darkness.

Those in this kingdom obtain their identity from a foul spirit pleasuring their *'body of sin'* in their 'moment-to-moment life. *This interaction IS 'their life'.*

Physically breathing and living by its senses, its perception of Good and Evil as it relates personally, is what the *'Child of Wrath'* calls its life.

For the believer, who has been translated from the Kingdom of Darkness into the Kingdom of God's dear Son, the Holy Spirit's presence on His revealed word is life.

There is God's grace for us *as we transition* from walking after our carnal flesh and mind which is hostile to God, to following the Lord Jesus. We know this scripture, amen?

> *"For I know that in me (that is, in my flesh,) dwelleth no good thing: for to will is present with me; but how to perform that which is good I find not." Romans 7*

That *'no good thing'*? We will see it is our very little soul, or the life in the flesh this scripture is addressing. Recall Jesus saying, *'The prince of this world cometh and has nothing IN me?'*

He was sinless, we were not. He is the spotless Lamb of God sent by God, to deliver us from the life lived after the flesh and its mortal consequences.

He is able to save those who come to Him as He is their High Priest, their advocate, their deliverer.

For those who do not draw near to Him, but hold back waiting for Him to do something, anything for them? This is an evil heart, and denying God when He tells us it is in our coming TO Him that we are delivered.

Born-Again, Delivered, and…?

So Satan has used his religious 'somebodies' as his access to us and religious strongholds were developed within us as we began in the spirit, but were lulled back to walking after the flesh. This occurred as Satan's ministers preached their lifestyle through verbal, and non-verbal representations. They have conveyed walking in and after the flesh is… permissible. Today, some of these miscreants tell us God's grace is sufficient for all manner of loose living.

That was and is not a *'good thing'*.
These seemingly mundane carnal exemptions become religious strongholds containing the strength of religious spirits in your life, your soul. These ingrained beliefs contrary to God's word AND spirit then become....
    Your identity, not Christ living in you.
Submitting to God, is seeking Him in spirit and in truth. Your identity based on your mentors, your teachers?
It becomes shaped just as theirs was based on the religious word they received with the spirit on it.
This might be hard to accept, but the spirit on that word? That spirit has became the entity you identify as *'you..'*
Wrong, error? When Peter savored the things of men more than God, <u>HOW</u> did Jesus address him?
Just as the Pharisees knew God's word, and debated from knowledge, they were identified by our Lord as unholy adulterous hypocrites. Not only that, but Jesus also stated their lineage *was no longer of Abraham*, but the devil.
Yet they had no intention of having the devil as their father, amen? But just as their disciples had no intention of becoming twice the child of hell that they were, that became their identity.
So when we regard our honorable intentions as being our excuse? That is not an indicator that we are drawing from the right spirit, the right source, amen? That old familiar hiss that accompanies those intentions?
It is *"Thou shall not surely die..."*
Living by *'another'* word is establishing a sense of righteousness that is based in the soul, or self. Righteousness based anywhere other than the gift of God through faith in what God accomplished at Calvary is demonic. Those walking in their religious soul's strength crucified Christ then, and they grieve the Holy Spirit present-tense.
Being called of their father the devil was God's word, God's view, and determined their future.
That should scare the hell out of the knowledgeable religious

man. It really should. You also have just been identified from God's point of view.

If you have learned from man _apart_ from the Holy Spirit, you have been conformed to fit that bill. This also fits the believer taught by man, mentored by men being ordained by man apart from the Holy Spirit. They have become twice the child of hell their mentor is.

Can we understand that now?

A religious spirit ruling a man only accepts what strengthens it from its own approved sources.

Brokenness, humbleness before the Spirit of Truth is unknown.

King David knew the Holy Spirit. When David was confronted by God's man Nathan on adultery and murder, David broke before God.

Not so King Saul. That man had taken God's anointing and ruled as though God would be lost without him. It was HIS time to rule, Abraham had HIS time, this was King Saul's time to establish HIS place!

Has Satan told you, "This is YOUR time?"

You did not resist that word did you? It fit what you wished to hear, the groundwork had already been laid in your pride, your gifting and your being '*chosen*'. Psalms 68:18 applied to *EVERY* other gifted person.... not you.

Brother, can we hear a call for repentance? Or has our rule been enjoyed so long that we are of the same spirit as King Saul?

If so, what God had given us has been removed and given to another., The evil spirit that inflames your soul is a counterfeit to the '*gift of God*'. But it makes you feel special, right?

King Saul following a different _word_ in his heart received a different _spirit_ than King David. The murderous spirit that worked through Saul was the same spirit that crucified my Lord. Again, true brokenness and repentance were unknown by him also. If God attempts to speak into our religious life from another source, a fallen spirit manifesting as religious pride will keep us from accepting what is being stated. Debate, contention, and anger will be present. Satan will not let you go without a fight.

We need to humble ourselves before God, or otherwise we will be known as the Pharisees, the scribes who did not know the time of their visitation.

The result was a brokenhearted Jesus weeping over them and their followers foretelling their destruction. Yet, as with them, resisting the Holy Ghost has become the religious *'norm'* as you live your life *'claiming'* you are led by Him.

This is being stupid, or what the men who translated the KJV called *'being without understanding'*.

What does it take for God to get our attention? If these words are too much, maybe we should just listen to John the Baptist's verbiage when he addresses those knowledgeable religious hypocrites, or hear Jesus calling them the serpent's seed. We cannot differentiate their time as being different from ours. Because it is the same spirit that builds us up religiously as we possess no power with God, at all.

You, have just been located in your *'power with man'*, but *'no power with God'* ministry. The strength of your powerless religious beliefs are the entities that will share their eternity, with you.

Hell was not created for you, but them.

Do not go, instead go before God, renouncing the hidden works of darkness, and learn to abide in Christ remaining in the Holy Spirit. Consume His word for His life, the spirit on His revealed word is your deliverance.

The true disciple? He will hear the Lord speaking to him, correcting him from just about any source. The source may not even know it was being used!

But that is the point, God gets the glory, not the source.

This is also true of God's servants. They will reject your accolades, and possibly your gifts if your soul is wanting to *'buy itself off'* so you *'feel'* you have fulfilled righteousness. God's servants know that God is to be the only recipient of praise and worship. Those who try to gain favor are corrected immediately, before the Lord Jesus Christ. God's patience has been ours as we in ignorance have traipsed after Christless cultural churchianity and its messengers. His grace remains sufficient for those who have a heart after God. If we choose to not take God's word to heart, or if we preach it, teach it, and see it as applicable to others, but not to us? Then our darkness is that great darkness Jesus warned us of.

God's patience for this willful sin has departed.

Every single individual has participated in the Kingdom of Darkness from within their own being, their flesh and blood soul. If we are not walking in the awareness of God's Holy Spirit we are STILL operating in the Kingdom of Darkness, relying on God's grace to cover that wickedness or evil.

If we do not think this is applicable to us, here is a question. Is there anyone who is not guilty of speaking from the evil one?

> "But let your 'Yes' be 'Yes,' and your 'No,' 'No.' For
> whatever is more than these is from the evil one."
> Matthew 5 (NKJV)

Our time here, on this earth, in this wilderness boils down to this. We will either die to our self, its ruler and his temporary earth dwelling identity, or we will die to God resisting the Holy Spirit.

If we think as a believer we are exempt from Satan's wiles through our flesh and blood soul, or that the grace of God covers willful sin, there is understanding coming that will tear down that stronghold. Paul writing to believers (Romans 8:13) tells us by the Holy Ghost,

> *'...if we live after the flesh we will die'.*

That is the very same word God delivered to Adam.

> *'If you eat of that tree, you will die'.*

God did not call His son Adam dead, just as Paul did not say we who are born-again as children of God are dead.

The Apostle warns us just as God did Adam,

> *'If you walk after the flesh YOU WILL die.'*

As a Christian, born of God, having received the power to become a son of God, if we resist that power and choose to walk after the flesh, we will die. Again, in this same chapter in Romans God tells us that sin in the flesh is condemned. This is God's word, amen?

When we acknowledge Jesus as our Lord we declare He has purchased all aspects of our life *inclusive of our time* to Himself. We are not our own, we are bought with a price per 1 Corinthians 6. Being redeemed FROM this world, this world with its culture and amenities is not to be our focus, the place where we find our life. Our new life is found in the word of God as revealed by the Holy Spirit IN us.

This is *that New Creature* born of God, not man.

If we cannot consume God's word for life, or we cannot abide in His presence it is because our carnal focus is in direct agreement with an entity influencing our mind, our will, and our emotions. This is occurring from within our precious soul. We are going to see exactly what the problem is, we will see it defined scripturally, spiritually and God will witness His word to you in your heart.

We will then have a decision to make. Because with this understanding, this knowledge we will choose to be obedient to abide in Christ, or we will choose to retain our carnal mind being an acknowledged enemy of God.

Brute Beast Number One- Cain

Cain presented a sacrifice to God that was unacceptable. Cain was following a '*word*', a thought process from within his (dead) soul as he presented an unacceptable offering to God from the cursed ground. This cursed offering was rejected, and Cain?

Cain is a type of the preacher who knows flesh and blood will not inherit God's kingdom, but walks in the flesh presenting his ministry, not caring if God likes it, or not. It is not about the offering nor is it about God. It is all about him, his will, his ministry, his... image.

That is the '*Cain Syndrome*'.

Being absent a heart after God, we take God not accepting what we offered to Him, as God rejecting our image, personally.

Again, this describes Cain. It was then that God told him if he did well he would be accepted. But Cain? He never changed what he offered. He later departed the presence of God, never seeking to return.
There are pastors, church leaders who have sought the Lord and when their carnal soul was rejected?
They have said they tried.
Their soul was not accepted, at all.
The image they required God to accept as proof of their religious value to Him was rejected.
Never changing the offering they departed.
This may be hard to hear, but the strength of that religious pride? It is Satan himself. And just as Cain, these ministers then built their own walled city, their church, and began trading in men's souls.
This is not fun and games, eternity is at stake, and we are NOT wrestling with flesh and blood. When we go before God and we are not able to come into His presence, we need to change what we are offering. This entails us learning to *'follow the Holy Spirit'* through actually seeking the Lord. We must be diligent, in faith, and not pretentious.
Why?
Because just as Adam, God only receives what came forth FROM Him.
When we were born-again of God, we had believed and accepted that Jesus was our Saviour, our Redeemer and we passed from death to becoming a child born of God's incorruptible word and God's spirit. God then received the child born of HIS word, and HIS spirit. This is God's flesh and God's blood of the New Man, amen? And that which OUR parent's birthed is now counted dead, buried, right?
Now, we must take God's word <u>we are born of</u> back to Him. If God meets us as we take His word that *'Christ is made unto us righteousness'*, that is the place He will lead us from to grow Christ in us, and us in Him.
If we have been in Churchianity thirty years, we must

understand that our knowledge, our position does not impress God whatsoever.

Back to Cain.

Cain in following the prince of the power of the air in his mind and his emotions became volatile. He murdered his brother and left the presence of God. It is in the last verse of Revelation 18 that we see the entities working through Cain. Cain *was intoxicated* with Babylon, she was manifesting through his precious flesh and blood soul as he pleased and promoted his agenda, his plans, his validation.

This is the same soul, the same flesh *'in which dwelleth no good thing'* Satan will tell us is saved.

Just as Cain, we are hearing from a murderess who has us in her scope's crosshairs.

Cain being influenced by his enemy, a fallen foul spirit now works through his *physical* bloodstream.

Through Cain's bloodstream this foul spirit becomes Cain's identity as he fulfills its purpose. Its murderous intent was manifest when a righteous man and his seed was removed from the earth, and *Cain is now the only one seen as the brute beast*.

The foul spirit, the fallen evil one walks away with Cain being identified as the brute beast, the man who murdered his brother.

To Cain, obtaining right standing with God was less important than the self-righteous, self-approving word he heard through the life of his flesh. That word made his younger brother his blood sacrifice.

Brute Beast Number Two- Korah

Korah, or Core, was a minister in the tabernacle in the wilderness. Per Jewish history, Korah, the first cousin to Aaron, was jealous over the High Priest position. Korah, just as Cain was hearing another's word from *within his flesh wherein dwelt no good thing*.

Korah was hearing he was much too talented to be a follower.

Korah's sense of being worthy of leadership was received from a foul spirit infusing him with the self-perception of being much too smart and too eloquent just to be a supporter. His view of himself went from being a servant of God in the tabernacle to actually deserving to be THE Man in charge.

Korah, sitting in the assembly, wants that wireless microphone. If he just could address the people, they would be following HIM!

He can do better, *much better* than the speaker.

Korah was being seduced through his mind and emotions by his enemy to glorify himself. Unseen, but equally as amazing was that the entity that worked through him also worked through others to support its agenda. That foul spirit drew accomplices in other Israelites *'bodies of sin'*, gathering them to him to conspire.

Babylon was at work through Korah's soul, and the souls of others as she shared her glory with him so he could be something more to Israel; A *REAL* leader.

So Korah delivered Babylon's special message of grace, that EVERYONE in Israel was holy.

> (Wow, I have heard that recently. Satan speaking through his Coloradan messenger related everybody on earth was saved as Jesus paid the price for ALL sin. Jesus in John 3 is ignored as He tells us that he that does not believe is condemned already.

Bypassing the word of God, like children at a buffet heading for the sweet treats, the people including 250 *'princes'* in Israel, famous men, men of renown loved that man.

They then confronted Moses for taking too much on himself. But it was Korah who was found guilty of biting off a bit more than he could chew.

But hey, moving on, his funeral? It occurred along with his family's and... *was it ever spectacular!!!*

Those who supported him, they met their end, albeit differently it was similarly expedited.

Being influenced by his enemy through his flesh *wherein dwelt no good thing*, Korah had identified with the foul spirit working through his soul making its purpose to misdirect Israel, his *very own career move*. Korah bent the knee and worshiped the enemy of his soul. Bending the knee, bowing? It is looking to another to get your ministry, to be glorified from a different source, men.

Korah cooperated with God's enemy in an effort to mislead God's people. Again, the foul spirit walks away, and *Korah is left identified as an eloquent brute beast*.

To Korah, God's word, God's calling and order was less important than the self-righteous, self-approving word he heard in his own dead soul.

Dirt man Korah had his return to dirt, expedited, really fast tracked.

Brute Beast Number Three-Balaam

This man was a gifted non-Jewish prophet, he was *not* a covenant son of Abraham. Just as spiritually uncircumcised ministers today see ministry as a path to honor and an abundant lifestyle, Balaam is their elder brother.

Balaam in his precious little soul heard a word that his *'gift'* was his path to a more prosperous lifestyle. This word came from a fallen spirit from within his soul, his life in the flesh *wherein dwelt no good thing*.

That word was a king's request could be a great financial blessing if he worked this in the right way!

Per 1 Samuel 8, the king's support is taught as the tithes due everyone in charge of their own kingdom from their subjects. King Balak was likewise due 10% of his people's increase, that should satisfy anyone, amen? Just a portion of the King's 10% would be enough to satisfy Balaam's soul.

Add honor and accolades, and he might just be able to afford to lose his talking donkey. In short, Balaam's status and finances could see a big improvement if his prophetic gift would be accepted.

Following the god of this world in his flesh and blood precious soul, Balaam disregarded God's word to him in the spirit. Balaam went from arguing with his disrespectful donkey, to engaging the king's messengers.

Balaam worked diligently to put his prophetic gift, his ability to see in the spirit, in front of the king.

Finally, Balaam found himself in front of king Balak.

Balaam then delivered God's word which was not pleasing at all to the king, whatsoever. But having worked so hard to get here, Balaam could not let this go. So Balaam in his glory grab, in prideful stupidity, counseled Balak on how to get the Israelites to bring a curse on themselves. The king listened, and followed Balaam's instructions. Balaam now had credibility with the king, his ministry was accepted, and he now could be supported by the people through the King's 10%.

Balaam had followed the god of this world, the enemy of Israel's king. Just like Korah, telling people what they want to hear, even in opposition to God Himself can be the key to successful ministry, amen?!

Again, the foul spirit walks away, and *Balaam is left identified as the brute beast that argued with a donkey.*

Balaam's demise? We will get to it shortly.

Balaam, Korah, and also Cain all ended up sharing a condemned spirit's identity and its future as their very own. Not taking God's word over their precious little, short-time souls, they are now known as brute beasts, prime examples of the 'Children of Wrath'.

'Child of Wrath', 'Beast', or 'Child of the Most High'? Which identity is it that we desire to possess?

We would of course desire to be known as a child of God, amen? But that would depend on whose word we heard, and followed.

Are We, Different Than 'Them'?

Can we be accountable in truth before God?

When we pray, and when our offering to God is not accepted have we as Cain got up and left?

When our prayers do not get anywhere, have we said we tried, and then depart never returning, never changing our offering? This is a hard heart resisting the Holy Spirit.

In not yielding to God, do we in our heart then hate the righteous man when God accepts *'them'*?

Faulting God saying *we tried*, in not changing our heart or our offering we are of the same spirit that drove Cain in hatred to murder.

Is this too many questions, or are we open to the Holy Spirit to be corrected? It is better we examine our hearts, judge ourselves and be open with our Father on our errors, shortcomings, and mistakes.

He already knows, when we own them before Him, He can lead us from that place to where we become reliant and empowered by Him.

Do we desire to be accepted by men, to enter our ministry? Have we waited on God, and when we did not receive the direction, or the timing we desire, have we instead taken the advice of our followers, or religious leaders?

In learning scriptures, do we desire the accolades of men and the appearance of *'having it all together spiritually'*?

If so, we are on the same track as Balaam, and Korah glorifying their selves delivering the message people pay to hear.

People absolutely eat up self-pleasing words, amen?

Do we as those *'gifted morons'* really think God does not see our heart?

If so then we are without understanding. Being blind we think God is a tool for our ministry, a faceless someone we can market.

Korah? His demise was immediate.

Balaam actually survived a few chapters before dying by the sword of the Israelites. Balaam died in the company of those he had found honor among, he was unceremoniously slaughtered right along with the kings of Midian.

Is that a clue as to why we should abandon that soul pleasing spirit, deny our soul, take up our cross so we have a different future?

Balaam now joins Cain, along with Korah having his identity permanently etched alongside theirs as brute beasts. *'Brute'* in the Greek means destitute of reason, absurd, unreasonable. But to each of these men, the path they took at that point in time was, to them, prudent.

EVERY single one of us gets these options, many along with that whisper, that lie that *'This Is Our Time'* to prosper....

Prudent? Remember the serpent was more subtle than any beast of the field? That word subtle is also defined as... prudent. When God tells us one thing, but when it makes more sense to us to follow our reasoning, we are on the same path as our soul-brothers Cain, Korah, and Balaam.

Loving God, or.. Not

To the one who truly loves God, we are going to look at this brute *'Beast'* as an entity we renounce as we personally follow Christ. We will also identify the flesh and blood soul as the *'Child of Wrath'* and one more, the *'Body of Sin'*. As believers we will identify the source of strength, as Satan's access through the life of our flesh and how he has quietly, subtly endeavored to remain an integral part of our identity.

Does this sound wrong?

In Revelation 18, Babylon is identified as responsible for all those slain, but Cain is tagged as the *'murderer'*. When in rejecting following the Holy Spirit a man is tagged as the *child of wrath* in fulfilling the desires of the flesh and mind, whose word, whose identity is he taking?

Just as the Great Whore Babylon, this *'beast'*, this child of wrath has been hidden in plain sight, concealed by her *'ministers of righteousness'*. As you are walking after the flesh, it has defined your reality, your life, and has shaped your world.

This beast, this child of wrath is the embodiment of the Kingdom of Darkness, and manifests that kingdom through the souls of the dead, those who walk after their carnal soul and its mind satisfying its wishes.

Paul understood this and wrote to those at Ephesus, but not in the same manner he addressed those in Galatia.

Remember, the Galatians had started in the spirit and fell from grace trying to please God in their... flesh? Paul never addresses those in Galatia as being *'In Christ'*.

Paul, by the Holy Ghost however addresses the *'faithful in Christ'* at Ephesus. Now we can understand why he addresses their *'walking after the flesh'* as being something that is *behind* them. This brings clarity to Paul addressing them as being *'In Christ'*.

> *"And you He (God) made alive, who were dead in trespasses and sins,*
> *in which you once walked according to the course of this world, according to the prince of the power of the air, the spirit who now works in the sons of disobedience, among whom also we all once conducted ourselves in the lusts of our flesh, fulfilling the desires of the flesh and of the mind, and were by nature children of wrath, just as the others." Ephesians 2 NKJV*

This *'spirit'* that works through the sons of disobedience is the *'principalities and powers, the spiritual wickedness'* that believers *'wrestle with'*.

In 2 Corinthians 10 we are told to,

> *'...cast down imaginations, and every high thing that exalteth itself against the knowledge of God, and bring into captivity every thought to the obedience of Christ...'.*

Every thought? Is that not a *soul-centered* clue? The absolute need for you, and I to walk in the awareness of God, yielding all to the Holy Spirit who is our life is being revealed.

This spirit of disobedience referred to in the 2nd chapter?

It is the life of the flesh that influences every individual who has not learned to follow and walk in the Holy Spirit.

The god of this world is the *'one'* who intimately fulfills the carnal man's desires of his flesh and mind. The carnal believer is not exempt. Those principalities and powers that we wrestle with? It was in pleasing our-selves they gave us carnal validation, and satisfied us with the feeling of being someone. These spirits work through people's minds and emotions, in their bloodstream making them feel accepted and loved, or rejected and pushed aside.

It drives some to suicide and others to commit horrendous acts. Satan has seduced individuals with the belief they will be happy with wealth and recognition.

Others are convinced they are lost without it.

This is the life, the soul of your flesh.

To those at Ephesus, to those faithful IN Christ, Paul tells them this;

> "we ALL once conducted ourselves in the lusts of our flesh, fulfilling the desires of the flesh and of the mind, and were by the nature the children of wrath."

The child of wrath is the identity of this fallen spirit with hell being created for it, not for you. Yet those aligned with it not only get to share its identity, they also get to share its future. Understand this, that would not be God's decision or choice.

That decision would have to be made in opposition to God, in resisting Him and rejecting the leading of His Holy Spirit. In resisting the Holy Spirit we are NOT in Christ, we are NOT faithful in Him. There are no exceptions. In our willfully following a fallen spirit pleasing ourselves we will be known as the children of wrath. Fact.

Your House, Divided

At 26 years of age, a young man entered into a relationship with God that astounded him. He became aware of the Holy Spirit's indwelling presence as a power he could not describe. He heard the voice of God speaking from within his spirit, the words broke his heart as the words dealt with church leadership and severe judgement. He experienced God providing for him, and of possessing authority he did not understand. He also was put in positions of conflict where he was ignorant on how to proceed, which baffled him.

This happened multiple times, leaving him conflicted. One night he was invited by a brother to attend a meeting. Sitting in the back of the assembly he heard the Lord describe where the speaker had missed it. Acknowledging the word, he sensed conflict grow between him and the speaker. But in trying to sink into and disappear into the chair, the minister called him to the podium.

The minister told him they were going to cast a devil out of him.

As they laid their hands on him, they instead began blessing him, asking God to increase him. On the way home, he shared with the brother what the Lord had told him. Two weeks later, that brother told him the minister had confessed where they had missed God. They identified their error as what the young man had told the brother, and repented.

It was comforting to know, but how to proceed was never grasped. Ultimately, fear of man, respect for men would be exposed as ruling him. It was at that point he stumbled, falling hard, losing his intimacy with God.

In his endeavoring to return, he then committed Cain's error.

It was many years later the man returned to the Lord not regarding the cost. Loving the Lord, desiring to walk with Him in the intimacy they had shared, he did not understand what hindered him from entering this place with God, again.

He was asked to work in a church.

When asked to speak, he could not prepare a message. Initially frustrated, he learned he would receive God's word to speak on the way to the building, or on the walk to the podium. It was then in church he would deliver God's word, and God watched over it. Often men would come to the altar in tears as he was speaking, but the intimacy with God by the Holy Spirit that he had known, was still absent.

The Personal... *Beast*

He did not understand the '*why*' but he refused to quit seeking His Father's constant presence. '

One Sunday after church service the young minister had gone out to lunch with the pastor, a visiting evangelist and their wives. As they ate dinner, the young man became aware that everything he ate was separated from its life source. From the vegetables to the meat dishes, everything was dead and incapable of sustaining lasting life. He thought, 'What an odd way to see food'. Concluding dinner, he then reached for a piece of cake. All of a sudden, shocked, he 'saw' a creature, a beast reaching for the cake just as he did. The beast's body was exposed sinews and muscles, as a powerful beast without skin. The eyes were half open in a guise of humility, the nose was eaten back as void of skin, the fingers were long and claw-ike. The creature's demeanor was, 'Give me what I want, leave me alone, and I will leave YOU alone.'

He knew this creature was somehow related to him, in the sense it looked similar to him, sharing his facial structure, and at that moment it shared his appetite... he did not understand at that time what it was.

That would take... decades.

In Romans 8:1, the Holy Spirit through Paul tells us,

> "There is therefore now no condemnation to them which are in Christ Jesus, who walk not after the <u>flesh</u>, but after the Spirit."

The Greek word for flesh is '*sarx*'. This word contains the following as part of its definition, the *"flesh as stripped of the skin."*

This defined the creature as its muscles and sinews were exposed, it appeared fierce with the potential for violence. Yet its eyes portrayed false humility, its eyelids were half closed in the non-threatening pretense of I will not be an issue, provided you do NOT challenge me.

Again, to live after the flesh, pleasing the body with its life even unknowingly is our yielding to a spirit working in and through the body. In Romans 8, the Holy Spirit continues to tell us that,

> *"For they that are after the flesh do mind the things of the flesh; but they that are after the Spirit the things of the Spirit.*
> *For to be carnally minded is death; but to be spiritually minded is life and peace."*

Carnally minded? That word translated carnally is again the word *'sarx'*, *"the flesh as stripped of the skin."*

This beast identified getting what it wanted as its requirement, as its fulfillment.

Prior to Adam sinning, Adam was naked and unaware of his body. Adam lived by every word that proceeded from God's mouth. Upon sinning, his *'eyes being opened'* there was an awareness of his body that had not previously existed. He became *intensely* aware of his flesh and blood self.

In Revelation 17, the inhabitants of the earth are *'intoxicated'* or drunk with the wine of the Great Whore's fornication. This fornication is her pleasuring and fulfilling the desires of the flesh and the mind as one receives her words. It was her spirit on the word Adam received that accessed Adam's soul in his blood, manipulating him to seek to save his-self.

> *This occurred from WITHIN Adam, just as it does from within his descendants.*

Adam's body had become the *'body of sin'* as the god of this world changed Adam's perception of life from God and His word to his life, his dead soul found in his flesh.

Adam?

He knew God's word that told him he would die if he ate of that tree.

Cain?

He knew the sacrifice God required.

Korah?

He knew that Aaron was the High Priest chosen by God, and that his assigned place or ministry was in the tabernacle.

Balaam?

He knew when he counseled Balak he was going against the

King of Israel he had prophesied to Balak about.

This Beast, This Creature?
It thrives in the darkness of disobedience, in the area where light is known, but has been denied for even a forgotten reason. It lives where there the soul of man is joined to Babylon in spiritual fornication, or being one with it. Any area where a man, believer or otherwise is fleshly minded, self-centered, identifying with the body as life apart from known obedience to God? This beast resides with the rule given it. Being religious, identifying your-self as a minister apart from walking in the presence of the Holy Spirit, you may sense God's spirit on His word, but will never encounter God's power personally.

Your house is divided.

The young minister? His house was divided in his marriage. As he continually sought to save it, he never committed his rebellious wife to God, to her heavenly Father as the fear of losing her ruled his soul.

As Gideon, he knew better, the word of God was clear.

But the day-to-day struggle blinded him as fear of loss never entered his.... mind.

He had surrendered his first wife to the Lord, he had released her to their Heavenly Father. He had been told to let her go. The pain in his soul when she passed was excruciating. Not being willing to trust God to enable him again, he struggled, and strived to save this relationship. In the end, he was told,

"You will let it go, now, in the hospital, or in the morgue,
but you will release her."

He did.

The beast, the life of the flesh finds its identity found in earth living, in calling the wilderness its home through a disobedient compliant soul, as Adam, as Cain, as Korah, as Balaam...

This beast thrives through anyone who follows a desire regarded as more important than God's will.

Another Beast?

The writer recalled a similar creature *(beast)* described by a man called to be an apostle. This man was powerful in Christ, IN Christ he was a real threat to religion, to Babylon, and God was mightily using him. This man described an encounter with a similar beast calling it a demon. That creature had told him,

> *'Stay out of my kingdom!'*

That man later publicly told God repeatedly he did not want a ministry that would have put him in the crosshairs of religion.

> *He was to have taken the oversight of pastor's souls.*

That was his calling. God would have made him capable, instead, this man stated repeatedly, *'I do not want this.'*

It was later that Babylonian ministers then *required him to submit to them* and their oversight.

Satan is like that, he will seduce you, and then as you please your-self, he will endeavor to crush you, conforming you deeper into his image.

That *'beast'* that had told him to "*Stay out of his kingdom*"?

That beast then brought in his Kingdom of Darkness ministers of righteousness to manifest and <u>maintain</u> his existing rule.

The word of God manifested as the *'divided house'* began to fall.

The downward spiral had begun, and great was the fall of it.

In this tragedy his wife died, cancer.

The church then began a cyclical pattern of repeating his teachings, holding meetings, and what-not. And where previously there had been an awesome presence of God, where no one had gotten sick, now divorces and death began to manifest as the Gates of Hell prevailed.

> *Satan does not want that man serving God, that would be extremely destructive to his kingdom. God's word to that man remains true, recall the son that told his father no? And then repented? He returned to his father's will, his father's field, and completed his work.*

The enemy had arrived to steal, kill, and destroy, and as with

Adam found an accomplice desiring to save his soul.

The preservation of self, the saving of one's soul initiated a path of destruction even as he taught the flesh and blood soul was to be trained. That was him complying and staying out of that creature's religious kingdom. His knee was unknowingly bent, and his kingdom?

It was not the Kingdom of God, it became his own rule as he set up his *'scriptural'* order, relying on flesh and blood reports to give others the illusion of him hearing from God.

When drawing on a *history* of power with God, replaces present-tense power with God? You are no longer yielding to Jesus as your head real-time present-tense. Now, the message of Samuel to King Saul regarding a change in ruling is apropos. Even Samuel being heartbroken could not turn God's heart to accept a man appearing humble who was still great in his own sight. King Saul was an uncorrectable and arrogant ruler whose false humility found its end through his own weapons. Again, the fallen spirit walked away and King Saul was left with the identity of *'thou hast rejected the word of the LORD, he hath also rejected thee from being king'*.

Destruction of the Beast

When the soul, the life of the flesh is reckoned dead, and the Holy Spirit on God's Word becomes our only life, this beast, this creature's access is removed.

It is counting our physical body as dead, and its relationships after the flesh as dead. It is in loving the Lord with all our heart, soul, mind and strength that we are enabled by the Holy Spirit to abide in God's tangible Holy Spirit.

Too much?

If so, then we cannot follow Jesus nor be where He is per Luke 14 and John's gospel, chapter 12. That explains the powerlessness living in Churchianity, why 6 out of 10 man-called, man-approved self-called pastors are addicted or struggling with pornography as they fecklessly preach on the power of God. This is why 4 out of 10 pastors fall into adultery after, AFTER entering the ministry.

Powerless living results when we think we are following Christ without ever being crucified with Him. *'Thinking'* we are good people, *'thinking'* our intentions are acceptable, we are as Peter telling Jesus He does not need to be crucified. Preserving our flesh and blood soul/life puts us in the category of being Satan's messengers.

It is ONLY through yielding, following the tangible Holy Spirit that our members on the earth can be *'mortified'*. This is further understood when we see the *'body of sin'* being crucified as opposed to the '*body of sins*'.

> "Knowing this, that our old man is crucified with him, that the body of sin might be destroyed, that henceforth we should not serve sin." Romans 6

This pointed again to the body with its life again as being the issue, the source of... sin. Not serving sin, would be our not finding our life in our body of sin, but in the Holy Spirit, amen? As the man, older now went before God regarding this creature, this beast, the answer was simply,

'It is the life of the flesh.'

It is the life we lived after the flesh, Paul stated, *'we all once conducted ourselves in the lusts of our flesh.'* No one is immune to this beast working through them as they please them-selves.

As stated, Paul addressed those *faithful* in Ephesus who are *'In Christ'*. He relates that in their *'past'* they lived following this beast, this prince of the power of the air.

But those who are *'In Christ'* have crucified the flesh with its affections and lusts, Galatians 5.

In the *'body being counted dead'* the only life a saint has left is in the Holy Spirit.

Also in Romans 8 we hear God's word written to believers, those called to be saints. The Holy Spirit through Paul relates that if we live after the flesh we will die. We do have decisions to make, amen?

This beast? It is a parasite to the creature we told God we buried. It is attached through the bloodstream manifesting

as the life of the dead soul. It produces the awareness, the enjoyment of life in our flesh that is dead to God.
That is a 'wow statement'.
Your life in the flesh, if not animated by the Holy Spirit, has another source that gives you that sense of *'being alive'*. This entity makes the awareness of our dead flesh and blood soul our identity, that self-image which is so precious to us. It is the image that must be adored, pleased, protected and preserved. This entity is the absolute enemy of your eternal soul that is found in God's word and spirit. It not only opposes the child born of God, but it also mocks him just as Ishmael mocked Isaac.
This *'beast'* is to be shut down, denied, and not to be regarded in its entirety through counting the body with ALL of its affections and desires... dead.

Pastoral Beasts
Are we an earth dweller, an inhabitant of the earth? Or have we been crucified with Christ, buried with Him, raised and seated at God's right hand IN CHRIST being dead to our flesh OVER principalities and powers? Are we walking in the awareness of the tangible Holy Spirit, in our NEW LIFE? Or are we carnal, religious, living in our *'own strength'* claiming TO WALK IN THE HOLY SPIRIT by a faux faith apart from the witness of His presence? That is what Jesus referred to as *'great darkness'*.
As a *'minister'* the patience of God has departed this foolishness.
There is no sacrifice for this sin, this mockery from this point on. That is the word of my Father to you, personal and direct. You entered His land, defiled it and made His heritage an abomination, God's word to you is to repent before Him, His people... or not.
The decision has already been made, your sin is retained, judgement follows a short span given you to repent.
There is an anger burning in the heart of God that is not to be played with. This claiming to walk in the Holy Spirit without

yielding, without paying the price to abide in Him through following Him is a lie.

This yielding to a foul spirit pleasuring yourself in ministry declaring it is the Holy Spirit is the error that will never be pardoned.

Argue it, debate it, by the spirit of God I must tell you God's patience has departed this foolishness. God is spirit, those who worship Him must do so in spirit and in truth.

If we think these *'beast'* references are just too much, Jude would be a good read as Jude details this destructive creature and your church leaders it works through.

He describes those who,

> *'have gone in the way of Cain, and ran greedily after the error of Balaam for reward, and perished in the gainsaying of Core.'*

Let us look at 2 Peter. This *'beast'* is again found in references identifying religious leaders what we would recognize as pastors, worship leaders. The commonality is that both then and now they have rejected taking up their cross.

God's word...

> *"But these, as natural brute beasts, made to be taken and destroyed, speak evil of the things that they understand not; and shall utterly perish in their own corruption;*
>
> *And shall receive the reward of unrighteousness, as they that count it pleasure to riot in the day time. Spots they are and blemishes, sporting themselves with their own deceivings while they feast with you;*
>
> *Having eyes full of adultery, and that cannot cease from sin; beguiling unstable souls: an heart they have exercised with covetous practices; cursed children..."* 2 Peter 1-12

Concluding, Pastor, church leader, board member?

Accountability follows immediately.

Before God, walking after the flesh is now choosing to spiritually commit adultery in your body and the price will be exacted...

as God is not mocked.

'MUSTARD SEED FAITH'

In Luke 17 the disciples had asked Jesus to increase their faith, and He responded,
> *"If ye had faith as a grain of mustard seed, ye might say unto this sycamine tree, Be thou plucked up by the root, and be thou planted in the sea; and it should obey you."*

Real working faith, even what is regarded as *'Mustard Seed Faith'* is extremely rare. When we consider Noah among billions, or the Israelites in the wilderness we see the rarity. Among those eyewitnesses to God's power who were delivered from Egypt? Other than Moses, out of approximately 6 million Israelites, only Joshua and Caleb possessed a confidence in God and His word.

With this history, Jesus poses this question in Luke 18,
> *"Nevertheless when the Son of man cometh, shall he find faith on the earth?"*

Man's religion minimizes the reality of real working faith in God as it teaches faith not as an experiential reality from walking in the spirit, but as metaphors. To them the tree being plucked up and planted in the sea, and the mountain being removed in Matthew 17 share metaphoric similarities. Satan, speaking through his religious ministers, tells us they are merely symbolic of troubles in our lives.

The reason?

Your life, your flesh and blood soul is their market.

You need to have unsolvable problems, it is their job security... nice, right? In your need to solve your life's problems, you must *'seek to save your soul'* for them to have this market.

Your life's problems? Your job issues, or your financial goals/

difficulties? Per the god of this world, these are the mountains in your life that mustard seed faith can remove.

Wow, does that sound right?

Do you remember when you committed your life to God? You had repented of your sin and believed Jesus paid the price on Calvary for it. When you believed, you were born from above, you also believed Jesus was raised from the dead to justify you. You were then baptized, and you told God... that you buried your old man.

Is that accurate?

In this commitment you told God you were going to follow Jesus, right?

But to follow Jesus means we actually follow Him, not just... say we do, or that somehow we are.

Following Jesus is absolutely not joining a church believing that replaces scripturally following him.

But what does this have to do with our '*mountains*' or life's problems?

Jesus speaking in John 12,

> "He that loveth his life shall lose it; and he that hateth his life in this world shall keep it unto life eternal.
> If any man serve me, let him follow me; and where I am, there shall also my servant be: if any man serve me, him will my Father honour."

If we are going to follow Jesus, we need to understand what following Him entails. We must as He told those who heard Him then, '*Count the cost*'.

When we read of our Lord, we see His purpose, His motivations, and what His singular goal was in His time here.

That may sound complex until we read His word, yielding to the Holy Spirit to reveal it. We then understand everything Jesus went through was He would be able and capable to assist us in our taking that very same route He took.

Jesus actually spoke from His experience, He taught from His reality of following AND walking in the Holy Spirit.

That reality is to become ours in our '*following Him*'.

Now understanding Him takes on a new light. As we follow Him, we can expect His assistance as we focus on Him. Recall *'Seek ye first...'*?

If we want to get our bills paid first, get our marriage 'lined out' first, or overcome our addictions first, we will have 'metaphoric' mountains that will *NEVER* be removed.

Why?

Because His enablement is for His purpose, His goals, not our carnal needs or desires.

Jesus had mountains. Peter had mountains. Family needs were the eldest son's responsibilities. Peter had a fishing enterprise, and it appears his mother-in-law may have resided with him.

But all of this fades at a particular event...

We read of Jesus of Nazareth and of Him growing in wisdom, and physically maturing. In Luke 2 He grows in favor with God and man, but then something happens that changes, <u>everything</u>.

Jesus is baptized by John.

Jesus is baptized in the Holy Spirit at Jordan.

Then everything in Jesus' time here, from this very point changes drastically.

It is from this point on that we have a clear picture of Jesus. Everything that took place up to this point is not amplified on, or detailed.

Why?

Because it is from Jesus was baptized in water and in the Holy Spirit where Jesus identifies with us in our becoming sons of God. This is also where we identify with Him as the ONLY One we follow THROUGH the Holy Spirit.

At His baptism, Jesus fulfilled all righteousness.

From that point on, in entering the wilderness He *continued* fulfilling all righteousness.

Hebrews 2 details that it pleased God to make the captain, the pioneer of our salvation perfect through suffering. As our pioneer, Jesus suffered what we must suffer in order to lead us through the mortifying of our members on the earth to

become sons of God. That was Jesus fulfilling all righteousness for us being inclusive of loving not His flesh and blood soul unto death.
Are we grasping the picture, the narrow path past the strait gate we must take in following Jesus?
In Hebrews 5 we get a picture of Jesus in that wilderness,
> *"...in the days of his flesh, when he had offered up prayers and supplications with strong crying and tears unto him that was able to save him from death, and was heard in that he feared;*
> *Though he were a Son, yet learned he obedience by the things which he suffered;*
> *And being made perfect, he became the author of eternal salvation unto all them that obey him."*

Jesus needed saving from death?
What death would that be?
The word of God tells us if we walk after the flesh we WILL die. Walking in the Holy Spirit is NOT done with finding a metaphoric *balance* to serve God and please ourselves or Jesus would have told us so, amen?
Jesus details that clearly. Jesus relates that to follow Him, everything of the flesh needs to be abandoned, died to.
This is our suffering with Christ, this is also where in resisting, grieving the Holy Spirit... *we deny Him.*
The wilderness was the place Jesus died to His flesh and blood soul relations. He died to His flesh and blood love of Joseph, Mary, His brothers, sisters, and to His own life also.
This was done as He picked up His cross and followed the Holy Spirit, pleasing our Father who is Spirit. Jesus despised His own flesh and blood soul in order to walk out obedience to His Father. It was only then He grew in the power of God, as He denied His flesh and blood soul, denying its inputs and familial relations.
Tested, proven, Jesus then exited that wilderness in the power of God.
Now, Jesus walking in the power of the spirit, maintaining

or keeping favor with man is not part of His walking in the Holy Spirit. Recall, being baptized in the Holy Spirit changed everything in Jesus' world? Now? No longer obtaining favor with men, God His Father is His singular focus. In fact, pleasing men would be diametrically opposed to pleasing God.

Wow... every seminary degree, every certificate of accepted approval from man is a documented issue with God.

Again, wow... Jesus said you cannot have the approval of men and the approval of God.

Disagree? Let us read on.

The presence of His Father, in the Holy Spirit is the ONLY life Jesus now identifies as real living.

This Jesus is the One we told God we would follow when we fulfilled righteousness, and were baptized into Him. Our walking in union with God in the Holy Spirit is what God sees as all important, He sees it as life.

Back To *'Mustard Seed Faith'*.

So, in regards to your *'metaphoric mountains'*, your finances, your problems, your flesh and blood issues of this world.

What of them?

What did Jesus tell the rich young ruler?

What did Jesus tell the man that *'wanted'* to follow but first had to go deal with family responsibilities? His dad was dead or dying.

Did Peter abandon all and follow Jesus? John, James, the others? Or did they negotiate a time to meet up and discuss the *'mountains'* in their lives?

Religion, Churchianity apart from Jesus Christ has deceived you with a false gospel. All the mountains, all the issues in your unburied life cannot be resolved by giving more seed to that ungodly seed based faith ministry. You are playing a spiritual lottery with the house winning every time.

That big complex, those great locations? If you give more, will you be blessed more? Will you curry favor with the *'leaders'*?

Your soul is being manipulated, your emotions are in play as

you hear testimonies, and people glow with the testimony that they gave all their funds and only then did God bless them.
You buy into it, you dig deep and give until it hurts because God loves a cheerful giver.
But, when you are not blessed, you correct your heart and try again...
The House wins every time...
Then you attend a meeting in another town, and that same cheerful glowing testimony is produced by that same cheerful glowing person word-for-word, and you realize this is not God, this is clever marketing.
This is a program to fund their business.

The Mountain Remains
Has your faith in God taken a hit as your prayers, your requests have not moved your *'mountains'*? Jesus told us in Matthew 6:33 to seek first the Kingdom, or reign of God and all the things the Gentiles strive for would be added... we must decide.
Is God's word true, or not?
You must decide for your-self.
Have you wondered why your faith to move your *'mountains'* seems to be... inoperative?
A young man, a believer was living on the *'skid-road'* of a town, drug addicts were present, his neighbor a spiritist teaching metaphysics.
Broke, he cannot afford his half of the rent that amounted to $25 per week.
He had a metaphoric mountain, amen?
The prodigal son had the same issue, broke, possibly living in a pigsty, eating pig slop.
Yet Jesus did not refer to either of these situations as *'mountains'* to be moved by his faith!
That would be inane.
Disobedience had landed that young man in dire straits, as with the prodigal son desiring to have his own life apart from His father.

Their mountains?

Regardless of their prayers, the confessions of their faith, the taking of God's word, these metaphoric mountains identified by the disobedient, will remain. These items in our lives that are immovable?

They remain until the issue between the believer and God is removed by... the believer returning to obedience.

The young man walked out his front door one morning, and *'his senses'* returned. He spoke to the Lord directly. Uncensored, *"If you will let me work, I will work my butt off, pay my bills, and return to your will."*

That afternoon he received a call from a man in another state requesting help. He responded, within one month he ended up in Alaska with more of an income than he had ever consistently made.

The prodigal son? We know that story. Instead of praying about your mountains, asking your Heavenly Father to bring you to your senses might be more productive.

The point?

Your mountains, your problems?

If you are hearing they are metaphoric mountains we need faith for, your preacher, your minister of righteousness is preaching another gospel.

This false gospel pleases your soul as you fellowship others who likewise wallow in their struggles. We can call this wonderful place our church home, our church family who supports us as we perpetually struggle with our... issues.

However, God ALWAYS watches over HIS word.

If our prayers about finances, marital issues, work issues are not being answered, we need to repent, abandon our self-righteous ways and seek God. We need to ask Him to bring us to our *'senses'*.

God's word is true, if we line up with God in spirit and in truth, He will move heaven and earth for His child. But to the disobedient, Psalms 50 is a good read.

"God is not a man, that he should lie; neither the son of

> man, that he should repent: hath he said, and shall he not do it? or hath he spoken, and shall he not make it good?"

Again, if our prayers are not being answered, it is because there is something on OUR end that is wrong. Something must change and it will NOT be my Father.

Going to the religious looking for answers will be a dead end. Why?

Jesus is unknown by Satan's ministers of righteousness. In claiming to have a relationship with God, today's cultural pastors and church leaders mirror their counterparts, the self-righteous scribes and Pharisees.

In their impotent theology, their mountains are their personal problems they teach mustard seed size faith can remove. This is our present tense real-time reality. These children of the devil act like they are doing God's work.

Just as before, the believer is as the Israelites being afraid of being kicked out of the Temple, disfellowshipped. Today, the fear is losing your support group, the people who make you feel loved and accepted.

Personally, we must prefer God's acceptance witnessed by the Holy Spirit, only. He was sent to the obedient to come alongside, be their Comforter, amen?

Reverencing Satan's Messengers

Man pleasing through church leadership reverence had been ingrained in me from 2 years old. It was a tough road to get free, but the freedom before my Father is amazing.

Today's scribes and religious leaders, pastors have their soul centered mountains that will remain unmoved.

Over one-half struggle with pornography, four out of ten have had sexual intercourse with someone other than their wife since entering the ministry. They have marital issues and financial issues they call *'their mountains'*. Their sin laden frustration remains hidden from view as they hypocritically present being *'spiritually together'* before you, their target audience, their market.

As the Pharisees did not recognize life when He was right in front of them, those ordained of men glory in their knowledge and their position with men. But unknown to them, what is highly regarded among men is nasty, and despicable to God.

You will not be told you buried your old life, and now your New Man, your New Creature, your victory is ONLY found walking in the power of God, the Holy Ghost. There will be no accurate reference to your carnal self, your life, your *'body of sin'* being crucified with Christ. There will be no reference to your desires, whims, and wishes being crucified with Christ. In this façade of religion presented as Christian living there can be no being raised up in Christ walking in New Life found in the presence of the Holy Spirit.

The Dance

They have this dance called the *'Pharisaical Sidestep'*. We just slip back to walking after our flesh, fulfilling the desires of our mind and sidestep. As we bypass the truth, man's explanations are now easily digested requiring no accountability to our actually possessing or understanding *'Mustard Seed Faith'*.

The Pharisees perfected the *'sidestep'*, making God's word of no effect through their traditions. Today, it is the same god of this world marketing God's word to the believer through Churchianity, its contemporary religious belief system.

Jesus?

He is not part of their charade.

In Luke 17 after referring to the sycamine tree being planted in the ocean with minuscule faith, Jesus continues,

> *"But which of you, having a servant plowing or feeding cattle, will say unto him by and by, when he is come from the field, Go and sit down to meat?"*

The word *'but'* Jesus uses connects the context of mustard seed faith, the tree, with this context regarding a servant. Jesus does not differentiate the servant fulfilling obedience from the sycamine tree itself being obedient! The tree, obedient? *"...and it should obey you."*

The tree obviously has no self-will, but the servant does.

Yet the tree is declared to be obedient as it responds to *'Mustard Seed Faith'*. The servant as the tree is also considered obedient responding to the commands of his master. Is there something we are to learn from the tree, the servant, or what we say?

Or is the Mustard Seed itself, supposed to be seen as powerful real faith exercised in this physical world walking WITH God? That would be a *'wow statement'*, amen?

Could faith which comes from hearing God, speaking by His life, His spirit, His word actually impact the creation held together by the power of His word? If so, then we are talking about a spiritual reality that supersedes the reality of our soul-centered life with its issues we told God we died to in baptism.

> (Hmmm... can it be? Is it possible we have also looked at the cross as symbolic, being buried with Christ as a metaphor? Then we could never, ever have been raised up seated at God's right hand in Christ above all principalities and powers. Again, hmmmm..)

In Matthew 17, we have an identical situation. The disciples had been unable to deliver a child from his bondage. A demon had not obeyed them. Jesus did not identify the demon as a metaphorical mountain, or the mountain as a demon.

Jesus said exactly what He meant.

The disciples were not struggling with personal issues, they had left all. They questioned Jesus as to why they were unable to cast out this demon. Jesus' response,

> "Because of your unbelief: for verily I say unto you, If ye have faith as a grain of mustard seed, ye shall say unto this mountain, Remove hence to yonder place; and it shall remove; and nothing shall be impossible unto you."

What does a mountain, and a demon have in common? Unbelief is being addressed resulting from a failed encounter with a demon, along with a reference to talking to a mountain. Faith in God will impact EVERY area of our walk here. *'The just shall live by faith'* is not to be confused with carnal Christianity fulfilling its carnal desires through faith. Self-professed theologians, carnal Satan induced experts on Jesus say that Jesus did not mean a literal mountain.

Again, Satan's messengers reduce God's words to metaphors, symbolism, men's traditions/theologies and make it of no effect. If you have done this? What you say has no power but in seducing the souls of men. You have a fire coming your way that should cause you to fear. Let us move beyond men's carnal reasoning, instead of reducing Jesus' words to *'metaphors'* or calling them *'hypothetical'* let us do something really different. Let us take Jesus' words as Him telling us the straight truth.

Let us take Jesus as speaking from His real-world experience as He walked in the power of the Holy Spirit.

Wow, that would be different, amen?

It will be shown this is exactly what Jesus did, and what we are to do. Now we will see it is OUR faith as with the disciples being exposed for what it really is!

Unbelief was called unbelief.

Doubt was called doubt.

Churchianity has that dance step handed down called the *'Pharisaical Sidestep'*.

Accountability to truth goes out the window as our precious lost soul we seek to save cannot handle it. Resisting the Holy Spirit is now covered with great service planning, and seductive live music.

Really. Can we grasp how ignorant this is? Yet, this truth is where our faith is revealed as mental assent only, the product of our seduced soul.

It is odd, is it not?

We say we love the Lord, but then we resist the Holy Spirit.

We please our-selves, not God and that is why we do not have His tangible presence.

We are serving the god of this world that pleasures our carnal flesh and blood soul.

This is adultery, pure and simple.

We have decided NOT to abide in Christ, as the cost to pleasing ourselves, our wife, our children, our... whatever is a cost we will not pay.

We do not as in ever, wait on Him in the assembly, humbling ourselves not moving, until He moves.

We do not have nightly prayer meetings where there is no preaching, just waiting on God, correcting our hearts, straightening out relationships in His body.

We do not come before Him, acknowledging it is IN Him we are cleansed of all sin and all unrighteousness to worship Him as He is worthy.

It remains odd, doesn't it?

We believe He has risen from the dead, all powerful, but He cannot be waited on, or trusted to show up where there are 2 or 3 and manifest in their midst as they wait, on Him.

Jesus is the Head of His church...

But OUR church?

Our pastor feels pressure from his lord to get things going, that would not be Jesus pushing him, amen?

That would not be the Holy Spirit. It is the god of this world working through our beloved pastor.

He must get things going, with a prayer of course, or he will not be seen as competent and in charge.

Now that does not sound like anything of God, right?

But you will pay Babylon as she requires payment for her services...she requires it of you for you to keep her identity....

In all this mockery, we resist the Holy Spirit who is our life and then in stupidity wonder why our uncrucified, unburied lives, our struggles, our problems just seem to be perpetuated in that same life we told God we... buried.....

Stupid is an offensive word, but what is way worse than being stupid, is continuing a path that is wrong because our precious little soul is offended, unhappy.

Denying our precious little soul is what following Christ is all about. Seek to save it, you lose it. Count it dead, get over it and get with God. Before God, this is the straight truth.

Do we really want to challenge God's resolve?

Our excuses, reasonings, suppositions and hypotheses are being exposed for what they are.

Do we have real faith? Or is it just a faux faith religious pretense? Pharisaical stupidity is our declaring we walk in the Holy Spirit absent His power, His presence, stating it is by the same faith our *'metaphorical'* mountains are being removed.

The emptiness of our confession reveals the soul-pleasing god we are serving. The money you spent on seminary teaching built strongholds that harbor great darkness. The time you invested will make it hard to walk it back and kneel before God, asking forgiveness for not seeking Him.

> *Again, God is no respecter of persons, not knowing Him*
> *personally is our telling Him we have better things to do*
> *than deny ourselves, take up our cross and follow Him*
> *in the Holy Spirit.*

We are not walking in the power of the spirit because we willingly chose a different route to obtain our kingdom. We also bent a knee to the wrong god to take that route. God has this sacrifice that covers that sin, it can be yours.

> *The cost is your life, your ministry, your flesh and blood*
> *relations, all have to be counted dead to come into His*
> *presence, seeking His kingdom, His rule, His reign.*

This got really simple, really quick. Lies and hypocrisy are exposed, and we have a choice. We will either repent, be open and honest from our heart before God humbling our-selves, or we harden our religious man-taught hearts. One has the power of God in our future, the other? It has our willful sin being retained and judgement following hard on its heels.

Jesus had left all, at Jordan's baptism He had died to the family He had been born into, and began dying to His own soul also. Jesus began not pleasing Himself, He being baptized into the Holy Spirit followed hard after the Holy Spirit. That point has been made that we cannot do both, we cannot keep our old life lived in its strength and follow Jesus. Jesus tells us except we do what He did, we cannot follow Him.

For references, we have Luke 14:26,27 and John 12:25.

Leaving All, From the Heart

Counting your-self dead, is doing EVERYTHING in your time here as unto the Lord, not as unto any man. That would be placing our entire time, what we have seen as *'our life'* in God's hands. For us to walk in the Holy Spirit requires we have faith, faith in God. Otherwise, as the Israelites we cannot obtain the Rest God has promised us, we cannot cease from our labors as we handle *'our unburied life'*. We labor as we *'think'* we are to thrive in this wilderness with all the things of Egypt at our beck and call.

That is not faith, that is an evil heart of unbelief.

In contrast, Jesus following the Holy Spirit had His soul dealt with in the wilderness. It was only then Jesus departed that wilderness in the power of the spirit.

Jesus is speaking from this reality when He discusses the sycamine tree, or the mountain. To speak of this topic from a theological point of view, from man's reasoning accepted as divine inspiration?

Paul calls it the foolishness of man's wisdom.

We are going to see the sycamine tree and the mountain in Matthew Jesus referred to are real, not metaphors.

They are actual physical parts of His creation.

In Colossians,

> *"For by him were all things created, that are in heaven, and that are in earth, visible and invisible, whether [they be] thrones, or dominions, or principalities, or powers: all things were created by him, and for him..."*

The sycamine tree, as the mountain were created *'for Him'*. Neither God, nor His Son Jesus, nor His sons are subservient to them. Au contraire, ALL of creation is subject to God and His word. In fact, God STILL to this moment upholds all things by the word of His power, amen?

Do we remember Paul telling those in Corinth they were carnal, and walked as... men? Being occupied with the things of this world, as mere men we are subject to its elements. This is the seed that fell among thorns, amen?

Likewise, being carnal we are under the principles or rudiments of this life. From this dead perspective the sycamine tree being plucked up, or the mountain being cast into the sea illustrating faith MUST be viewed as metaphors.

Recall Jesus telling Nicodemus about being born-again?

The second time Jesus tells Nicodemus,

> *"Except a man be born of water and of the Spirit, he*
> *cannot enter into the kingdom of God."*

Being born again is needed to see the Kingdom of God, but being born of water, the *'washing of water by the word'* is essential, as our unregenerate mind, our carnal living in our strength will result in our NEVER entering God's Kingdom, ever. Because God's spirit, His Holy Spirit lives through the word of God made alive in the believer.

This is becoming a New Creature.

Debate it, or get with God's Holy Spirit and allow a transformation.

Before God, in hearing men we have denied our Master as 2 Peter describes us. In loving ourselves, not God we have denied the Lord who purchased us. In denying we are bought, in our not being His servant, we have no authority, zip, nil, nada, hindi, none.

But in our pride, we will not be denied! In our self-righteous carnality we will declare we have our ministry, we have our constituents, we have our responsibilities, we have pressure to keep it going.

These are the tools Satan uses to keep us obedient to him, the true master of our religious soul as we seek to save it.

Apart from the power of God, our strength is from a different source.

From our soul, our strength is in debate, arguments, and in studying to shut-down those who would dare to contradict us. By the spirit of God, I tell you that you do not know who it is you are dealing with.

Repentance is the word this day, the hardness of your heart is going to be removed. It will be removed by you in your brokenness before God, or through imputed sin.

Those are your choices. Sin retained is exactly what happens when God's judgement occurs.

It begins at God's house, amen?

> "And whosoever shall fall on this stone shall be broken: but on whomsoever it shall fall, it will grind him to powder."

Unbroken, in man imparted ignorance we must teach *'Mustard Seed Faith'* separate from the *'Servant Message'*. As we teach others we separate our issues as being under God's grace, because we struggle. We then teach others that if they had *'Mustard Seed Faith'*, very small faith, extremely small faith, THEIR life's situations would be handled. In our teaching of others, we excuse ourselves in blatant hypocrisy.

Repentance anyone?

In our reading this, are we going to see a great message we can preach as God's word and receive additional recognition for being *'someone'*? Do not be that scriptural bastard. Instead, be correctable as a humble and contrite heart God will NOT despise. We must correct our hearts before God.

Back To That Sycamine Tree

In many ways it resembles a Louisiana Water Oak. Massive branches, with large roots spreading over the ground it is a formidable natural structure.

What did Jesus say about that large sycamine tree to one with 'Mustard Seed Faith'? *'It would obey you'*.

An obedient tree sounds far-fetched, amen?

In our being blinded by Satan's fallen compatriots through his amazing, well groomed, well-spoken ministers of righteousness we forget the events which resulted in Jesus' disciple's amazement.

> "But the men marvelled, saying, What manner of man is this, that even the winds and the sea obey him!"

If Jesus had told the disciples that with mustard seed faith, they could control the wind and waves, Satan's ministers of righteousness would be teaching Jesus did not mean *'literal waves'*. They would preach about *'Mustard Seed Faith'* controlling the *'winds of adversity and the waves of depression'*!
Repentance anyone?
But Jesus is not at all like... them. Jesus, the Son of God, is relating real world truths to His disciples. Jesus is relating to them His reality, can be their reality.
Jesus told the water to become wine, it obeyed Him.
Jesus commanded the loaves and fishes to multiply; they obeyed Him.
Jesus walked on water as did Peter.
Why?
It was His servant.
God is unchanging, His rare, extremely rare servants stood out as they walked in His authority.
Moses' lifted his rod, then he stretched out his hand over the Red Sea, it parted in obedience.
Moses commanded the earth to swallow up Korah, it obeyed him.
Elijah told the widow woman her meal and oil would not run out. Both obeyed him.
Repentance anyone?
Jesus on the Mount of Temptation was tempted to command a stone to be made bread.
We now understand the stone would have obeyed Him, amen?
But in being proven by God Jesus knew His Father's voice and His Father's ways.
It would be in our not knowing His voice we would not walk WITH Him. We would have taken a different route.
That would be following the god of this world AND GLORIFYING ourselves in... our *'ministry'*.
Jesus waited on His Father to glorify Him.
The true servants of God need no glory, God is the One doing the work and is worthy of the glory. In our being a vessel that

is used, we are to be like the sycamine tree... we do not receive glory for obedience.

Can we grasp that?

In the end, neither the sycamine tree nor the obedient servant get any glory for doing what they are... told to do.

The water that was turned to wine did not '*glory*'.

The quiet wind and waves did not '*glory*'.

Likewise, a servant of God knows it was not HIM that went to Calvary or healed anyone in his strength. It is Christ who receives ALL glory.

There is much more, but the bottom line is this.

Are we redeemed? Are we born of the spirit to walk in the spirit?

Do we see the martyred deacon Stephen as preaching one message and losing his life? Do we see him missing out on having children, grand-children not having a full life?

If so, we are sooo deceived.

If we minister we have life because we are breathing, not having the ever present witness of the Holy Spirit who is our life? Then we are nothing more than cleaned up, well-groomed tucked, untucked charlatans, just chaff for the fire.

Same Jesus

This same Jesus who told His disciples if they had faith as a mustard seed they could command the tree, the mountain? He also told them this,

> "Abide in me, and I in you. As the branch cannot bear fruit of itself, except it abide in the vine; no more can ye, except ye abide in me."

Jesus told the eleven disciples who had been cleaned by the word He spoke to abide in Him.

> (Cleaned by the word? Do we recall that conversation with Nicodemus?)

He told these eleven to remain in Him. In John 14 Jesus had told them He would come to them in the Holy Ghost. Where two or three are gathered in His name, Jesus will manifest

through the Holy Spirit.
Can we just accept that? Believer, can we just accept that our being in the presence of the Holy Spirit we are encountering the Godhead? Our choosing to abide IN HIM is our being in Christ and encountering God, the Us who created everything?! Christ is made unto us righteousness, that in itself means we can enter His presence and remain! We are to have a conscience free from sin, guilt, and shame as we abide in Him.
It is in the Holy Spirit Christ is made unto us wisdom.
It is in the Holy Spirit Christ is made unto us justification.
It is in the Holy Spirit we are in Christ and have passed from condemnation to life.
It is through our abiding in the Holy Spirit we are not in the flesh but walking in NEW life.

> *"For in him dwelleth all the fulness of the Godhead*
> *bodily. And ye are complete in him, which is the head of*
> *all principality and power:"*

If we do not remain in Him, He will not remain in us, God's word. Do we think *'abiding'* is automatic? Have we been told we are *'abiding'* because we... believed?
Jesus *never* confused believing with abiding. Jesus actually means what He says.
Contrarily it is that man with fingers in your wallet your wife adores that tells you that you are great, and God's grace covers your life lived pleasing yourself.
Sounds a bit like the serpent and the woman in the Garden, does it not?
Jesus? What does HE say?

> *"If a man abide not in me, he is cast forth as a branch,*
> *and is withered; and men gather them, and cast them*
> *into the fire, and they are burned."*

Outside of Him, possessing *'beliefs, teachings'* living by the traditions of man the word of God is made of no effect and our metaphoric mountain? Or the hypothetical sycamine tree issue? They remain unmoved as the flesh and blood soul is... powerless.

Abiding in Christ occurs when we make a home for Him. This is why He said,

"Remain in me and I will remain in you."

If we do not 'abide in Him' He cannot remain in us. Listening to words that please our carnal religious soul we will gravitate to Satan's ministers who tell us God's grace covers our carnal living.

That lie we will ride until we come to a screeching standstill before the Lord... guilty of willful sin.

Being repetitive, earlier in this chapter these questions were asked, they remain relevant in the same manner.

Do we have real faith? Or religious pretensions?

Pharisaical stupidity is our declaring we walk in the Holy Spirit absent His power, His presence, stating it is by the Mustard Seed Faith our *'metaphorical'* mountains are being removed.

For us to declare we are abiding in Christ because we believe is the same error of stating the sycamine tree is a metaphor for our struggles.

Too much? Let us hear Hebrews,

"So I sware in my wrath, They shall not enter into my rest.) Take heed, brethren, lest there be in any of you an evil heart of unbelief, in departing from the living God."

To accept Jesus died for our *'body of sin'* and redeemed us from death to live pleasing ourselves is being of the same evil heart, sharing the same bad, bad perspective as the delivered Israelites.

Remember God's word,

'If you live after the flesh, you will die'.

Not *'you are dead'*, but that you will die.

God is not mocked and honestly, in living after the flesh, our future looks like hell. When we do spite to the spirit of grace, it is because we do not accept the price He paid, was the price we owed. Our being delivered from bondage is our having a redeemer, someone who has given us life. Having a redeemer is having someone as our *'savior'*. It is identical to honoring a father, a mother who initially gave us life. These people are worthy of being honored. Honoring someone in this case is fulfilling righteousness, doing what is right. Doing what is right is *'fulfilling righteousness'*. It is living for the One who saved us from death.

The evil Israelites?

They did not grasp this.

> *"Let us therefore fear, lest, a promise being left us of entering into his rest, any of you should seem to come short of it. For unto us was the gospel preached, as well as unto them: but the word preached did not profit them, not being mixed with faith in them that heard it."*

As faith comes by hearing, and hearing by the word of God, not taking what God is telling us and receiving it as life, is our rejecting faith in any form. Not hearing what God is telling us, is rejecting God, resisting His Holy Spirit, and following the wrong spirit, as it twists God's word. A few verses later in Hebrews we are told that we must labor. Labor involves our making an effort, amen?

> *"Let us labour therefore to enter into that rest, lest any man fall after the same example of unbelief."*

Abiding in the Holy Spirit initially is extremely difficult. It is described by my Lord as becoming as a baby, a little child as it is a brand New Life in Christ. Strong crying, strong pleading occurs as we transition from what we want, what pleases our dead soul, to what pleases God. As stated, the faith to make this transition is rare, extremely rare. If we remain steadfast, we will lose our soul-centered near-sightedness, and begin as our Lord to hear our Father's heart.

Purchased, and...?

In our being bought with a price, we are born from above, not to do our will but the will of Him who has redeemed us. However, in order to be obedient to God, we must be able to trust Him. In our being faithless, uncrucified, not buried with Christ, we develop our ministry, not our relationship with God in the Holy Spirit. And the glory we receive? As Balaam, we

have prostituted our gift and served another. The accolades, the honor? It is our only reward, God's mouth to our ears.
Not possessing faith in God, we instead put our faith in men that they will accept our presentation, our offering. We rely on their grace to overlook our slip ups and foibles.
Our offering?
It is our presentation of being knowledgeable AND spiritual. That is being a Malachiah priest. Check out your description... Malachi 2:3.
Not being under authority is the result of not trusting God. Faithlessness is not counting your soul dead and relying 100% on God's word and Spirit. As Ananias and Saphirra you hold what you committed to God back, in case things do not work out with God. That is why you preach and teach YOUR lessons, YOUR presentations, based on your reasonings and theology.
John the Baptist appropriately described you and the spirit you are of;

"You generation of vipers..."

This IS the warning for you to repent of the wrath that is not delayed.
Jesus described His church as foundationally different. He referred to it in different terms, with a different authority, and a different administration. But that is a completely different subject.
In conclusion... Following man, following man's teaching, even attending the *"Twice the Child of Hell Seminary"* obtaining their ordination only gets you the eternal identification of being a brute beast, as Cain.
Learning to drop all the Holy Spirit will not participate in, is living by God's word, with His Holy Spirit making His word our reality.
That is life, that is living, that is going from faith to faith, strength to strength, and appearing before our Lord in Zion.
Abiding in Him will result in possessing the very life by which all things were created. The result? Mustard Seed Faith...
The key to this potent faith has not been included in this

writing, just the steps in that direction.
The key?
It will be revealed by the Holy Spirit and its simplicity?
It will amaze you.
But the cost?
It is the same price Jesus paid in becoming a Living Sacrifice...

THE TEMPLE...
OF GOD?

God created man in His image, a living soul. The religiously *'saved'* man, the *'born-again'* Christian sees their life lived in the flesh as saved, their soul as redeemed, in the image of God.

However, this flesh and blood soul is lost when we seek to save it. As stated previously, it is not saved, nor will it ever be. This is not the uncorrupted living soul God created, pre-fall in His image.

According to God's word, believing our flesh and blood soul, our life lived after the flesh will be saved, is believing a lie, a different gospel.

Recall, flesh and blood will not inherit the Kingdom of God? Or that corruption will NOT inherit incorruption? If our flesh and blood life will not become incorruptible... What then of its redemption?

Flesh and blood living, is referring to our identity, the who we are in this flesh and blood body as our life. Identifying our life as in our flesh, is our valuing what our parent's birthed, nurtured, loved (or not), as *'who we are'*.

However, its only value per God's word, is in it being a living sacrifice.

If we see it differently... What then would be the need for a living sacrifice?

And why would there ever be a need for us to be born... again? If our flesh and blood life is saved, if that soul can be saved, there would never be any need to be born-again of God. Recall John 1:13?

> "...Which were born, not of blood, nor of the will of the flesh, nor of the will of man, but of God."

We can even call our life lived in the flesh, satisfying ourselves approved of men religiously as living in the spirit. That would be so true, but it would NOT be God's Holy Spirit.

Following the god, the spirit of this world as Adam is preserving and living pleasing our... selves. This occurs even as we accept and are accepted religiously by our peers. Consider Jesus in being baptized, or in Him being raised from the dead, how did His Father refer to Him?

Was it, *'Behold Our Son'* referring to the flesh and blood sinless flesh and blood soul born of Mary?

Or was it, *'Behold My Son in whom I am well pleased'* referring to His Son by whom He created all things?

The latter would be referring to Jesus, the Word of God made flesh living by the Holy Spirit. That is a different life, a different soul than the sinless soul than Mary had produced.

This is referring to the Last Adam, a New Creature. How could it be... a different life or soul?

As detailed in the previous chapter, 'Obtaining God's Soul,' it would have different blood animating different... flesh. As the life of the flesh is IN the blood, Jesus the word of God made flesh lived by the Holy Spirit flowing through the word made flesh, manifesting the very soul of God in the physical body prepared Him.

Romans 8 explains this, "*...shall also quicken your mortal bodies by his Spirit that dwelleth in you.*" Jesus' body was '*quickened*' or animated by the indwelling Holy Ghost.

This per Romans 8 is the result of Christ in you, with you being dead to the flesh or the body of sin.

Jesus died to the soul that Mary birthed from His baptism. Death to His natural man was accepted in its finality. He counted it dead and took to following the Holy Spirit as His life. *Contrast that* with cultural Churchianity...

When we baptized someone? They got wet, they received a certificate and maybe someone took them out to satisfy their soul at dinner.

Contrast that with Jesus' baptism.

Too much? Is He our example?

From baptism Jesus lived by EVERY word that proceeded from the mouth of God, following hard after the Holy Spirit. Have we heard that taught? Again does that sound too stringent, too hard?

> *Well gosh darn it, could that be why He walked in the power of God and the church which we are, does not?*

Being a living sacrifice, was not done in Jesus' strength, it was done in... get this, the enablement, the power of the Holy Spirit. The One and the Same Holy Spirit sent to.. those who are obedient.

This was what enabled Jesus to put on incorruption in His resurrection. Being raised from the dead, Jesus was living by the same word of God, the same Holy Spirit that He walked the earth in His body, the living sacrifice. It is in eating His flesh, and drinking His blood we have eternal life, this is EXACTLY what He told us in John's Gospel, chapter six.

This is how Jesus, being sent by God, lived by the Father. Your flesh and blood body, its Adamic reality?

Instead of relaxing IN IT, waiting for God to do something, it is to be reckoned dead, and become a living sacrifice with the fire of the Holy Spirit on it.

It is your choice, and my choice that we make before God, personally, individually. That is not my opinion, this is God's word.

There must be a major transition from the false foundation of chilling in our first-born soul as a *'believer'* calling it living.

That transition is called Calvary. It is essential to count the body of sin crucified WITH Christ for us to follow Jesus.

When we repent and accept Christ as our Saviour, our past sins are forgiven, amen?

Are we then at that point *'translated'* back into the pre-fall still imperfect sinless flesh and blood undying pre-sin Adamic state? If not, why not? Because that soul, the dead flesh and blood soul will not inherit the Kingdom of God. I am being redundant as this point cannot be overstressed.

The Temple
Jesus went through everything we must go through. From His baptism forward He walked out what we must walk out in order to assist us as we abide in the Holy Spirit. This abiding in Him enables us to lay aside everything in obedience through His strength in the Holy Spirit, not our carnal religious ability. That ability? It is called self-righteousness.
Good luck competing with Job on that one.
Being our example, it was in being filled with the Holy Spirit, then following the Holy Spirit living by His Father that Jesus became the Temple of God. Jesus identified His body, the word of God made flesh animated by the Holy Spirit, as the Temple of God to be raised up in incorruption.
Jesus, nor the apostles ever identified their flesh and blood bodies, as becoming the Temple of God apart from the Holy Spirit. In being born-again of God, of God's incorruptible word and spirit, this body is to possess the indwelling presence of the Holy Ghost on God's word.
As God will NOT anoint flesh, as NO flesh will glory in His presence, this reveals the body with its life accepted as a living sacrifice, only. Seriously.
At this point, it is relevant for us to review and count the cost as Jesus stated. Counting the cost enables us to make that commitment to count that dead thing, that first born soul as dead.
This goes against everything in us, as the life of the Adamic flesh is not... God's spirit.
If you disagree, just move into the tangible presence of the Holy Spirit and remain, abide in Him. If a war is present, if there is wrestling present, where does that struggle stem from?
Why is it called the '_body_' of sin?
Why was the '_Son of Man_' lifted up?'

Are these not clues?

We can recall out of the millions of Jews exiting Egypt, only two, Joshua and Caleb entered the Promised Land (*other than the Levitical priesthood tribe*).

Noah stands out from billions, so when we look at the '*cost*', understand that true faith in God, is the exception to the rule, the rare item, the precious fruit that God is looking for.

For me?

How to possess true faith in God had been hidden from me. Raised in Churchianity, I was powerless to live victorious. I desired to, but there was no power in the gospel presented to me. I could not accept that living in my strength calling it Christ was anything less than my living self-righteously.

I stumbled, I fell, I crawled, as I could not get up and walk before God in the Christian life as presented. I failed family, I failed friends, I just... failed very miserably at being a 'good Christian' in my strength.

I was the very reason Jesus went to Calvary, right brother? There was no one more despicable than I was.

Yet it was for me Jesus paid my price so that I can stand righteous before God based on Him...

> *You told me at the funeral you wished I had died, as*
> *'y'all loved my wife'. I am not blaming, or faulting you.*
> *You were correct, I more than deserved death, but Jesus*
> *took that place of condemnation for me!*

Now this life is His, His life is MINE!!!

It is a NEW LIFE!!!

This message is His, and I unashamedly declare that absent the presence of my Father in the Holy Spirit both you and I are life-less. Please forgive me for the pain I caused you... I was desperately in need of God, and did not know how to come into a relationship with Him at that point.

I was then reduced to the place that without the presence of the Holy Ghost I was dead. I now thank God for that tribulation, and I now know as my reality that abiding in Him is my life, and the length of my eternal day!! We, you the reader and I both must recognize the Holy Spirit as God, we must understand the necessity of His tangible presence to present our body a living sacrifice.

Being born of the incorruptible word, and in receiving the Holy Spirit as the earnest of our inheritance, our bodies are to be the Temple of God in holiness. But before we exclaim, awesome, amazing, or hallelujah let us consider a few things.

Let us hear God, speaking to Ezekiel in chapter 8 very directly regarding the Temple;

> "Then said he unto me, Son of man, lift up thine eyes now the way toward the north. So I lifted up mine eyes the way toward the north, and behold northward at the gate of the altar this image of jealousy in the entry. He said furthermore unto me, Son of man, seest thou what they do? even the great abominations that the house of Israel committeth here, that I should go far off from my sanctuary? but turn thee yet again, and thou shalt see greater abominations."

We have received the earnest of our inheritance, the Holy Spirit and are also declared now to be God's inheritance.

We are NOT to grieve the Holy Spirit, we are to understand He contains the Godhead and fellowship Him in love.

This is our becoming His place of rest....

If we are obtuse, living after the flesh we can declare we are the Temple of God, we are God's sanctuary, but that in itself does not ensure divine protection, nor that we will inherit God's promises.

Recall Hebrews 4?

God destroyed the earthly temples due to their disgusting filth they imposed upon Him. Their ambivalence towards God pushed God away from His own house. Grieving God, vexing God was the result of their self-centered stupidity to put it bluntly.

What we likewise may have done in ignorance was covered by grace, but now when we defile it knowingly?

There is no sacrifice that covers willful sin, but a certain fearful

looking forward to judgement.
Accountability follows this understanding.
Before we knew we were to abide in the tangible Holy Spirit, God's patience, God's grace covered an abundance of sin.
But now?
The Holy Spirit is telling us that as He used to be an unwilling participant in all we did?
Our flesh is now to be the unwilling participant in following the Holy Spirit.
Next time you sit down to enjoy a television show, try to enjoy it in the presence of God's tangible Holy Spirit. If you cannot, God is enduring it just as He endured the filth the Old Testament priests threw in His face. In Malachi 2, God returned their excrement giving them a facial with it not stopping there. He then threw them on the manure pile.
Do we desire that identity?
We do have a different covenant, but an unchanging God, amen?
The apostle God called and sent, the apostle Paul, tells us this;
"...If any man defile the temple of God, him shall God destroy; for the temple of God is holy, which temple ye are.
Let no man deceive himself. If any man among you seemeth to be wise in this world, let him become a fool, that he may be wise." 1 Corinthians 3
This word just got personal. This is no longer *'corporate'* at all. Being the temple of God, the responsibility is on the reader and the author what we do with it. If we defile it, allowing the spirit of lust, greed, idolatry *(covetousness)* in it, or sell out Christ in pleasing man instead of God? God's word is abundantly clear.
Being the Temple of God means our body is to house the holy presence of God. In this, do we believe it is automatic or does faith involve our actual participation?
In the scriptures below, Jesus is talking with the 11 disciples. Neither the 5,000 or the 70 are present, Judas has departed. Again, for us to state this scripture includes us is to identify

our level of love, of commitment as the same as these 11 disciples. This also means we as them cleave to the tangible Holy Ghost, and drop all that hinders His tangible presence. Otherwise, we are willfully seduced and deceived. Jesus is speaking with His disciples....

> *"Now ye are clean through the word which I have spoken unto you.*
> *Abide in me, and I in you. As the branch cannot bear fruit of itself, except it abide in the vine; no more can ye, except ye abide in me." John 15:3-4*
> *"If a man abide not in me, he is cast forth as a branch, and is withered; and men gather them, and cast them into the fire, and they are burned." John 15:6*

Can we understand why it is our part to abide in Christ? Are we to be the place of rest God has desired? Or are we going to take all the creator has provided and as the Israelites in the wilderness, focus on our carnal appetites?

Can we see the necessity of abiding in the tangible, Holy Spirit? To not abide, is to deny Jesus Christ.

To not abide is to put our back to the life of God, the Godhead in the tangible Holy Spirit.

As stated previously, we know that God is no respecter of persons, right?

The excuse of '*I did not know?*' It is now exposed as an evil heart of '*I did not seek you. I had better things to do*'.

These disciples had been cleansed. Jesus had given them the word His Father gave Him. As Jesus lived by every word that proceeded from the mouth of God by the Holy Spirit; the disciples were now being instructed to do the same.

They were told just as they had followed Him; They were soon to follow the promised Comforter, the Holy Spirit inclusive of the Godhead abiding in them. This would refer to the Father, the Son, through the Holy Spirit!

> *"At that day ye shall know that I am in my Father, and ye in me, and I in you." John 14:20*

The disciples knew the tangible presence of the Holy Spirit, it

was not '*faux faith*'.
> "And I will pray the Father, and he shall give you another Comforter, that he may abide with you forever: Even the Spirit of truth; whom the world cannot receive, because it seeth him not, neither knoweth him: but ye know him; for he dwelleth with you, and shall be in you...." John 14:16-17

Jesus stated if the disciples loved Him, they would keep His words. They would abide in Him. He then states that His Father will love them and '*we*,' meaning the Father, the Son will abide in the disciple by, or via the Holy Spirit. Jesus just stated the Godhead is to abide IN us through the Holy Spirit, this results when we keep His words!
Keeping His words is doing what He is telling us, amen?
> "...he that loveth me shall be loved of my Father, and I will love him, and will manifest myself to him.
> Judas saith unto him, not Iscariot, Lord, how is it that thou wilt manifest thyself unto us, and not unto the world?
> Jesus answered and said unto him, If a man love me, he will keep my words: and my Father will love him, and we will come unto him, and make our abode with him."

Do we remember why the world could not receive the Holy Spirit? It was because they could not '*see Him*'. Yet Jesus is telling His disciples it is in the Holy Spirit that He will reveal Himself to them.
Being repetitive, the five thousand who followed Him to get their bellies filled, are not there.
The cost? They might miss dinner...
The seventy who rejoiced in their '*power in ministry*' are absent. The cost? Maybe their peers would not accept them, better to '*assemble with the troops*' at the whorehouse next Sunday... (Jeremiah 5).
For us to not forsake all to follow Jesus in and through abiding in the Holy Spirit excludes us from ANY and all promises made to those who do, amen? This remains true regardless of what

the Satan's apostle tells you...
Accountability follows.
Jesus is telling those who have forsaken all to follow Him, to remain IN His presence through the tangible Holy Spirit. They '*knew*' the Holy Spirit as He dwelt with them, and they had been cleaned through the washing of the word.
These were the cleansed vessels that the Holy Spirit would soon indwell with power...
Jesus reveals spiritual life as a present moment-to-moment reality. The scripturally knowledgeable man will want to ascribe this living as occurring sometime in the future. Or the religious man will say he possesses it now by a faux faith, absent the tangible Holy Spirit. To state we are walking in the spirit apart from the Holy Ghost because we know a scriptural reference? Just because '*we think*' it does, does not make it accurate. That is God's word. That is what Jesus told the Jews;

"Search the scriptures; for in them 'ye think' ye have eternal life: and they are they which testify of me."

Thinking something is applicable to us because we know a scripture, is having faith in our scriptural knowledge. That is the error of religious pride and great darkness. There are two souls, two deaths, two resurrections, two fires. God tells us to choose His word and spirit, to choose eternal life. Following the Lord we are to be raised up in Christ and burn with the fire of the Holy Spirit...
But this is our decision, not God's, amen?
We need to choose the soul of God for life, or not. We need to pick our death, and our fire, as that will determine our resurrection.
Suffering with Christ is dying to ALL the Holy Spirit will not witness with His presence. If any man does not have, as in possess the spirit of Christ, he is none of His.
You can sense your lungs taking in air, you can feel your pulse, that is not faith, amen?
Do you actually think physically breathing is you possessing life?

To walk in NEWNESS of life is experiencing the tangible Holy Spirit, valuing Him more than your breath! This is living... as Christ IS our life. It is in this, it is in the Holy Spirit we receive God the Father and are following God the Son, amen? To say we live in the Holy Spirit apart from being aware of Him, is saying God's presence is not discernable.

Seriously?

At the same time, the spirit of lust, of greed, of jealousy, of hate? These are all discernable, and tangible which we KNOW!!!!!! My Lord, why do we identify with the fallen spirits as our life? Why do we identify with principalities, powers and spiritual wickedness as our life, and deny the Holy God of all creation???

This is an indescribable idiocy...

In this understanding we just confirmed everything stated above. We have been dead walking after the spirit of this world by choice...

Now we see this as open hostility to God.

Before God, again, I tell you the truth, the patience for this idiocy has just departed.

My Father's House

The religious natural man would attempt to define God's word by the natural mind, or the known laws of physics. That would be the carnal mind that receives nothing from God, amen? Jesus declared;

> "In my Father's house are many mansions: if it were not so, I would have told you. I go to prepare a place for you. And if I go and prepare a place for you, I will come again, and receive you unto myself; that where I am (present tense), there ye may be also.
> And whither I go ye know, and the way ye know."

Jesus left to go prepare a place for His disciples following His resurrection.

Jesus then returned in the Holy Ghost on the day of Pentecost keeping His promise to His disciples.

The promised place was prepared, the blood had been applied to the Mercy Seat, and there was nothing separating the disciple from His Lord!

In the Holy Spirit, the way is manifest. For us to follow Jesus and abide in the tangible Holy Spirit, Jesus laid down some very stringent costs. Being redundant, these costs include suffering the loss of the first-born soul, to find the soul born of God.

Luke 14:26-28 and John 12:25-26 excludes our even having the capability to follow Jesus, except we hate our soul, our life in this world.

Our example?

Again, it is our Lord. Jesus' soul, Jesus' life in His blood, the life of the flesh? It was the accepted sinless sacrifice; it was denied in His walk here, and then it was poured out at Calvary. After being led by the Holy Spirit into the wilderness, the *'soul'* that came of the wilderness was the express image of God. That soul was the Word of God, animated by the Holy Spirit, and to this moment remains the very image of God. This is our calling, nothing less. If we disagree...

Are we to become perfect in a manner different than how Jesus became... perfect? (Hebrews 2).

Who do we think WE are?!

Jesus exited the wilderness walking in the power of the spirit, just as we are to do also in being raised up IN Him!

We know God has a soul, amen?

Now we can say, we are looking right at it! Jesus is the express image of His Father...

We have identified two souls, one to be counted dead from baptism, and one that is to be found.

It is James we read of the man that has *'two hearts'*, or minds. The Greek word is *'dipsychos'*, which refers to two souls. Having two minds, is wavering. James discusses the man who has *'two souls'* as being unable to receive anything from God. Trying to please God and fulfill your life in the flesh is now known as being *'double-minded'*.

Let us hear God's messenger Paul, whose prior identity was Saul of Tarsus.

> *"I beseech you therefore, brethren, by the mercies of God, that ye present your bodies a living sacrifice, holy, acceptable unto God, which is your reasonable service. And be not conformed to this world: but be ye transformed by the renewing of your mind, that ye may prove what is that good, and acceptable, and perfect, will of God." Romans 12*

We see the flesh and blood birthed soul as being only of value, in the manner in which Jesus offered it up in His walk here. That sacrifice became the Temple of God in power, after the first soul was reckoned dead.

WHITE CANE BLIND
and
Dead Drunk

When Adam sinned, spiritually he became blind. The serpent was no longer seen. Adam had died to the life lived in the spirit of God on His word in his pure soul. His dead flesh and blood soul now was the access point for the god of this world. Adam began living according to the unseen god of this world.

It was then Adam... *reproduced.*

Now *'his dead to god'* descendants hear the god of this world's words as their own *'thoughts'*, and accept his scenarios as their own *'imaginations'*.

Deceased Adam AND his descendants own these inputs as though they were their own, as they proceed from within their mind, will, and emotions, their deceased soul with its limited life-span.

The god of this world <u>is the fallen man's identity</u> in this world. Fulfilling the desires of the flesh and of the mind Paul describes those who live after the *god of their flesh* as the children of wrath in Ephesians 2.

Aware only of self, Adam is now snake-bit, intoxicated, poisoned with the awareness of his physical body as his only life.

Adam no longer is a living soul, he is a different creature, a beast now influences Adam's soul manipulating it though it were his own. No longer living by God's word, in Genesis 3:12 Adam would rather sacrifice his wife, than physically die.

Does that sound like a son of God? Or a child of wrath?

Babylon, the Great Whore has her first victims (Revelation 18:24).
Adam cooperating with the serpent has heard, believed and acted on another's word. Receiving the spirit on that word, Adam's physical eyes were opened to a different reality, Adam is now *dead drunk* on his carnal 'flesh-based' perceptions.
Dead to God and the power of God's word, Adam is drunk on his physical senses that are now his life. Following the thoughts flooding his mind, he is now consumed with saving his soul.
But God had this question for Adam, "*Who told him he was naked?*"
It was not Mrs. Adam, it was the god of this world, unseen and yammering away. Adam, and his descendants receive these thoughts, these words as their life, their reality, and as they do the god of this world has his place of rest in them. Their main concern is themselves, their possessions, and their validations. But when they die, they carry the stigma of the spirit they followed, their possessions, validations are lost as their own 'self' goes in the ground. The only way to see this, is God's way. They are drunk. That drunkenness is their being pleasured by a spirit they are following willingly.

> "*I will shew unto thee the judgment of the great whore that sitteth upon many waters:*
> *With whom the kings of the earth have committed fornication, and the inhabitants of the earth have been made drunk with the wine of her fornication...*"
> "*So he carried me away in the spirit into the wilderness...*" Revelation 17

In verse 15, the '*waters*' are described as the inhabitants of the earth. This is where we see the whore at rest, the earth that we have called home? We now understand earth is being identified as the wilderness.
That clears a great deal up, amen?
It is in the wilderness that God reveals who He is to His child. The wilderness is the place of being proven. Being proven

occurs before the experience of being raised up in Christ seated at God's right hand in power.

It is our departing the wilderness following the Holy Spirit that we walk in authority, in the rest God has provided us IN Christ.

If we are to be raised up at the right hand of God to rule, to reign, we are no longer identified as an *'inhabitant of the earth'*, but with those who dwell in heaven.

Again, departing the wilderness is *'entering into the rest'* that God has provided. This is where we cease from our own works, and all things are of God. This is where we walk in the Holy Spirit following Him just as Jesus did, and the apostles also in following Christ.

If not, we live on the earth in the wilderness with its inhabitants finding our validation, our purpose. And physical death? It is seen as the end of our precious little life.

But for the believer, the one who loves God, acknowledging being raised IN Christ is walking as a servant of God.

We are to be the temple where God joins heaven and earth through us to manifest His glory.

Per Romans 5, we are to reign in life, that life being in Christ.

> "...For if by one man's offence death reigned by one;
> much more they which receive abundance of grace and
> of the gift of righteousness shall reign in life by one,
> Jesus Christ.)"

It is through faith in what God accomplished in raising Jesus from the dead, that righteousness is imputed unto us and we are saved, (Romans 10:9) Believing that Christ is raised, is accepting we were crucified WITH Him, and our old man is now dead. Otherwise, we will still *'live in the wilderness'* we call earth as though it were the promised land.

Our reigning is walking in authority being raised in Christ with our flesh and blood soul counted dead, being a living sacrifice *under authority* with Jesus as our head.

Necessities

Our view of this world as home MUST be changed through the renewing of our mind.

Our view of who Christ is in us, of who we are in Him must become preeminent in order for us to walk pleasing to Him. We are not to love these physical bodies unto death, but count them as a living sacrifice for God's glory.

Now the correlation between the Israelites departing Egypt into the wilderness is understood. The correlation of Jesus going INTO the wilderness, then exiting in the power of God is understood. We who will walk in the power of God will grasp these truths and drop everything to come into an intimate relationship with our Father, in and by His spirit, His Holy Spirit through believing His word.

Now we see what a great salvation God has wrought through Jesus Christ! Now we see the deliverance from Egypt in a new light! We can understand hating our life in this 'world' the wilderness, to enter into life in Christ who is our rest! We can see it is in the Holy Spirit we exit the wilderness and are seated at the right hand of God, in Christ.

We can now understand Hebrews 4. What is the rest God has prepared if not our being raised up and seated at His right-hand through abiding IN CHRIST?!

Is this not where Christ sat down AFTER defeating our enemy? Is it not in walking following His presence we are delivered out of the wilderness? Is this not why in the wilderness, the Israelites NEVER walked in darkness? Was not God's presence by day a pillar of cloud, and a pillar of fire at night?

If we are in the wilderness, we are to walk in the light of His presence, not in the dark as those who know not God.

The Apostle John in 1 John 5 describes the world (the wilderness) as lying in wickedness. God through Isaiah chapter 60 tells us,

> "Arise, shine; for thy light is come, and the glory of the LORD is risen upon thee.
> For, behold, the darkness shall cover the earth, and gross darkness the people: but the LORD shall arise

upon thee, and his glory shall be seen upon thee."

Paul spoke with King Agrippa regarding His charge from Jesus,

"...To open their eyes, and to turn them from darkness to light, and from the power of Satan unto God, that they may receive forgiveness of sins, and inheritance among them which are sanctified by faith that is in me."

In Churchianity, we have not entered the *'rest'* provided by God from before creation.

The wilderness' cultural church is led by those whose chosen profession is being a pastor. One man at a bible school told me he considered being a pastor because he would have Mondays off. Barbers do also. Not being called by God, cutting hair would not have the greater condemnation.

Professional pastors may have the gift of God, as described in Psalms 68:18, but if they are not yet called, or sent by God... ..they are at this very moment in absolutely the wrong place, at the wrong time. IF they were called by God, they would serve Him in fear, and reverence. Instead, they present their word studies, or motivational speeches.

These men, these false ministers are the precious stones that bedeck the Great Whore.

"And the woman was arrayed in purple and scarlet colour, and decked with gold and precious stones and pearls..."

These precious stones were to have been the temple of God but have *'bent the knee'* and taken the easier deadlier route receiving their temporal kingdom.

"And I saw the woman drunken with the blood of the saints, and with the blood of the martyrs of Jesus: and when I saw her, I wondered with great admiration."

To be absent from the body is to be present with the Lord, amen? So this *'woman'* is guilty of the blood of those she has murdered, but she cannot be drunk with the blood of those who have passed. They are present with the Lord, amen? However, we find she is drunk with the blood of the *'martyrs'* of Jesus Christ. The life, or soul of the flesh is in the blood per

Leviticus 17:11.

The Great Whore is drunk with the blood, she is intoxicated with the very bloodstream of the souls of the saints. Those believers who believe they can serve God and still live in this world are committing adultery. James lays this truth out plainly.

> *"Ye adulterers and adulteresses, know ye not that the friendship of the world is enmity with God? whosoever therefore will be a friend of the world is the enemy of God."*

This is the filthiness that has made its presence known in heaven, as Sodom likewise did. This is the fornication and adultery believers are committing with her as they live pleasing their souls, living after the flesh apart from the Holy Spirit.

The word martyr refers not only to those killed by her. It is also referred to as a '*living witness*'. Jesus told his disciples if a brother trespassed against them and would not hear them, then to '*take with them one or two more, that in the mouth of two or three witnesses (martyrs) every word may be established*'. The word witnesses is also translated martyrs from the same Greek word.

So we see the Great Whore is intoxicated with those who are the witnesses of Jesus Christ, but have not been crucified unto the world, neither the world crucified unto them.

These '*temples of God*' will be destroyed.

> *"And they that are Christ's have crucified the flesh with the affections and lusts.*
> *If we live in the Spirit, let us also walk in the Spirit."*
> *Galatians 5*

These believers are '*one*' with her in adultery and fornication as they find their religious man pleasing '*life*' in her. This occurs apart from them being seated at God's right hand in Christ.

These are the earth dwellers who find their life, their home in the wilderness.

They are not to be confused with those that inhabit the heavens seated in Christ.

A disciple of Jesus being on the earth, is a citizen of heaven. In not loving our life in this wilderness unto death, we remain, we abide IN Him, seated at the right hand of God.

Recall those who in the wilderness sought to save their lives, their souls? They died there with an evil heart withholding faith in a God who had revealed Himself multiple times as their deliverer, their provider. That was written for our admonition, our learning, amen? The Israelites faith? It was in their prudence, in their wisdom, in their attempts to save themselves that they perished in their wilderness.

We can learn from them, right?

In Genesis 3:1 we find Adam through willful disobedience followed the one from whom he derived his wisdom.

Reasonable AND Prudent

God through Moses defined the serpent in one word. *'Subtil'*.

Subtil is being prudent, it is doing what makes sense, being reasonable.

Wow, prudent?!! Wise? Subtil? This articulate serpent was defined as *'more subtil'* of all the beasts. It made sense to Adam, to follow Satan's word even though he knew... God's word.

Would we do that?

In our intellectualism, would we do what *'makes sense'* as opposed to putting our precious reputation and *'our life'* in peril?

Recall the Israelites being trapped at the Red Sea?

Not a very wise route fleeing bondage, amen?

Not prudent, nor reasonable. Not at all... subtil.

God's ways are above our ways, God's ways are higher than ours.

This is why God calls the wisdom of this world, foolishness. Theology is blind men describing their theory of what *'God hath said..'*

Otherwise God's word would be recognized as revelation by

His Holy Spirit in the power of God.

God's word does not make sense to the flesh and blood soul that has been raised under the god of this world. Bible Schools and Seminaries that declare the Holy Spirit an *'emotion'* are totally dead to the tangible Holy Spirit and close to committing the sin that is not forgivable. If they remain uncorrectable, their leaders will be revealed by God as the bastards they have chosen to be.

Jesus called their counterparts in His time here the serpent's seed, fools, and children of hell.

God is spirit, yet they have reduced their god to the image of their wonderful, revered, and respected leader whom they worship...

And their leader?

He loves it.

White Canes... Everywhere?

The inhabitants of the world are the equivalent of citizens with sunglasses, white canes wandering as bestial entities in their souls tell them what they see, what to think, and how to respond. As the blind listen, and as it makes sense, they follow the god of this world.

Dead drunk on the word of another, blind as to who they follow, they receive Babylon in their hearts and minds. They join with her spirit on her word, uniting themselves with her. They are intoxicated, blind, walking in adultery, and fornication. Being factual, the truth is the world lies in darkness.

Men approve men ordaining self-called pastors to market the soul pleasing message they purchased. This is ministry, this is business. In following these blind church leaders who are dead to God, we follow the spirit that shares her glory with them. The result of the blind leading the blind is they both fall in a ditch.

All a ditch is, is a rut. All a rut is, is a grave, with both ends kicked out. Walking in death, til they lie down in death, those who follow man can never exit this grave.

Wandering the world in a rut is NOT going from glory to glory, faith to faith through the Holy Ghost.

Our ability to exit the rut is found in our abiding in Christ, the tangible Holy Spirit on God's revealed word. Accepting Jesus as being the light of the world, it is now our *hating our prior existence, our history, our walking apart from God in the world*. Our past was detestable in walking after the prince of the power of the air. Jude talks briefly about '*hating the garment spotted by the flesh*'.

If we relish our past we are as the delivered slaves, the Jews in their longing for Egypt.

They were extremely unwise as they in their lust for the food they had previously eaten, willfully withheld faith in God.

Being an overcomer we now recognize the tangible Holy Spirit ON God's word... as life! We need to remember, whatsoever is not of faith, is sin, or missing the mark. How would we respond, if the Holy Spirit revealed our jobs, our reliance and trust in the world's financial system was our faith in Babylon apart from God? What if this was revealed as our walking '*blind*'. Would we begin to acknowledge Jesus as our only provider in all we do? Would we become His servant on our job? Would we consume His word and submit all our ways to the tangible Holy Spirit acknowledging all our needs are already met '*in Him?*'

Or in a time of testing, would we '*redeem*' ourselves, our finances and '*get religious?*' If we do not see the Lord as our provider, if we do not see Him in our provision, and serve Him in what we do, this is evil.

The word of God is true, it is IN Christ that we are complete and have need of nothing, not religiously so, but through our abiding in Him.

The Jewish leaders had God's word which had been delivered through Moses. Recall death had reigned from Adam to Moses? The entrance of God's word was to bring light and life, the key ingredient being the '*entrance of God's word*'. Without being yielded to the Holy Spirit which gives life to the word, the Holy Spirit had no entrance. God's word then became a dead letter to these heirs of God.

The Israelites without being yielded to the Holy Spirit were in darkness. Those covenant children of Abraham chosen of God had God's word, but that word did not do them much good. Knowing God's written word, while resisting the Holy Ghost is denying the very power of God. In this, the Israelites were repeatedly defeated, dispossessed and struggled under other rulers, being conquered and despised.

Can we identify with them?

In hindsight we can say they were disobedient, and that they lacked faith in God, but to them?

They worshiped at the temple, and God's laws were part of their everyday life! They searched the scriptures, and per Jesus, they thought in the scriptures they had eternal life. They were full of God's word, yet impotent, having no power with God. But hey, that was okay, because after all they *like us drew their validation from each other*, not God... amen?

With that we can understand them completely.

As professional ministers not sent by God use their spiritual demeanors coupled with the knowledge of God's word, they exercise authority with men, not God. Just as with the Israelites, so it is with them... God's word is prevalent, yet powerless.

When we pick and choose the word of God that applies to us and willfully avoid, ignore what the Holy Spirit is saying? We exist as a god with no fear of God.

As we have no fear of God, Satan has no reason to fear us as we possess *no authority* over him.

This knowledge removes the hedges of God's protection. That understanding should really cause us to hit our knees! Contrast this understanding of God that Jesus had with the understanding of our present-tense real-time religious leaders.

"...*Who in the days of his flesh, when he had offered up*

prayers and supplications with strong crying and tears unto him that was able to save him from death, and was heard in that he feared..." Hebrews 5

Jesus had the wisdom, the need to go before God, yielding to the One able to save Him from death. Should that not cause us to get extremely serious with God?!

Reverential fear is missing in our temporal life here because we do not even recognize our God. We do not even know the Holy Spirit, as we have been taught by word and example interacting with Him is non-essential.

We have grown so accustomed to grieving the Holy Spirit, IT IS OUR LIFESTYLE....

The live music worship band, the dancing, banner waving sounds more like the worshippers of Baal, or the delivered Israelites prancing around the golden calf.

Jesus was alone and in fearing the One who has the power after He has killed to also to cast into hell, Jesus was heard.

Never do we see Him backed up with live music manipulating souls. Babylon, rock on, your sins as Sodom's have reached into Heaven. When judgement comes, you can pray, you can rebuke the enemy, all to no avail.

As with Noah's generation, as with Sodom, as with the disobedient Israelites in the wilderness, once judgement began? God honored the decision they had made to their own hurt.

This is one of God's ways.

God is today, *this day* telling us to depart Babylon, we need to hear what the spirit is saying to the church.

Or not...

Those that are wicked, let them be wicked still, it is of no consequence to the believer seated at God's right hand.

Jesus has said, Let the dead bury the dead. Jesus also declared those that do not believe are condemned already.

Have you heard about THAT Jesus?

Jesus never chased down anyone asking them to please, oh please reconsider Him.

The word of God that proceeds from God's mouth, never placates the natural man's soul in its ease, or in its self-centered living. Ever.

The things that happened to the Israelites, happened for our admonition, upon whom the ends of the world has come. To be here on this earth at this time, is an amazing opportunity for those with ears to hear. Noah had faith in God, as did Moses, Joshua, and Caleb.

These men were not heard or respected in their generations, but before God they stood out...

Jesus Walked Out Equality WITH God

Baptized in the Holy Spirit at baptism, led of the Holy Spirit into the wilderness, dying to sinless self by the Holy Spirit... it was only then Jesus exited the wilderness in the power of the Holy Spirit.

Every word that proceeded from His lips after that, was the word that God was present tense speaking.

That would be Jesus walking in union with God His Father, amen? Walking in union with God, is walking by the same word God is speaking. This includes the Holy Spirit present to perform the spoken word. Does this sound a bit like the power of creation? God watched over that word, as it was His word, amen? Why? Because very simply...it was.

> "Let this mind be in you, which was also in Christ Jesus:
> Who, being in the form of God, thought it not robbery to
> be equal with God..."

What would be equality with God? Equality here is being *'in agreement'*.

Being equal is as four sides agree being *'equal'* in length, not being different.

Being equal with God is agreeing with God that walking in or after God's tangible Holy Spirit is life, His life in you. This is walking in the light.

The simplicity is this.

We are to have this same mind be in us, that was in Christ

Jesus. This mind? He became of no reputation becoming a servant, making another's will, His will. In making His Father's will His will, He identified with His Father's purpose for Him.

Jesus understood the cross lied ahead, He understood He was to take on the sin of man. Jesus identified with His Father and entrusted His soul... His life that He had with His Father from before creation to God His Father.

This is radical to me.

Having taken on a body, the life of that body was to become the sacrifice for sin, and this body made in the likeness of man, was also to manifest the exact representation of His Father. In this, His flesh and blood first soul made in the likeness of sinful man was to be died to, to reveal God.

This is the *exact reverse* of what had transpired with the first Adam. This had to happen.

<u>The first Adam</u> died to God and became a servant to the god of this world preferring his flesh and blood soul, or life in the flesh.

<u>The Last Adam</u> died to His flesh and blood soul to become the servant of God walking in the Holy Spirit.

For you, and I to walk in the spirit and take on the mind of Christ, we must acknowledge our body as Paul did his; It contains no good thing. It is only in the tangible Holy Ghost that we agree with God, and become One in Him. In Him, in walking in the Holy Spirit we are not in the flesh, but in the spirit, in union with God IF we suffer as Jesus did, the circumcision of the flesh.

This is our covenanting WITH God.

This is where having consumed God's word, we follow hard after the Holy Spirit understanding HE IS OUR LIFE! Abiding in the Holy Spirit, is our not grasping at equality with God, but making this body His temple, His place of rest, His place of abiding.

With Him abiding, as He did in Jesus He then has a place in us, through us, to work as He did through His only begotten Son.

Being 'One' is both parts being made complete. In being 'One' equality is not an issue, as 'wholeness' is realized.

> *Jesus died to bring forth fruit after His kind, amen?*

I am to be 'One' with God through the Holy Spirit, just as each member of His body. This is my family, the family of God. These are those who take up their cross and make the very presence of my Father their life. The body they have in this wilderness, this earth? It is not their priority, God's presence on His word is their life.

Jesus told us clearly;

> "God is a Spirit: and they that worship him must
> worship him in spirit and in truth."

Now we understand Jesus being '*equal*' with God is Jesus abiding in God's tangible Holy Spirit.

Walking in the tangible Holy Spirit, is possessing the very Spirit that God is.

As stated, it is in becoming ONE with God in the Holy Spirit that wholeness is found, equality is not an issue! This is how Jesus lived by the Father. Jesus counted the physical flesh and blood soul as literally deceased, and offered it up to God through the spirit of holiness.

Put simply, Jesus did what Paul tells us to do. Jesus shut down the affections, and the validations of the flesh through the Holy Ghost.

Even sinless desires were brought into subjection to the Holy Spirit as He fasted for forty days. Jesus of Nazareth died to His flesh and blood soul...

At the wedding at Cana, His mother was addressed as a person of no personal importance, '*woman..*' When His family came looking for Him, He asked those He was teaching,

> "Who is my mother? and who are my brethren?
> And he stretched forth his hand toward his disciples,
> and said, Behold my mother and my brethren!
> For whosoever shall do the will of my Father which is in
> heaven, the same is my brother, and sister, and mother."

Jesus died to His flesh and blood soul life as a living sacrifice to come into agreement with God.

That agreeing?

Jesus acknowledged that His life was God's spirit on God's word. Walking being full of the Holy Ghost, it was God in Christ, amen?

What is the difference between God the Holy Spirit, and God the Father? In that they indwelt Jesus and He lived by the Father, Jesus showed us *how to walk with God.*

Are these just words, can we grasp what is being said?

Jesus became God's word made flesh. The only words that issued from His mouth were His Father's... His Father in Him did the works.

Sacrilegious?

When was Jesus filled with the Holy Spirit and when did the Holy Spirit dwell on Him, and when did the Holy Spirit indwell Him with power?

Did the disciples have the Holy Ghost dwell with them, and then *IN THEM* in power?

Did Jesus learn obedience?

And lastly; Is Jesus the Son of God?

If so, then He endured correction, as God chastises EVERY son He receives. Hebrews 2 reveals Jesus was tempted in all points as we are, this means Jesus walked the very path we must walk, to come into sonship with our Father! Recall John 1, we, you and I also have this power to 'become' the sons of God?

Allowing the same mind in us that was in Christ, is not thinking it robbery to be equal with God as we become a servant of God, and drop everything He will not witness with His presence to abide in Him.

Jesus is our example, our pattern. His flesh and blood body that Mary had birthed was pure, sinless. Jesus understood that this body was to be offered up to God as a living sacrifice. From His baptism to the cross it was not regarded, it was not prioritized. The tangible presence of God the Holy Spirit was His only life (John 8:29). If this is too much, then we can just *'study it out...'* We can intellectually research this, amen pastor? We can make

the biblical *'Jesus'* a historical study, part of the eschatology class we took, or possibly just one subject in our hermeneutics class?
Or maybe Jesus can be a *part of our life*, like our career.
We have a house, cars, spouse, children, two dogs, our church, our ministry *and we have Jesus.*
Whose disciple are we?
Whose child are we, really?
Are we a child of heaven, or a child of wrath?
What is our concern, do we have any?
I know, too many questions, but before God the answers from your heart have already been heard.
The soul is deceitful, desperately wicked per God through Jeremiah. We can religiously believe what we think, and what we say is true. Yet God sees the reality of what word, what spirit we really receive and... act on.
Living in the Holy Spirit requires a few things.
One, a genuine love for God that encompasses being concerned about the things that concern Him.
Another requirement is the willingness to accept God's Holy Spirit, as being in the presence of God, Himself. IN that God is love, He is gentle, not forceable, He will not require that you abide in Him. Yet abiding in Him evidences your love to Him, and He will evidence His approval with His presence. His approval, His presence will be how He leads us.
Finally, learn the fear of God, learn what it is to fear Him, as He is holy. No flesh can glory in His presence, and as Paul tells us, we are not in the flesh but in the spirit if the spirit of God indwells us. That would be the result of our abiding in Him, amen?
I would ask the sincere believer, submit yourself to God, fear Him in His holiness, consume His word and abide in Him. You are to be His dwelling place, His place of rest...

> *It is in this abiding IN HIM He will move heaven and earth to bring you into His fullness.*

MENE, MENE, TEKEL, UPHARSIN

KING-PLEASING

The Israelites had left Egypt and were on the move. Besides hearing of them as a great multitude, the other nations also heard what had happened in Egypt. They knew God had dried up the Red Sea for the Israelites to cross, and how Pharaoh's army had drowned while attempting to follow them. Balak got the news, and heard they were coming his way. Balak knew those who had withstood the Israelites had failed, Balak was smart, he knew he needed a bit more help... Balak also realized his fight was not against mere men.

Balak reached out to the prophet Balaam the prophet to curse the Israelites.

God also reached out to Balaam and told Balaam not to go.

Balaam? He had options!

For Balaam? Money, honor with a king, and possibly more hung in the balance.

What to do...?

God attempted to preserve Balaam by warning him. At one point, an argument ensued between Balaam and his mute donkey (2 Peter 2) as God worked to draw him back. However, the financial reward, the approval of a king outweighed his fear of God. Against his dumb mount's better judgment, Balaam departed for his payday and honor from a king...

Stopping for the night, God quizzed Balaam on what he was doing. A brief discussion ended with God telling Balaam, *if* the men call you, go with them.

Uncalled by the messengers, Balaam on his own initiative arose early and went with them, unsent.

That exceptionally massive word *"if"* is an important word

that proceeded from the mouth of God to Balaam.

That word *"if"* was a word he could have lived by.

In Revelation 2:14, Jesus details Balaam's error. Simply, the offer of money and ministerial recognition was more valuable to him than pleasing God.

> *That would be silly, right? Even a third grader knows if God says, 'Do not do it,' you just don't do it, amen?*

Upon not being able to curse Israel, Balaam instructed Balak how to get the Israelites to sin and bring a curse on themselves. Balak revealed that the Israelites would succumb to human lusts. Give the Israelites a little recognition, the offer of sex, and then food offered to idols as part of the festivities and then? These Israelites would bring a curse on themselves.

This teaching, this ministry to King Balak was done to receive personal honor, and finances from the king.

Pastor, is it possible Balaam had a chariot payment due? Or is it possible he owed tuition to the School of the Prophets for his credentials? Or possibly, could it be that Balaam's wife did not approve of their lowly living, possibly she wanted a more prestigious man?

Whatever the reason, Balaam sold himself, pimped himself out, and sold out God.

This error is no different today as adulterous ministers today spiritually roll with their mother in bed, pleasing the Great Whore, and being pleasured by her sharing her glory.

Nasty? I am soo glad you agree... God is finished with both of them.

Any assembly apart from yielding to the Holy Spirit, having as its literal head Jesus Christ has another spirit over it. If the Holy Spirit is not yielded to, waited on, the spirit that services the pastor in his self-seeking, self-pleasing is now manifesting seducing the souls of that man's church.

Disgusting, revolting?

This describes the fornication and adultery taking place today that God hates, intensely. Her sins as Sodom's have reached into heaven, if you stay with her, you *WILL* partake of her plagues.

Pastor, John the Baptist quizzed the temple leaders on who it was that had warned them to flee. You can answer that question easily. The Lord Jesus Christ, is telling us to come out of her, leave her, to not partake of her judgements.

But, as Balaam, the honor, the adoration, validation, not to mention our chariot payment is due, amen? Maybe your wife desires a *'little augmentation'*?

This will cause us to scoff, laugh, or ridicule, amen?

But when your plagues come?

> "...He that sitteth in the heavens shall laugh: the Lord shall have them in derision. Then shall he speak unto them in his wrath, and vex them in his sore displeasure. Yet have I set my king upon my holy hill of Zion."

Being in charge, being as a king, is an extremely fragile position. Preaching and teaching *'no one is perfect'* and God's grace covers a life lived after the flesh, is being a contemporary Balaam.

'Your' kingdom can grow, the king's tithes for the support of his house (1 Samuel 8) may increase, but as with Balaam, you have an appointment with the Lord of Hosts, Jesus Christ, that is *already* scheduled.

> *(As believers, we cannot be cursed, but being "drawn away" or enticed to please ourselves is the trick of an enemy set on destroying God's people...)*

Instructed by Balaam, King Balak sent his beautiful women and charismatic princes to Israel and enticed the Israelites into sexual sin and to eat things sacrificed to idols. Drawn away by their lust the Israelites sinned, and the judgment of God followed.

That is, until a Levite in holy anger skewered a Jew and his Midianite sex partner with a spear to the ground.

That stayed the plague. Someone, one man stood for God, ONE MAN! Out of all Israel, one person got God's attention.

The Levitical priesthood was born.

Can we hear the heart of God? Who is it that will leave their personal interests, count their dead soul as dead, crucified and buried to live in Him? The price is paid, who will covenant with Him? In Isaiah 9, everyone, every single person in Israel was a hypocrite.

In Ezekiel, God looked for ONE man to stand in the gap, there was not one.

No joke, today, in the midst of this debacle of man run, man pleasing, self-called men persuading churchianity, can God find ONE man that will abandon their dead soul, abide in His HOLY SPIRIT and walk with Him?

For those who think they have their life *'really going on'*. For those in ministry who believe they are doing the work of God? Apart from living in the tangible Holy Spirit, proven by God, sent by God, being an approved by God living sacrifice, you are deluded.

This is not a fun word, nor an easy word. But it is an accurate word.

> *This is a warning, hear it, or not. God's approval, is the witness, the presence of His tangible, very real Holy Spirit.... without Him, you are dead meat.*

Back to another example of dead meat, Balaam...

This prophet Balaam, this gifted man of God, was not operating as a servant of God. This prophet being enticed by finances and having his gift recognized sold out God on the sly, paying for it with his life.

Not a wise trade.. but at the time it seemed to be without consequence, it seemed like a good idea, it appeared to be reasonable as the financial reward was... *tangible*.

God's Gifts

God has given gifts to men, even to the rebellious. The fivefold giftings of God: The Apostle, Prophet, Evangelist, Pastor and Teacher are His gifts to the church. These gifts of God, the ones He uses?

They are the servants of God. They are Christ's having crucified the flesh with its affections and lusts.

The others?

In Revelation, the church at Ephesus could not bear those that were evil. They even tried those, they actually tested those who proclaimed to be sent by God, and found them to be liars. Wow, can you see that? A Pastor or evangelist states God sent him. You wait upon God, you hear what he is preaching and there is NO witness of the Holy Spirit! At that point, someone needs to leave.

At a *"church"* in Colorado, the self-called minister promoted by the self-called pastor as a *'supernatural man of God'* presented a message, quoting and presenting scriptures that did not even exist in any translation!

Upon meeting with the *'pastor'*, and his elder, their conclusion was;

> *'Yes we acknowledge he was not truthful, but there was some good we could take away'.*

In Revelation 22, among those outside the city of God are described.

> *"For without are dogs, and sorcerers, and whoremongers, and murderers, and idolaters, and whosoever loveth and maketh a lie."*

Other translations define *'maketh a lie'* as living in hypocrisy. Declaring one thing, and living another. This assembly in Colorado did not rise to the heights of the saints at Ephesus.

Instead they sank to the level of the *'Priests of Excrement'* in Malachi.

The excrement those priests offered to God, has been met, matched and possibly exceeded by these uncorrectable bastards who claim to be the ministers of God.

Self-called, self-sent men with the approval of men evidenced by their certificates and diplomas, does not equal being sent by God.

As today, unsent by God, ministries as Balaam obtain validation from men preaching and teaching the message they are paid to preach.

As Balaam, they are making an adversary in God as warnings

have gone unheeded. Making a friend of the prince of the power of the air is a poor trade from following after the King of Kings, your Heavenly Father, on an individual personal basis.
The Israelites went from a position of being blessed and highly favored, to judgment.
God went from being pleased with the nation as a whole and individually, to not being able to look upon their sin.
It was Balaam who had the greater condemnation, amen?
Yet Balaam's sin is not restricted to those in leadership, as king pleasing is idolatry. When a believer desires to find favor from anyone in leadership in lieu of pleasing God, it is idolatry. Idolatry is our spiritually bending the knee worshiping another to obtain what we believe we need.
This is identical to a wife looking to another, forsaking her husband to get her *'needs'* met. God calls it spiritual adultery. If this sounds nasty, it is and God takes this idolatry thing, this adultery very personally.

Daily Pleasing God

In the workplace, how do you serve God while earning an income? If you cannot serve God and Mammon, how do we do it? How does a woman yield to her fallible husband as unto the infallible Lord?
What does God's word tell us?

> *"And the King shall answer and say unto them, Verily I say unto you, Inasmuch as ye have done it unto one of the least of these my brethren, ye have done it unto me."*
> Matthew 25

We acknowledge the Lord Jesus Christ in every aspect of what we do, doing what we do, as if He were the personal recipient. Correcting our heart, as our response is to Him even in the most negative encounters. We do what we do, endeavoring to *'abide in Him'*. This is day-to-day and moment-to-moment living with faith in God, in operation as our choice.
If we are serving God, looking to Him as we do what we do as unto Him, he will receive it. In serving Him, He may also

restructure what we do at work to please Him. After all, he is our Lord, right?

A young man seeking to please God in all aspects of his life acknowledged it was not his life anymore, but the Lord's. His employment was working for a construction firm. As he worked, he realized it was not his own time, because if God owned his life; his time also belonged to God completely.

He worked '*piecework*'. The more work he performed resulted in more income for him. The Lord dealt with him, teaching him to do the hardest parts of his job first and the easiest parts last. This was the reverse of how he had previously worked. He changed how he performed his work, attempting to keep the same pace, as usual acknowledging God in what he did, acknowledging God as his provider. Whatever work was assigned to him, he did not as previously evaluate it to determine his income, but he performed it as unto the Lord. About this time, he also realized his relationships needed to be ordered by God. So, he quit talking with people unless God gave him something to say. Within a few months, the owner of the company asked him to manage the business. As a manager, every person he had ever witnessed to, except one, came and asked him for a job. He stated the experience humbled him as it was God showing him in serving God, God could promote him. He went from laborer to general manager, following the Holy Spirit.

He also related how God's blessings on him transferred to the company and took it from "*barely paying its own way*" to a financially stable position. When we do '*what we do*' as unto the Lord, '*here*' a man who dies receives our efforts. But '*there*' God receives them as a witness He is living.

The reality of this, exceeds the words used to express it! This principle in giving in the body of Christ, remains true.

This is inclusive of whatever we do, or say, to another can be a personal blessing to our Lord! Recall the righteous asking, '*When did we see you hungry, or naked?*'

It is the same with each word we speak, we need to understand

He receives it, as unto Him.

Radical?

Standing before the Lord, Jesus Christ, we will be in one of two camps, how much better that we hear, and we understand this today? With this in mind, understanding Jesus takes our actions to those that are His, as unto Him, let us return to Balaam.

Unrighteous, self-pleasing Balaam consulted Balak on *'spiritual warfare'*. In this case, spiritual warfare was Balaam showing Balak how to involve Babylon's spirit of adultery and fornication with the souls of Israel.

Balaam actually lived a few chapters before dying by the sword.

Idolatry and king-pleasing may seem like a shorter path to an easier life. But in impressing men's souls with your gifts, demeanor and social skills, God is not at all impressed. Yet in cultural churchianity, this is the only path forward. There is not another one offered.

It is in our not recognizing God as our sole provider, our savior, our mentor in reality that we must follow men who can teach us *'how to build our ministry,'* amen? In following men we will never take up our cross, nor abide in the tangible Holy Spirit. Instead, the commendations of man, their diplomas would be our path, and pleasing man would result in our having a successful ministry.

With this heart, we will identify Brother Balaam along with our religious mentors mourning him as a victim as we believe we can sow to the flesh and reap incorruption.

In this foolishness we will bend a knee and accept that flesh and blood can inherit a kingdom, it is just not the kingdom of... God.

It is the kingdom, and the god of this world that my Lord Jesus took a pass on.

Demise of the Ruling King

Prior to Jesus' birth, Israel did not have a king for

approximately 600 years. God had previously honored their request and gave them kings. Rejecting God as their king, personally, they then followed their kings in either keeping God's commandments, or not. But these kings were not the only one's held liable for Israel's sins.

Remember when the woman gave Adam her husband the forbidden fruit? Was the recipient given a pass on disobedience? Nope? We can see that being a hearer, being a recipient does not excuse us from being responsible to the truth. Adam was not given a pass for his sin because he did not pick the fruit.

Neither did following the lead of a king give the Israelites a pass on their '*sin*'. Can we then see our following our spiritual leader, a pastor in his error likewise does not excuse us the hearer?

> "...O my people, they which lead thee cause thee to err,
> and destroy the way of thy paths." Isaiah 3

God had repeatedly warned the Israelites not to worship other gods, not to eat things sacrificed unto idols, etc. God ultimately would destroy their temple, remove their King, and set other nations to rule over them.

In this, God was essentially saying,

> "I have now set over you those that you despise. Maybe now you will turn your heart to me. You will not follow those you reject and resist; it might be you turn your heart to me."

Who do we look to for approbation, for acceptance? And when God removes them? What will we do then? After many disciples departed, Jesus asked the remaining disciples,

> "...What and if ye shall see the Son of man ascend up where he was before?"

Can we keep our eyes on the prize, hold the words of God as true having faith? Are we going to be as Elisha, or as those who believe Elijah was taken up by a chariot and horses of fire? One inherits, the other has to swim back where they came from.

If we are looking for a man other than the Lord Jesus Christ to

follow in and by the Holy Spirit... It is absolutely not to be. Hello? Do we grasp this?
This is the Narrow Way, the Strait gate entry point: Abide In Christ, and He will remain IN you. The purpose of the Holy Spirit's ministry is Christ IN you, the hope of Glory.
Other *'ministries?'*
They will desire your commitment to their church vision, their business, their goals. The more you donate your finances and resources, the more the whore will be endeared to you.
Quit paying her, and watch her love dissipate.... amazing.
Her schedule of *'services'*, or *'servicing you'* is based in your... supporting her... Just an FYI.
Early on in His ministry, Jesus drove out those calloused, hard-hearted, covenant-breaking, self-serving people who made money in what He identified as *'His Father's House'*. He was jealous over His Father's House, the Temple. Irate, He drove them out.
He had been waiting for that day *for years*.
Isaiah 49 details the sheathed sword, waiting.
When reasoning together is rejected, when the wisdom of God is rejected, what else is left but a certain fearful looking forward... to judgement.
We determine God's response. God is an unchanging God. The covenant changed, His response to those who break covenant has not. Later, with His disciples Jesus detailed the future destruction of the Temple the Israelites were so proud of. Once known as the Temple of God, the place of His presence? It had been defiled. Those wicked husbandman had taken it over, and regarded the planting of the Lord, as their provision. That would be the work of Satan, amen? It would not be God, can we agree?
Instead of God's house, *it had become their house*.
Yet today, as then, the spirit that worked through those priests? It is back and has through man-ordained business men, false shepherds and false apostles taken over the vineyard, with its fruit now received as though it belongs to

them.

At that time, Jesus made a very clear distinction. Overlooking Jerusalem, he lamented,

> "O Jerusalem, Jerusalem, which killest the prophets, and stonest them that are sent unto thee; how often would I have gathered thy children together, as a hen doth gather her brood under her wings, and ye would not! Behold, your house is left unto you desolate…"
> Luke 13

No more was He jealous over the Temple as his Father's House. Jesus abandoned that structure and the Levitical Priesthood.

That man built temple, the man run temple was later destroyed in its entirety.

Do we really believe in building our ministry, in constructing our church building we have done a work for God?

But in our Lord fulfilling His Word, He raised up the true Temple in three days, and a change of priesthood occurred. Change in how His house was supported changed.

It IS a totally different house.

Jesus had exposed those who claimed to represent God, revealing the serpent's seed in the House of God. A man would no longer need a mediator other than the Lord Jesus Christ. God will not accept another as a go-between for Him and… You <u>or</u> me. Those who intercede for the lost, or pray for the body of Christ? They are not '*mediators*' or '*representatives*'. They are members of the body engaged in ministry IN the body.

Priests, apostles, prophets, and pastors are NEVER to stand between you and God, unless it is in private intercession.

Now as believers, individually we are to be the Temple of God. We are to stand before God as the church, individually first, and collectively submitted to Jesus Christ our Head in and by the Holy Spirit. And as the Body of Christ, we are to relate individually and personally to our Head, the Lord Jesus Christ, again; In and by the Holy Spirit!

Any man who does not represent the Lord Jesus Christ in and by the tangible Holy Spirit personally in any assembly

convened to worship the Lord?
He is not the servant of God, that man is now guilty of willful sin.
And that sin is *now* imputed.
The word is judgment.
We will either hear, or we can be as Lot's jovial sons-in-law.

An Empty Tomb
Jesus Christ is alive and well, and is vitally interested in His Body, you... The Church, the Tabernacle of God.

> *"For no man ever yet hated his own flesh; But nourisheth and cherisheth it, Even as the Lord the church.*
> *For we are members of his body, Of his flesh and of his bones..."*

Balaam did not think God saw his on the sly education of Balak to do evil. People who think God is not concerned with what they do, or that God gives them grace to sin, are stupid. I know, it sounds... crass. The translators used a more gentle phrase, *'without understanding'* in lieu of *'unintelligent, stupid'*.
But God has this thing with making His point. You can read of Israel's paramours, or of the Malachian priests facials and this point is clear. God does not mince words or cater to your soul-centered sensitivities, He sees the flesh and blood soul as dead, deceased.

How about that third grade clarity.

Along that line, hindsight shows Balaam to be willfully ignorant. I mean, you talk with your donkey and speak with an angel and still go against God's Word? Really? Is this the picture of one whose opinion of himself is radically inflated? Or is the picture of those who really just have no clue who God is?

> *"For the word of God is quick, and powerful, and sharper than any two-edged sword, piercing even to the dividing asunder of soul and spirit, and of the joints and marrow, and is a discerner of the thoughts and*

> *intents of the heart.*
> *Neither is there any creature that is not manifest in his sight: but all things are naked and opened unto the eyes of him with whom we have to do." Hebrews 4:12-13*

Just an FYI: Jesus Christ of Nazareth, the one with whom we have to do? He is addressing the *'Leader'* affecting HIS flock, HIS people, and HIS body. This is a good time to accept the Head of the Church as the Head of the Church in reality, or *'hit the door'*. Our Father is trying to preserve the reader who is in *'ministry'* just as He did Balaam. It is on the *'Leader'* after this.
Consider Ezekiel 34,

> *"And the word of the LORD came unto me, saying,*
> *'Son of man, prophesy against the shepherds of Israel, prophesy, and say unto them, Thus saith the Lord GOD unto the shepherds; Woe be to the shepherds of Israel that do feed themselves! Should not the shepherds feed the flocks?*
> *Ye eat the fat, and ye clothe you with the wool, ye kill them that are fed: but ye feed not the flock.*
> *The diseased have ye not strengthened, neither have ye healed that which was sick, neither have ye bound up that which was broken, neither have ye brought again that which was driven away, neither have ye sought that which was lost; but with force and with cruelty have ye ruled them'."*

Do we remember when the first-born of every family in Egypt was affected that did not have the blood of the lamb applied to the door frame?
The word I initially received was what happened in Egypt will pale in comparison with what God is going to do in His Body. That sounded so radical, I wanted to temper it, but I cannot. It is what it is. There is an anger, a zeal that is unmatched that is pending, that will impact every *'church leader'* in their house. When I say this is personal to the Lord Jesus, I am saying he is making it extremely personal with each and every leader, intimately personal. Each Leader will know the Lord of Hosts

has visited him. His reward is with Him.

The *'sheep'* belong to God. It would be better for a man to bind a millstone around his neck and be cast into the sea than to offend one of these little ones.

Judgment: Warning Signs and Man's Foolishness

A person has a 'scare,' a medical issue, an accident, something that makes them aware of their need for God. The individual humbles their *'self'* and breaks their heart before God, and the 'situation' is resolved.

Once the situation is over, they immediately give thanks and praise to God, but then the individual returns to their life. It was a wake-up call, as they say. But the foolish individual hits the snooze button and goes back to living as before.

Hebrews 12 relates chastisement *'yields the peaceable fruit of righteousness'* for those who receive it and see it as a *'learning moment'*. But to the obstinate and foolish, it is the precursor to a more severe penalty.

When the King of Assyria, Sennacherib (Isaiah 36), came up and took the fenced cities of Judah, he moved on to attack Jerusalem. But King Hezekiah humbled himself and prayed. So, God moved. An angel (one angel) of the Lord smote in the Assyrian camp over 180,000 soldiers. Sennacherib's armies left the attack and returned home where Sennacherib was then killed.

This was a strong message God had sent to King Hezekiah and all of Israel, that HE alone was God and worthy of from-the-heart consideration as the One to be feared.

When King Hezekiah later became sick, God healed the King. God had redeemed the nation from the destroyer, and God was their personal Healer.

Was there any like God that deserved all their worship?

Evidently not, because when Babylon sent representatives, Hezekiah desired their accolades and acceptance.

Afterward, Jerusalem incurred the judgment of God that God had relented in Jeremiah 26.

When the Word of God is delivered, we have two options. We can humble ourselves and search our heart before God. We can *'be open with the one with whom we have to do'*. The other option, which is used more often than not?
First you check with your-self, then your peers, and attack the messenger.
Which response will *'yield the best benefit for the Lord?'* Which response will further the will of God?
Which indicates a love for God?
If it is about saving your position, place, or reputation, it is about 'a*nother lord*'.
Moses was a man that murdered another man then ran for his life.
Later, he delivered the law that states a man shall not kill.
(*It is easy to judge this fellow. Any takers?*)
Elijah, was a bald man upon whom the anointing oil could never be poured, as it could not contact flesh. He was anointed by God in a powerful manner.
(*Bald! Does he think he is a prophet? It is easy to judge this fellow. Any takers?*)
Mary was unwed and pregnant with the Lord Jesus. Under the law she was to be stoned for bringing foolishness into Israel.
(*Mary, easy to judge. Any takers?*)
Jesus, born of fornication?
(*Easy to judge this fellow. Any takers?*)
The foolishness of God is stronger than the wisdom of men.
He that hath an ear let him hear...

> *Mene, Mene, Tekel, Upharsin; This IS the Word of the Lord to each church "leader" ...*

THE HEART OF GOD

For Eli's apathy, the loss of his sons, the loss of the Ark of the Covenant, and the loss of his own life, was the price Eli paid.
But what was the 'cost to God' from Eli's apathy?
What was the price God had to pay for Eli's turning a blind eye towards his sons' loose living?
When the heart of God is irrelevant, those who do not love God are in leadership.
Not caring about God, is reflected in our not waiting upon God, grieving His Holy Spirit and not giving a thought to it.
The natural man does not care, as long as his appetite is appeased, and he can fulfill the desires of his carnal mind.
Welcome to Balaam's world, and to Eli's mindset.
A man manifesting his gifting, or calling does not equate to him being obedient. Beware the man whose calling and gifting are his claim to ministry. This is a personality driven foul spirit masquerading as a minister of righteousness. If he is not speaking for God as God's mouthpiece with the Holy Spirit witnessing it, EVERY word out of his mouth is to make you as he is.
Yet, we are to be transformed into the image of Christ, amen?
The cost to God from those who learned from Eli was a nation of *'covenant children'* that did not fear God nor respect God's Word.
Under Moses and Joshua, God had those who loved Him leading the nation.
Under Eli? The nation did not revere God's Presence or HIS calling. God was unable to live among them and bless them.

God had to watch them struggle when all of heaven was on standby wanting to *"roll on their behalf"* but God could not.

This was heartbreaking. And yet this contains a warning for all those whose care for their life, and the concerns of their soul exceed any concern for my Heavenly Father.

Eli The Priest

During Eli's priesthood, the tragedies of God's heart, and the nation rest completely and entirely upon their leader Eli's shoulders. The result of Eli's apathy was Eli's offspring were perpetually banned from the priesthood.

There is more, in 1 Samuel 2 God told Eli that Eli would watch his descendants suffer for what he had allowed.

Remember we are surrounded by a *'host of witnesses'*? Besides those saints who have died to their bodies, we see that the rich man in torment, shared Eli's experience watching his family on the wrong road.

Being a leader in a church, in what Jesus clearly identifies as *'His Body'*, carries with it the responsibility to re-present Christ. It is absolutely NOT for you to instill your programs. This is not your choice, nor those you *'serve'* as they make your car and house payments, and buy your groceries. But if you are self-called, this of course would be no concern, amen?

You have your career path, your job.

Similarly, in Jeremiah 23, God declares that both prophet and priest are profane (*useless*). It is in his own House that He declares he has found their wickedness. Further, He states,

> "If they (prophet and priest) HAD stood in MY counsel, and caused MY people to hear MY words, they would have turned them from their evil way and the evil of their doing."

This is a promise to those called of God that He will honor HIS Word. When God's word is spoken, God has something to watch over. It will not return to Him void. So as we see the result of professional ministers in our communities, God has had *NOTHING* to watch over. Just as with the priests and the prophets in Jeremiah's time, they presented their view of what God was saying.

Yet it was not God's word.

Taking God's word and using it as a backdrop for ministry is the ministry of a profane and useless imbecile. God is not a respecter of persons.

God however does honor one man above another.

Does this seem scripturally contradictory?

Let us hear a portion of what God told Eli.

> *"...but now the LORD saith, Be it far from me; for them that honour me I will honour, and they that despise me shall be lightly esteemed."*

Those who seek God in spirit and truth, offering the living sacrifice with the fire of the Holy Ghost on it? That fire is God honoring them. Those who think their presentations of God's word are... acceptable. Those who exhibit their learning, wisdom, and oratory skills?

Say good-bye.

Send them flowers while you can.

In Exodus, God told the Israelites to take a good look at those who had troubled them, as they would see them no more, forever.

We decide our future with God through either surrendering our will, to do His will; Or we arrogantly believe we as a god in our kingdom can do His work, for Him.

If the Head of the Church sends a word to his bride through a messenger and that messenger adapts the word to his master's bride for the messenger's betterment with the bride, where does the liability lie?

Does it lie with the bride, or with the messenger?

The picture is clear, and the messenger has a very dim future. When the message is not from God, God's people are destroyed. In Ezekiel God reveals how violence proceeded from the Temple, God's house, and spread throughout the land.

In Jeremiah 23, *'ministers'* would *'steal'* God's word from one another in order to appear to be somebody to the House of God.

But this is inconsequential, whether a man is stealing another man's words or coming up with his own. He is cursed, without a message direct from the Head of the Body, he is not God's messenger.
God did not send him.
Consider this:
God had created Adam as His son from the dust of the earth. God gave him life, planted him in a gorgeous setting, and gave him His Garden to tend, with the blessing of ruling the earth in his future.
God had planted a holy seed, but God reaped a degenerate vine. God was not mocked.
This explains why one of Adam's punishments was to plant one thing and reap something entirely different than what he planted. This punishment reflected the sin.
Adam was reaping what he had sown. Adam had taken the blessing of God, the purity of what God had sown in the earth, and exchanged it for something vile in faithlessness. God is finished with those who have defiled His inheritance, Jeremiah 16:18, Ephesians 1:18.
In this same manner, this is also a clue as to God's judgments for those who violate the Bride of Christ.

> "... You absolutely will lie down in sorrow..."

Be forewarned that when this judgment occurs, it will be in your home and the sympathy card will not be a card that can be put into play. God told Samuel what He was going to do concluding with this;

> "At that time I will carry out against Eli everything I
> spoke against his family—from beginning to end."

God is a *'finisher'*. Judgment results from imputed sin. God's grace is His favor, His kindness, His mercy, His enabling. The sacrifice was offered, the payment for sin has been paid. Understand Jesus is NOT going back to Calvary, and His grace has departed from the arrogance and brazen professionalism of men. It is a fearful thing to fall into the hands of the living God.

God called fishermen, common people.
God did not go to the *'school of the prophets'* to call His disciples, nor to their pupils in their religious circles.
God called a red-faced shepherd boy who had learned to fellowship God while watching the sheep.
God called a man who fished naked, to be an apostle.
Do we really think in our 'gifting' God is blessed to have us?
> *C'mon now! Who do we think we are apart from the Holy Spirit, God's Presence?*

God had taken Abraham, a man who believed God and entrusted everything he was, and everything he had to God. God then created a nation from him so that,
> *'God could have a people'.*

Abraham's blessing would be that he had a seed. To God, the blessing was to have been that God would have a family.
They were to be His people, a nation, that the LORD God could dwell among, and He would be their God.
They would be HIS people. He had grown them, delivered them, fed them with manna, given them water from a rock, and separated THEM from ALL the peoples of the earth.
And for all this, they with their leaders turn to worship pieces of wood covered with gold?? And after giving Israel the Promised Land and driving out the inhabitants, this is what the Redeemer of Israel reaps?
When the people of Israel desired a king, as recorded in 1 Samuel 8, God told Samuel,
> *"...they have not rejected you, they have rejected me."*

God had desired to be their King in each of their hearts, to be held in a special place of reverence and love, not just corporately, but INDIVIDUALLY!
What will it take for us to GIVE God His place of REST???? God only accepts God, Adam only received back to HIMSELF that which was sent forth from him. Can we grasp the picture. or are we... *'without understanding...'*
This is a heart issue, not our judging after the flesh comparing our prominence in ministry. God offered His Son in our stead

that we would NOT walk after the flesh... It is not complicated.

New Race

> *"A seed shall serve him; it shall be accounted to the Lord for a generation. They shall come, and shall declare his righteousness unto a people that shall be born, that he hath done this." Psalms 22*

Not '*generations*,' but a generation, singular. Not '*seeds*', but a seed, singular. Do we now grasp this does not include our '*generational*' flesh and blood soul? God had seen the '<u>end of all flesh</u>' in Noah's time. In having a new race through Jesus Christ God has again announced the '<u>end of all flesh</u>'. Can we grasp this? It cannot be made simpler.

> *"The book of the generation of Jesus Christ, the son of David, the son of Abraham." Matthew 1*

Those who are counted worthy to obtain eternal life, will never die. This is the seed promised, the <u>generation</u> of our Lord, Jesus Christ.

Those bought by Jesus Christ at Calvary, those who have covenanted with Him through being crucified with Him, buried with Him, and raised IN Him? They are God's precious fruit of the earth. If you mess with them, you are messing with God personally as they are about His business. When you understand the heart of God, you will tread carefully.

Church Leaders are not to be adored, idolized or revered as though they were in God's place in our hearts. Church leaders who have accepted these accolades as though they deserved them are under God's judgement.

God has desired that '*place*' of adoration in the hearts of His people. But love does not demand. Nor does love seek its own, love has as for its desire the betterment of the one loved.

Love does not say, '*I'll do this for you if you do this for me*'. Love is not '*deal making*'. Love is '*covenanting*'. Covenanting is seeing another's life as though it were your very own. In times of trouble, you are there for them. In times of joy, you rejoice with them. In their being hung on a cross for you, you die with

them. You '*covenant*' with them.
> "*Then said Jesus unto his disciples, If any man will come*
> *after me, let him deny himself, and take up his cross,*
> *and follow me.*" Matthew 16

The cost? It was the price one would pay in losing what had validated them, comforted them, the cost was their own soul. Once they began to follow and paid that price through the Holy Spirit to walk in the spirit? After they were discipled? They are part of our mother, Jerusalem above Paul speaks of in Galatians. It was freely you received, freely you now give.

The other woman, the whore?

She will tell you if you can come up with the price, I am yours as long as you pay.

The tuition, her payment is in the current currency.

Come with your unbridled lust, your carnal desires, bring your desire for a profession, a career and learn how to manifest her kingdom through your educated soul. This is descriptive of the Babylonian Whore's sons, her '*ministers of righteousness*'.

Being '*decked*' with precious stones, she displays her assets, her '*ministers of righteousness*'. She takes their giftings, and markets them as she pimps them out to her assemblies.

> (God in no way condemns the believer, but instructs
> them to come out of her in order to avoid her plagues,
> her judgement.)

God had delivered the nation of Israel from bondage, cared for them, fed them, asking only that they would from the heart reciprocate His love.

It is no different today.

When we give God the leftovers of our time and love, it is because our '*Eli's*', the Leaders of Churchianity have communicated this '*is acceptable*' by their words and in their lifestyle.

God has been patient, and God's patience is often mistaken for apathy. Today we just call it God's '*grace*'. Do not be deceived. God's patience is gone, the ice is getting thin.

When God is disrespected, blindness, arrogance, false

humility, and special privilege are assumed by those in leadership and laity as their covering. God's words become *'hypothetical, positional,'* or *'for another time'*. God's long-suffering is taken for God's permissiveness.
Psalms 50 is an excellent read at this point. All that God said to Samuel was,
> *"Ever since I brought them from Egypt, they have continually abandoned me and followed other gods...."*
> *Strong words for those God had delivered. '...they have continually abandoned me...'*

Only hard-hearted, insolent individuals would read this, and take all that God has, that cost God dearly, and walk away as though it were nothing. They would take for granted the love of God as He patiently waited for those He loved to *'come to their senses'*.
That patience?
It is gone, absolutely GONE.
A man may put up with this in his home, from his wife. He may even take abuse and disrespect, not wanting to endure the ignominy of perceived failure and the pain of potential separation or loss.
> But understand that God is not like
> that man, whatsoever.

God is the Head of Christ. And never in scripture do we find Jesus having a problem with that.
Jesus is the Head of the man, while the man is the head of the woman.
Any cultural issues or gender issues we might have with that, is our issue. As God is an unchanging God. *(But I get ahead...)*
What can a man give to God? Does God require our feeding him? Does he need our funds to support him? If love seeks the betterment of the one loved, what is the object of *'our love?'* It really is easy to locate.
In whose interest have we worked for *'the betterment?'* While we can say we have no *'gold covered idol,'* can we say we have not sacrificed for our *'self-image'?'*

We can look at what we have spent our time/money on. If we can easily discern it, we should understand that it is very clear to the one who gave His only begotten Son for us.

Again, I refer to Stephen preaching to Israel's spiritual leaders who murdered him. He laid it all out very clearly in Acts 7. It was then Stephen concluded with:

> *"Heaven is my throne and earth is my footstool: what house will ye build me? Saith the Lord: or what is the place of my rest?"*
>
> *"...ye stiff-necked and uncircumcised in heart and ears, ye do always resist the Holy Ghost: as your fathers did, so do ye."*

In one sentence the problem is defined, exposing each leader, and each believer's heart. Proclaiming to love God, the Holy Spirit is virtually unknown as many claim to walk with Him by *'faith'*. Their faith? It is the mental perception that apart from any witness of the Holy Spirit, any conscious yielding to Him, He is directing their steps.

In this they *'think'* their self-indulgent, self-pleasing living is lived with His approval.

The issue is this.

This is the soul, the mind, the will, the emotions being seduced because when they *'think'* God's word is true, they call that mental assent their faith.

Before God, the Old Testament false prophets share the same position of the pastors and church leaders this day.

> *"For both prophet and priest are profane; yea, in my house have I found their wickedness, saith the LORD. Wherefore their way shall be unto them as slippery ways in the darkness: they shall be driven on, and fall therein: for I will bring evil upon them..."*

They say that those who fail to learn from history, repeat it. The false prophets loved to sweet praise of the people, from the kings to the temple-goers. Their words, their traditions, which were their theologies were finely honed to keep their position and support from the same. Put out of the priesthood, a man

who was used to the support and adoration of the people lost more than his meal ticket. The messages MUST be palatable, non-confrontational, and promise more of God, with less from the hearer than the other speakers.
Quick question...
>*When did God EVER send a man to tell everyone they were doing great?*

<u>When</u> did Jesus chase down an errant soul and tell them not to worry, God's love was greater than their living in sin?
Likewise, your beloved *'minister of righteousness'* will tell you, no worry, no one is perfect, God's love covers your self-centered living, your pleasing yourself.
Wrong tree, wrong fruit, wrong choice and the consequences are bad, really bad. Add to that, the timing of this lifestyle? It is close to pounding on the side of the ark, in regards to being the wrong time.
Enjoy the Gym, the Restaurant, AND..

Enjoy Your Church!
The culture of today's church is all about *'keeping you, the churchgoer, involved'*.
Check online for Pastoral positions and become educated as to what *'churches'* are listing as qualifications to become their *'hirelings.'* Gifting, culturally appropriate messages, energy, smile, these are all assets. Service planning, service design (*oh hallelujah-and we thought it was the Holy Spirit leading?*), and adding to the membership, are the *'paramount'* requirements.
If you cannot pull in more *'tithes-payers,'* then what good are you?
Check online for favorite sermon topics and you will get web pages of free sermons and blogs such as: "*How to structure your sermon title, to ask questions that people care about.*"
It is an industry!
It is NOT ABOUT GOD, nor about your soul being denied, in order to be saved.
Au contraire, it is about keeping your soul's attention, enticing

you to make it *'your church home,'* and making it easy to... give. *Did I say give? I meant to say give...*
This was also a first-generation church issue, as when Paul wrote to the Philippian assembly.
> *"For I have NO man like-minded that naturally cares for your state. For all seek their own, not the things that are of Christ Jesus."*

Another translation reads,
> *"All the others care only for themselves and not for what matters to Jesus Christ." 2 Peter 2:3 (NLT)*
>
> *"In their greed, they will make up clever lies to get hold of your money. But God condemned them long ago, and their destruction will not be delayed."*

And lastly, 1 Peter 4:17 (KJV)
> *"For the time has come that judgment must begin at the house of God: and if it first begins at us, what shall the end be of them that obey not the gospel of God?"*

The heart of man in bed being pleasured by the Great Whore is the issue.

The heart of God is expressed through the lifeless corpse of a beloved Son at Calvary.

Before Calvary, God had those who loved Him: Abram, David, Moses, Joshua, Enoch, they all walked with God. They may have had a revelation of God's redemptive plan, but they did not see the actual historical event.

We have the record, the event spelled out. And what is our heart?

As a woman despises her husband's toil all week and wants 'more,' are we not worse than that, in not giving to God our entire world, heart, mind, soul and strength? Are we just taking all He has given for granted and then asking for more?

Wisdom is understanding the love of God, understanding apart from abiding in Him, we can do nothing.

We do not have an 'edge', or an advantage over Jesus, who said that of Himself... He could do nothing.

RICHALLISTON

We are without excuse...

THE 'SIN' ISSUES
or
'Take Heed How You Hear'

The word of God tells us that the blood of Jesus cleanses us from all sin, so, which is it?
Are we sinful or sinless?

"If we say that we have fellowship with him, and walk in darkness, we lie, and do not the truth:
But if we walk in the light, as he is in the light, we have fellowship one with another, and the blood of Jesus Christ his Son cleanseth us from all sin.
If we say that we have no sin, we deceive ourselves, and the truth is not in us." 1 John 1 (KJV)

We who have believed and accepted what Jesus took upon himself at Golgotha believe he did so on our behalf.
Before God, I am a son of God belonging to the body of Christ through the Holy Spirit. When it comes to receiving God's word, I, as you must separate out our faith from others and walk in the Holy Spirit relating personally to our head, Jesus Christ.
Meaning this, our faith in God cannot be corporate, or church based. In the above scripture, we must each apply personal faith in God for what He is telling us. If our faith is in what our pastor, or our preacher tells us, it is not in God, but them.
Hmmm... Does that sound wrong?
That is Satan's work through his messenger getting you to follow his messenger, NOT the Holy Spirit. This produces that spirit of debate stirring in you, not the yielding to the Holy Spirit, asking Him to confirm His word. The group mentality,

the herd?

Those beasts are on the broad boulevard, not the narrow path. As the Israelites in the wilderness abandoned faith in God, Moses, Joshua, and Caleb did not.

We individually are to have our confidence solely in God. This is only through knowing our Saviour in and by the Holy Spirit, intimately.

Imagine living in Isaiah's time. God states through the prophet in chapter 9,

> "...for every one is an hypocrite and an evildoer, and every mouth speaketh folly."

If one were to identify with these people as *'their group'*, they would identify as being chosen by God. But in truth they did not love God personally. They drew near to God in their mouth, they delighted in approaching God (*great worship service by the way!!*), yet as them we would be lost. Being lost would occur even though we would be *'corporately'* accepted, God would see us individually as faithless.

Now as we see Caleb, Joshua, Noah, Abram and others, we understand walking with God is not based on others, it is based on a relationship with God, personally.

Again, I would encourage each reader, personally, privately to go before God in faith. To the extent that even if corporate churchianity does not believe God, you will accept His dying was just for you and you alone, and all past sins are forgiven.

It is that kind of personal faith that results in personal salvation and a personal relationship.

Church Lies

To the believer whose church tells them they are sinners, and that they, *'sin every day'*, reread the first sentence in the scripture we started with ending with

> "...the blood of Jesus Christ cleanseth us from ALL sin..."

The Word of God has this little qualifier:

> "...IF we walk in the light..."

What does "*walk in the light*" refer to?

Let's consider Abraham. Even when Abraham fell in fear, he fell forward and took even more ground in God. He did not retreat in unbelief '*back*' to daddy Terah's house. He continued in '*faith towards God*', towards the promises of God.

Is there ever a record of God dealing with Abram, or later, Abraham, for sin?

Is there a record of Abram, Abraham, sinning?

NO!!!

Was Abraham sinless?

Again, *NO!* But God never dealt with Abram regarding... sin. WHY?!!

Because sin was not imputed as he was not under the Law!!

> *(Paul taught this and was accused of preaching 'greasy grace', that we should sin more that God's grace would abound. The Apostle Paul got that lie straightened out in Romans 6.)*

Is this an excuse? No, this is the blessedness of the man to whom the Lord does NOT impute sin! When Abram deceived Abimelech, giving a false witness that Sarah his wife was his sister, he was '*moving forward*' in God's plan. His fear and the resulting deception were not imputed to him, as there was no law that declared, '*thou shalt not bear false witness.*'

God's grace was sufficient for him, and Abimelech, being warned, was preserved. Sarah was preserved also, and Abraham left with more than he came in with!

If we think that does not sound correct, consider this.

Abram in seeking to please God and inherit the promises was being delivered of all his fear. In delivering Abram, God was revealing Himself to Abram as Abram's shield, provider, and deliverer. Abram was moving forward in faith in the light he had.

> *This was his holy ambition that being of faith we are to share.*

The result was Abram being circumcised in his heart, and ears, resulting in him trusting God EVEN more. Walking in the light, is our putting our faith in God, making a personal decision to abide IN Christ, to remain in God's tangible Holy Spirit as our holy ambition.

This is not automatic, it will be our choice, our decision. Remaining in the tangible presence of the Holy Spirit, is consciously choosing to prefer to please God over... our own body with its life, our-self.

To declare we sin everyday as a carnal excuse to not live holy, is likewise our faithless decision to not walk in God's Holy Spirit. That is an evil heart.

This is not counting your-self crucified with Christ, being dead with Christ as YOUR LIFE! It is hanging on to the corpse, loving death and on the wrong road. Of course you have great company that make you *'feel'* good, that placate your soul with being accepted.

But it is NOT God's acceptance as witnessed by His abiding Holy Ghost. To us who are under the New Covenant, Jew and Non-Jew, Romans 6 says,

> *"...For sin shall not have dominion over you: for ye are not under the law but under grace."*

Grace is *'divine favor'*, not to sin, but to walk before God. This is God enabling us to walk in the Light, walk in truth as pre-fall Adam, naked and open before God with a pure heart. In this, we endeavor to fulfill the Word we have received from HIM in His strength, the Holy Spirit. This is having an honest and open heart before the One with whom we have everything to do. As we do, the blood of His Son cleanses us from ALL sin and unrighteousness.

So, we walk before God, not even conscious of making a mistake as we are looking personally, not religiously, to Jesus the author and finisher of our faith. In Hebrews 10, every time a sacrifice was offered, the individual was reminded he was a sinner. Christ was offered ONE time, for all our sin, so we can move forward in relationship with Christ by the Holy Spirit *with a conscience FREE of sin.* And we are of God,

> *"...who is made unto us wisdom, and righteousness, and*

> *sanctification, and redemption." 1 Corinthians 1*

How else can we *"with boldness enter the Holy of Holies?"* We cannot!!

It is only those who believe God, who are sinless before God in their conscience who can approach Him in FAITH through the blood of Jesus Christ! Any *'church leader'* that disputes this Word of God and cannot receive it is a heretic. He is to be avoided. He is NOT one of the gifts of God to the church.

Strong words? God is serious...

We are saved by faith, not works; we are saved by a faith that pleases God, a faith THAT works. How do we get this faith that works?

> *"Faith comes by hearing, and hearing by the Word of God." Romans 10*

Then let us add the understanding that the *'just shall live by faith,'* Hebrews 10.

For a minute, consider the word *'just.'* In this sense, it is meant that as you abide in Christ, you are *'justified'*, meaning the debt of your sin has been paid. You are righteous before God IN Christ. God's word.

In private, before God, no matter the issue, no matter our memory, we go before God and take His word back to Him.

> *"But of him (God) are ye in Christ Jesus, who of God is made unto us wisdom, and righteousness, and sanctification, and redemption:*
>
> *That, according as it is written, He that glorieth, let him glory in the Lord."*

Going before God in prayer, we confess HIS Word is true, and Christ is made unto us righteousness, sanctification AND redemption. This is *HIS* work, *HIS* word, our part is to believe, and we rest all we are on God, His word, His work! Our only part is to believe, *and abide in Him*! God witnesses this with His spirit, His tangible presence on His word as we believe Him over the memory of the flesh, or soul.

Faux faith is the assumption a person has a relationship with God, with no relating to Him in faith on His word.

Faux faith is declaring God's word without any witness of God's spirit.

This absence of God's approval, which is the witness of the Holy Spirit on His word, can be the result of ignorance. This would not mean one is not saved, it would indicate one of two things.

One; That the understanding of how to walk with God, has not been presented.

Two; That the understanding has been presented, and rejected.

The Apostles Doctrine

'Repent, Be Baptized, and Receive the Holy Spirit.'

As already addressed in this writing, this is the way of life. Dropping all to abide in the presence of the Holy Spirit, is the cost to follow Jesus Christ.

Remember, *'If we walk in the light, the blood of the Lamb cleanseth from all sin.'*

Being redundant, Abram/Abraham never had sin imputed to him, as the law was not yet given. Abram out of fear, had surrendered his wife to kings, twice. He produced Ishmael, endeavoring to produce an heir.

If we have from a pure heart, before God made steps we believed were *'of God'*, even in error, the blood of the Lamb covered that action. There is no error, or sin reckoned to us. In reality, everything we ever did in the flesh, is washed from us as we learn to abide in the tangible presence of the Holy Spirit speaking the same word He is speaking.

You were executed in Christ. Christ was executed on the cross, you in being crucified with Him are seen by God as physically lifeless. Your new life now is His presence, the Holy Spirit!

Your past? Condemnation? You cannot execute a dead man again!

> *(Did I just hear a Praise God? A hallelujah?!!! Keep this personal, every moment day and night with the One who gave His all for... you).*

Romans 8:1-2 depicts a life free of judgement, how can there be condemnation, if there is no judgement?! This understanding would not apply to the willfully disobedient.

> *"Therefore to him that knoweth to do good, and doeth it not, to him it is sin." James 4:17*

To those who walk in the Holy Spirit, God is our Heavenly Father. Jesus, our brother is the Son of God, and we are of the family of God, amen?

> *"For it became him, for whom are all things, and by whom are all things, in bringing many sons unto glory, to make the captain of their salvation perfect through sufferings.*
> *For both he that sanctifieth and they who are sanctified are all of one: for which cause he is not ashamed to call them brethren..." Hebrews 2:10-11*

What we see is this; It is all about the family of God. Our older brother, Jesus sent of God, is not only our example, but He paved the way for us, amen?

Being led by the Holy Spirit, we are God's sons per Romans 8. The blood of the Lamb perpetually cleanses us from ALL sin and ALL unrighteousness. We serve God and do noy *'buy into'* Satan's messengers or their *'Twice the Child of Hell Seminary '* educational contracts.

The disciples that followed Jesus, what tuition contract did they sign? What was the expense they were expected to come up with?

Did they take care of Jesus, did they pay His way?

We know the answer....

We are now looking at, God's ways...

Jesus told those who followed Him, freely you have received, freely give.

If We Sin After Being Born Again...

What does God tell us?

> *"My little children, these things write I unto you, that ye sin not. And if any man sin, we have an advocate with the Father, Jesus Christ the righteous." 1 John 2*

If you make a mistake, simply go to your lawyer, your advocate, Jesus Christ, and consider this. God loved you so much he gave his only Son...and Jesus in quoting Hosea 6, said *"I will have mercy and not sacrifice..."*
If you confess your sin, he is faithful and just to forgive you.
Believing God's love for you is knowing God wants His child FREE to stand before Him. Jesus went to Calvary so the believer would NOT have a conscience plagued by sin. That is amazing grace! How much sin does the blood of Jesus cover? ALL sin, with the exception of a particular sin against the Holy Spirit, which is not a part of what we are dealing with here.
Satan would have yus remain fearful and wallow in our guilt. This is a trick, a trap of Satan. I recommend this as a sincere prayer, stated as one word in a short single breath:

"*Father,forgivemeintheNameofJesusthankyousoverymuch.*"
Then move on, not having a consciousness of ever having made that mistake! And one more thing, never justify your mistake, when accused, press your lower lip firmly against your upper lip and thank God for Jesus being your justifier. That is not saying we are not to fulfil righteousness with one who we may have wronged. It is essential we learn to follow the Holy Spirit on God's word, and not our *'feelings'*.
For a few minutes, let's review the onslaught of,,,

'You know what you did!'

The attacks of Satan tell you that you are unchanged, always screwed up, and you are still a screw-up. The family and friends that remind you of your mistakes? Let's review what God's Word says. That is the rule, correct? This is the lesson for the self, the soul. For what saith the scripture?

> "Abraham believed God, and it was counted unto him
> for righteousness.
> Now to him that worketh is the reward not reckoned
> of grace, but of debt. But to him that worketh not, but
> believeth on him that justifieth the ungodly, his faith is
> counted for righteousness." Romans 4

And also...

condemnation, if there is no judgement?! This understanding would not apply to the willfully disobedient.

> *"Therefore to him that knoweth to do good, and doeth it not, to him it is sin." James 4:17*

To those who walk in the Holy Spirit, God is our Heavenly Father. Jesus, our brother is the Son of God, and we are of the family of God, amen?

> *"For it became him, for whom are all things, and by whom are all things, in bringing many sons unto glory, to make the captain of their salvation perfect through sufferings.*
> *For both he that sanctifieth and they who are sanctified are all of one: for which cause he is not ashamed to call them brethren..." Hebrews 2:10-11*

What we see is this; It is all about the family of God. Our older brother, Jesus sent of God, is not only our example, but He paved the way for us, amen?

Being led by the Holy Spirit, we are God's sons per Romans 8. The blood of the Lamb perpetually cleanses us from ALL sin and ALL unrighteousness. We serve God and do noy *'buy into'* Satan's messengers or their *'Twice the Child of Hell Seminary '* educational contracts.

The disciples that followed Jesus, what tuition contract did they sign? What was the expense they were expected to come up with?

Did they take care of Jesus, did they pay His way?

We know the answer....

We are now looking at, God's ways...

Jesus told those who followed Him, freely you have received, freely give.

If We Sin After Being Born Again...

What does God tell us?

> *"My little children, these things write I unto you, that ye sin not. And if any man sin, we have an advocate with the Father, Jesus Christ the righteous." 1 John 2*

If you make a mistake, simply go to your lawyer, your advocate, Jesus Christ, and consider this. God loved you so much he gave his only Son…and Jesus in quoting Hosea 6, said *"I will have mercy and not sacrifice…"*
If you confess your sin, he is faithful and just to forgive you.
Believing God's love for you is knowing God wants His child FREE to stand before Him. Jesus went to Calvary so the believer would NOT have a conscience plagued by sin. That is amazing grace! How much sin does the blood of Jesus cover? ALL sin, with the exception of a particular sin against the Holy Spirit, which is not a part of what we are dealing with here.
Satan would have yus remain fearful and wallow in our guilt. This is a trick, a trap of Satan. I recommend this as a sincere prayer, stated as one word in a short single breath:

"Father,forgivemeintheNameofJesusthankyousoverymuch."
Then move on, not having a consciousness of ever having made that mistake! And one more thing, never justify your mistake, when accused, press your lower lip firmly against your upper lip and thank God for Jesus being your justifier. That is not saying we are not to fulfil righteousness with one who we may have wronged. It is essential we learn to follow the Holy Spirit on God's word, and not our *'feelings'*.
For a few minutes, let's review the onslaught of,,,

'You know what you did!'

The attacks of Satan tell you that you are unchanged, always screwed up, and you are still a screw-up. The family and friends that remind you of your mistakes? Let's review what God's Word says. That is the rule, correct? This is the lesson for the self, the soul. For what saith the scripture?

> *"Abraham believed God, and it was counted unto him for righteousness.*
> *Now to him that worketh is the reward not reckoned of grace, but of debt. But to him that worketh not, but believeth on him that justifieth the ungodly, his faith is counted for righteousness." Romans 4*

And also…

> *"Know ye not that the unrighteous shall not inherit the kingdom of God? Be not deceived: neither fornicators, nor idolaters, nor adulterers, nor effeminate, nor abusers of themselves with mankind, nor thieves, nor covetous, nor drunkards, nor revilers, nor extortioners, shall inherit the kingdom of God.*
> *And such were some of you: but ye are washed, but ye are sanctified, but ye are justified in the name of the Lord Jesus, and by the Spirit of our God."* 1 Corinthians 6

If you owe someone a debt, who is anyone to declare your obligation to that person but the one you owe it to? If that person forgives the debt, who is another to declare it unforgiven? Are they not challenging the character of the one who forgave it? Let's look at it another way.

Let's review two scenarios;

> *One: let's assume you have majorly messed up your life. You have done everything wrong since you were 4 years old. You 'shot up' peanut butter under the kitchen sink as a child; you were interred in juvenile detention; you received adult convictions and have a rap sheet so thick that it rivals an old Sears catalog. But you come to God, convicted of sin by the Holy Spirit, and you are born again by the Spirit of God.*
>
> *Two: You were born again at seven years old, convicted of sin, and you gave your life to Christ. Since that point, raised in cultural churchianity, you 'rebelled' and lived a life doing as you please. You always loved God but did not know how to live the life that was preached, never having learned 'how' to do it from the heart. Faking it never seemed to be able to last very long. Now you are in your thirties and have a history of failed relationships. The church hates you, and you are endeavoring 'to abide In Christ,' having tried all else and failed.*

As you attempt to serve God, all the memories of failures flood your mind, and you feel helpless. This remains the lesson for

the child of God in addressing the enemy.
Step one: The First Question you ask is:
What saith the scripture?
If we are going to deny the soul, we are going to have to give our soul, our mind, our will, our emotions, our heart, the Word of God.
This Word of God is living.
It is NOT up to you to make it work. THIS is God's Word, and it is ON HIM!

> *"... whom he called, them he also justified; and whom he justified, them he also glorified.*
> *What shall we then say to these things? If God be for us, who can be against us? He that spared not his own Son, but delivered him up for us all, how shall he not with him also freely give us all things? Who shall lay anything to the charge of God's elect? It is God that justifieth.*
> *Who is he that condemneth? It is Christ that died, yea rather, that is risen again, who is even at the right hand of God, who also maketh intercession for us." Romans 8*

We will tell our soul, our mind, and EVERY other entity listening in:

> *"Father, your word states I am forgiven, I am justified, and the blood of the Lamb cleans me from ALL sin and ALL unrighteousness!!!*
> *This is YOUR word, and on THAT basis, I am forgiven! Christ is made unto me salvation, redemption and righteousness, and I come boldly before you and thank you!"*

We, then, have taken God's word and believed it. Now we stand on it, meaning we take it to our heart. We set our mind on God's word, reading it, and thinking on it. If we do not understand something, we thank God we will, because we trust His Holy Spirit to reveal it.
Being '*accused*' we understand it is Christ who died. He paid my price. He picked up my debt. If someone or some entity has an

issue, let them take it up with God. I will not defend myself, or open my mouth to justify myself.

If God justified me, who is it that can condemn me? It is God that justifies; this is so very critical, and important to grasp. If we justify ourselves, God cannot and will not.

This is faith, entrusting our entire life to God's hands.... Any attempt by us to *'explain why,'* to give a reason why we are not to be questioned or scrutinized concerning why we did what we did, is removing God from justifying us as we *'take the job.'*

Keeping our peace is difficult as the soul, the self, needs to defend itself. Keeping a mouth closed and a heart before God while being accused is trusting God, not your own righteousness, not the look on your face, but God, to justify you.

You may find you will endure this for a time, and then God will deal with those who came at you, breaking your heart. Because when you keep your heart before God, you forgive, your righteousness is of God, and your desire is that your accusers would have that love for God in their hearts.

As Stephen was being stoned, he requested God, *"Lay not this sin to their charge!"* We accept what Jesus did at Golgotha as a finished work; there is NO more sacrifice for sin that is needed. So, we walk before God, with no consciousness of making a mistake, or mistakes, looking to Jesus the author and finisher of our faith...

God's Word is true, we will accept no substitute.

What About Willful Sin, or Disobedience?
> *"For if we sin willfully after that we have received the knowledge of the truth, there remaineth no more sacrifice for sins,*
> *but a certain fearful looking for of judgment and fiery indignation, which shall devour the adversaries.*
> *He that despised Moses' law died without mercy under two or three witnesses:*
> *Of how much sorer punishment, suppose ye, shall he be*

> *thought worthy, who hath trodden underfoot the Son of God, and hath counted the blood of the covenant, wherewith he was sanctified, an unholy thing, and hath done despite unto the Spirit of grace?*
> *For we know him that hath said, Vengeance belongeth unto me, I will recompense, saith the Lord. And again, The Lord shall judge his people.*
> *It is a fearful thing to fall into the hands of the living God."* Hebrews 10

Willful sin is knowing what we are doing is wrong but doing it anyway.

Balaam is an example in the Old Testament; he did what he was told not to do and paid with his life.

In the early church Ananias and Sapphira knew better than to lie to the Holy Spirit. When they did, they paid with their lives.

So, willful sin is a serious issue, and not to be engaged in. There will be a consequence. Still, God is patient, as love is patient. 2 Corinthians 5

> *"...To wit, that God was In Christ reconciling the world unto himself, not imputing their trespasses unto them; and hath committed unto us the word of reconciliation."*

Remember the woman caught in adultery? Do you think she *knew better*?

Recall the man that lay by the pool thirty-eight years. Jesus told him to go and *sin no more* lest something worse happen to him. Both have the appearance of judgment for willful sin.

True story:

> *A pastor of a small country church outside Seattle had a contentious wife. To put it bluntly, he spent more time in a small shop next to the house than in the house with her. The pastor had told his wife a few times she "was out of order" in causing an argument that would result in his leaving the house.*
> *The Lord put it on a young man's heart to pray for her. He knew the nature of how he was to pray, and he*

was very concerned for her. He asked God if he could speak with her. When he received the peace to do so he entreated her as a mother. He spoke carefully to her on her responsibility to God to yield to her husband as unto the Lord. But she kicked him out of the house, and he left quietly. Shortly thereafter, she had a diabetic "scare."

About two weeks or so later he pulled up to a stop sign and the word of the Lord came to him. He started weeping and the word he received was, "that as Sennacherib came against Jerusalem, and was turned back only for a stronger nation to return, that something so hard was coming on this woman, that the former thing (the diabetic scare) would be forgotten." That afternoon he stopped by the parsonage. The pastor's wife was sitting on the sofa, head down, elbows on her knees. She had rolled her car, her body was beaten, but there was not a broken bone. The young man at that point had the power of God come over him, and he delivered exactly what God told him too. Exiting the parsonage, walking across the yard, the pastor grabbed his shoulder and spun him around, accusing him of possessing no compassion.

The young man told the pastor the entire story of what he had heard from the Lord. The pastor asked if his wife was going to be okay. The young man related exactly what the Lord told him, 'I cannot give you her life til the morning.'

Only one quarter mile down the road, the Lord released the woman, and the young man knew she would be okay. Returning the next day, he told the pastor what had happened. The pastor weeping, told him he had got it taken care of with God. God is so merciful...!!!

Another story:

In the church that same young man attended, one of the couples was a woman and her husband who 'followed'

> her. The husband would not talk or interact with anyone when she was around.
> The same young man was the adult Sunday School teacher and had invited the couple to his home for lunch. At the Sunday afternoon lunch, prior to the couple arriving, the young man prayed, and took authority in his home as head of his home under Christ. He stated before God, whatever ruled that woman's heart would have no access into his home.
> The couple arrived, and instantly the woman stated, "I do not feel any freedom to talk." The young man stated, "Relax, let the peace of God guide your heart."
> A couple more times, the woman related she felt no freedom to speak as the young man attempted to engage her husband in conversation. Her husband refused to speak, even as the man related God had established him as the head of his home.
> The woman became irate, and later she went and communicated a lie to the other elderly church ladies, attempting to split and destroy the church.
> The problem became serious, per John 20, the young man retained this couple's sin in Christ. Approximately three weeks later, the husband's head was crushed on his job, and the woman departed the church.
> This husband had made no attempt to fulfill what God had required of him as the Head, Christ's representative in his home. His penalty matched his error.

Willful sin has consequences, pastor.

But where sin abounds, grace does much more abound to the correctable, the contrite. For those hypocrites who would state that God's servants do not impute sin? What is it you do when you 'mark' someone as contentious and disfellowship them? What did Paul tell the church in Corinth of the man who had taken his father's wife?

God is finished with your hypocrisy, your confusing my Father's patience with His grace is no longer being accepted.

That warning is your freebie...
Both events involved a man, being responsible to God for their wives. One covered his wife in prayer. The other?
Keeping his wife happy cost him dearly.

> *"Behold, to obey is better than sacrifice, and to hearken than the fat of rams. For rebellion is as the sin of witchcraft, and stubbornness is as iniquity and idolatry."*

A repentant heart calls for mercy. An obstinate heart calls for correction, then judgment. The same one who tells us to forgive those who trespass against us also forgives us our trespasses when we ask. The woman caught in adultery was forgiven. The man that lay by the pool was forgiven.

The contentious wife of the pastor was forgiven, and she lived to be an elderly woman who graduated into eternity from old age!!

If we want mercy, we need to be merciful. Consider Jesus, who related,

> *"Ye judge after the flesh. I judge NO man. And yet if I judge, my judgment is true: for I am not alone, but I and the Father that sent me."*

Peter at Cornelius' house,

> *"...but God hath shewed me that I should not call any man common or unclean."*

Jesus had no opinion apart from his Father. Peter also was instructed not to prejudge.

Peter had asked Jesus how many times he must forgive. *"Seven?"* Jesus responded, *"Seventy times seven"*, not literally 490 times, but referencing Daniel 9.

Forgiveness should be granted until the end of the seventy weeks of Daniel's prophecy is fulfilled. So, we walk before God, not conscious of making a mistake, or mistakes, but looking to Jesus, the author and finisher of our faith.

What About Bondage

What occurs when we seem to have no choice, when it is, *'I*

cannot stop myself?"
The Israelites had served in bondage.
If we have any bondage in our life, we should keep in mind the Israelites in Egypt were still identified as Israelites!
Even in their bondage, they remained the inheritor of God's promises as the chosen of God!
We can be a child of God, the seed of promise, and be in bondage. But just as the Israelites, who in the middle of their bondage had called upon the Lord, we need to call on Him. Not just after, but also in the middle of our bondage in the midst of our shame and pain, we need to ask God to deliver us, and he will.
An event to illustrate this point:

Many years ago, a young man was sick in a basement room in Denver, Colorado. He rented the room by the week, and he had run out of money. It was below 20 degrees outside, and there was snow on the ground. He worked construction, and he had no work with snow on the job site. No work meant no income.

He called his parents to borrow some funds, and they told him they had turned him over to God. They would not be sending him any money. He thanked his mom, knowing he was the one who had asked, and he had been ready for yes or no.

His old 6-volt Chevy van would not start, and he was burning up with fever. He got angry and was very upset. He had forgotten he had asked God to deliver him of a debilitating bondage in his life, to the point of asking Him to deliver him from it or take him home. He had told God, "I have no control of this bondage, and if I have no control, I cannot bring it in subjection to your Spirit." In the middle of an "episode," in his shame he cried out to God, stating, "I hate this. Please deliver me or destroy this body." In that basement, in his despair, enduring the fever and his lack of funds, in anger he got up and picked up his Bible to throw it against the wall.

As he lifted up the Bible, he "saw" the Israelites in the wilderness, and he "saw" what God had desired. He put his Bible down and he thanked God he was God's son, that God was his father, and that a man who did not provide for his family was worse than an infidel! He then thanked God that God had already provided ALL his need In Christ!!! And that he would rather die in this room knowing God than to never have known him. The Holy Spirit came in, and he fell asleep awaking in the A.M. rested, healed, and delivered of all his bondage. As he slept the temperature outside was warming, the snow melting.

He walked outside and asked God, "What have you done?" The Lord replied, "I've set you free." But he knew he would not be free long if he did not surrender his life to the Lord. He re-committed his life to the Lord right then.

Deliverance by God always has a purpose. In this story, the young man wanted the freedom to bring ALL his life before Christ. God delivered the Israelites with a strong hand, revealing His power and His ability to the nation so that the Israelites could serve Him.

God did not deliver them to *'continue on their own path'* God's plan was their freedom to live before Him as His chosen people. The only way to remain *'free'* is, once delivered, surrender your life, daily denying your soul in subjection to the One able to watch over you.

Bondage happens when we deny Christ and *'please'* ourselves. A person delivered and not *'re-committed'* to Christ is on a route that will end up being seven times worse, per the Lord. As stated at the beginning, each soul will have spiritual oversight. One of two kingdoms will be served.

A nation delivered and allowed to continue in their own way to do what is right in their own sight would return to bondage, as that is what put them in bondage to begin with. Sin puts us in bondage; the one that sins is the servant of sin.

Undelivered and the Why

If a person desires deliverance from alcohol or drugs, for freedom to live *'his life,'* he remains in bondage. Desiring to be free of bondage is the desire to be free of a cruel taskmaster. We do not always consider how we got into the cruel taskmaster relationship. Pleasing ourselves led to this bondage. Whether in being unable to control our appetite for food, alcohol, drugs, television, or pornography, it all starts with satisfying a self-pleasing desire and not being open to the spirit of God's correction.

At any point we wish to count ourselves *'buried with Christ'* and live a life in the spirit. It is our counting the flesh dead and buried, so we can please God that deliverance is ours.

God's love to each and every single one of us contains the power to deliver us into His peace, His freedom, and allow Christ IN us, the hope of glory, to be revealed.

So that we can walk before God, not conscious of making a mistake, or mistakes...

Instead we look to Jesus, the author
and finisher of our faith...

THE REALITY OF LOVE

Abraham, Moses, Joshua and David stand out as having a love for God. This love for God, is revealed in their loving His... presence.

This revealed their heart, and the use of their time. When you love someone, you do not want to be apart, as being apart is painful.

For those who confess they love the Lord, they also believe the blood of Jesus Christ cleanses them from ALL sin. That means they are made righteous, acceptable in Christ, amen?

We recall that the veil was torn, top to bottom between the Holy Place and the Holy of Holies, allowing us unhindered access into the Holy of Holies, God's presence in the Holy Spirit. This access is mine and yours *to use at our discretion*, anytime as disciples, as believers who love their Lord.

Yet, from moment-to-moment we are doing what we *'love'* in reality, what really pleases... us.

So in all honesty, transparency,

To say we love God is not the same as
actually... loving God.

God's love to us is expressed at Calvary as He removed all hindrances that would separate us from Him. For us to actually love God is to consciously on purpose with intent abide in His tangible Presence.

This is to be our holy ambition.

Prior to the flood, God strove with man. God wooed, and strove with the heart of man, in an effort to redeem them.

In stark contrast to Psalms 1, man's heart was wicked and full of violence, even as they *'called on the name of the Lord'*.

Their focus, their love? It was... their lives/souls, their selves.

> "They did eat, they drank, they married wives, they were given in marriage, until the day that Noe entered into the ark, and the flood came, and destroyed them all.
> Likewise also as it was in the days of Lot; they did eat, they drank, they bought, they sold, they planted, they builded..." Luke 17:27-28

Today, it is the same scenario and our only part is simply to change our focus from pleasing our-selves to pleasing Him.

Abiding In Christ is a LIVING place.

Our being a church member, or having a religion requires no faith as it produces acceptance from men as we 'just show up' with our support. God is near our mouth, and far from our heart as we live lives believing God accepts our carnal living apart from Him.

Abiding In Christ requires a love for God that exceeds the love of our-self. That love brings us before the Holy Spirit and our life begins to be changed into His image.

These results are life-exchanging, never to be repented of.

Abiding in Christ is sharing the same love, the same heart our Lord has for His Father. Jesus lived by the words he received from His Father and the Presence of His Father was ALWAYS with Him (John 8:29).

Without the Father, Jesus acknowledged He was powerless, and he was so comfortable with that...why?

Jesus had abandoned His powerless sinless blood and flesh soul in the wilderness. With denying His flesh and blood soul, He also shut down its inputs, its desires having any sway in His reality.

The desire to please His soul, or to please men was what He had died to, in denying His flesh and blood soul.

Jesus lived out what He taught, being the greatest in the Kingdom of Heaven required this.

Loving God more than His mother, sister, brethren, and His own soul also, He walked out His Father's teaching.

We can recall Him calling His mother *'woman'* at Cana, or referring to those who heard God's word and kept it as His family. His *'brothers and sisters'* were not outside, they were in that room with Him, a new family, a new generation was being recognized.

Loving God is identifying with God as our Father, our life-giver, recognizing that apart from His spirit, His Holy Spirit we have no life. He is the One who has provided all our needs, and our life. He who will love life, will love God, His Word, and His Holy Spirit.

The Enabler

God had sent His Son, and soon Jesus was going away. He had been with the disciples for 3½ years, day in and day out. He had lived, eaten, slept, and traveled with them, relating to them the words he received from his Father.

To abruptly leave them, abandon them, does not fit the character or the nature of a loving Father.

Jesus told the 11 disciples who had left all that he would send them a Comforter,

> *"Even the Spirit of truth; whom the world cannot receive, because it seeth him not, neither knoweth him: but ye know him; for he dwelleth with you and shall be in you."*
>
> *"I go to prepare a place for you so that where I am, you may be also."*

This reference to *"Where I am"*, is Jesus telling His disciples that as He lived in the Father so they are to abide IN CHRIST. We are to have our citizenship, our life in Heaven *now, present tense* finding it IN the tangible Holy Ghost.

When the disciples received the Holy Ghost, they followed hard after the Holy Spirit as Jesus their Lord had shown them. In loving God, as Christ had shown them, they did not love their lives unto death.

That explains their demises, amen?

They grasped the reality that God is spirit and seeks such to worship him in spirit and in truth. The flesh does not profit. For those disciples who love God, we now clearly see why the carnal, self-centered mind and life lived after the flesh is hostile to God. It is the exact opposite of His image expressed by His Son, amen?

At this point, we understand with great clarity why prayers centered in self-gratification, centered in friendship with the world, go unanswered, per James 4.

Renewing our mind is accomplished as we by the Holy Spirit begin to consume His word, speak HIS word and LIVE His life in and by the Holy Ghost.

In Romans 8 we hear,

> *"God bears witness with our spirit..."*

'Bears witness' is 'to corroborate'.

What is it to corroborate? It is to *'acknowledge that what the person is saying is true'*.

Can God corroborate our words that Jesus came in the flesh? Yes!

Can God corroborate our words that ALL our sins have been forgiven and Christ is made unto us righteousness? Yes!

He is called the Spirit of Truth for a reason.

As we take God's word back to God and abide in Christ the witness of His presence on our words is spirit and life. This is abiding in Him.

This is our choice, and ours alone.

Each and every one of us has a choice, to be to God what ONLY YOU or I can be to Him.

There is a *'faux'* faith that Satan has snared Churchianity with. It is based on the teaching and the inference to each believer they have done all and are *'waiting on God'* to do something.

This teaching declares the listener to *'be full of the Holy Ghost and seated at the right hand of God In Christ'*. The teaching is that it is a finished work, and daily struggles are normal and to be expected.

Galatians 5:24 does not factor in.

One self-called Pastor stated, *"After all, we are in the flesh, we are to enjoy it!"*

The inference is that a believer can, *'live out his life doing as he wills, what pleases him, and the sacrifice of Jesus covers him'.*

Like Eli's sons, sleep with whoever you want, then go to church and offer your sacrifice. The sin is what the sacrifice is for!

One Colorado pastor told his youth group that by being nice to each other, they just might *'get lucky'*. No joke...

But as they tell you to just *'do your best, no need to be concerned'* keep one thing in mind.

Before God, possessing a carnal mind, living after the flesh is enmity, hostility to God.

Jesus' flesh was the veil that was torn top to bottom so we can have access into the Holy of Holies and remain in His Presence.

The false messenger teaches by word and lifestyle as long as you *'go to church'* supporting his *'work for God'* ministry doing your best, you are saved.

After all, we are only... human.

This *'excuse'* is being parlayed into the growth of men's kingdoms as people are told,

> "We are all messed up. None of us walks sinless before God, and if anyone thinks they do or can, they are wrong."

Yet in Hebrews 10, if we have a conscience of sin something is wrong.

The author states with the continual offering of sin sacrifices, the ones making the offering could never be made perfect, or mature. We are to have a conscience purged from sin, and unrighteousness. If not, we are as those under the Law who could never be made perfect.

> "...because that the worshippers once purged should have had no more consciousness of sins."

God said that as if our having a consciousness of sin is a bad thing! The truth God is revealing is we cannot be made perfect if we are always reminded WE are a SINNER! You are to have no more consciousness of sin or sins IN Christ! No more consciousness of sin? REALLY?! YES!! As in sinless? YES!!

Tell me, how *ELSE* can a believer *"have boldness to enter the Presence of God?"*

The leader who is preaching that you cannot live before God without sin is '<u>NOT</u>' a true Apostle, or Prophet, or Evangelist, or Pastor, or Teacher of God'.

These ministry gifts are to present the believer perfect and mature IN Christ.

These FIVE Gifts of Christ TO the church are for the maturing of each believer IN Christ.

When you come to maturity IN Christ, you are walking with God in and by the Holy Spirit and are functioning, actually functioning in the Body of Christ in relationship with the Head of the Body, Jesus Christ.

The ministry of the Evangelist, Pastor and Teacher is to be continually diminished, and even potentially end in your life.

Does this sound wrong?

Again, what does God's word tell us?

> *"And he gave some, apostles; and some, prophets; and some, evangelists; and some, pastors and teachers;*
> *For the perfecting of the saints, for the work of the ministry, for the edifying of the body of Christ:*
> *Till we all come in the unity of the faith, and of the knowledge of the Son of God, unto a perfect man, unto the measure of the stature of the fulness of Christ:*
> *That we henceforth be no more children..."* Ephesians 4

'*Till we* all come... unto a perfect man?'

What happens when the child of God matures into sonship?

What is supposed to occur as a child grows up, they need a nanny until when...?

The gifts of God were given in your life until Christ is formed in you and you walk as part of the body in obedience to the Holy Spirit. This is where you have entered the rest God has provided, and God has a habitation IN YOU!

In the Body of Christ, the '*administrative gifts*' are to present you mature, or perfect '*In Christ*'.

Are we following this?

A person entrusted with a child's care who does not help a child learn and mature is not *'helping'*. As children of God, we are to grow and mature into a relationship with God IN Christ where we individually *'walk in the Spirit'*, obedient to the Head of the Body, Jesus Christ Our Lord.

When you read the Word, you see the *'Fivefold gifts'* are part of the Body of Christ. Those who possess them are not to be using them. They are to be used by the Holy Spirit in being obedient to the Head of the Church... just as those who hear them are. Their function was never to *'have a following'*, but to deliver the Living Word of God to the believer so the believer would INCREASE in Christ. As this occurred, the Ministry Gifts input might actually decrease in the believer's walk as the believer grows in relationship with Christ.

Recall Moses,

> *"...would God that all the LORD'S people were prophets, and that the LORD would put his spirit upon them!"*
> *Numbers 11*

Not self-called, not self-seeking, there was no desire to rule, but bring God's people into fellowship with God!

Korah was of a different spirit, just as self-called, unsent ministries today. *Oh how the people loved that man.*

If you desire Korah's ministry, go for it but the worms will not die, neither shall the fire be quenched... still worth it??! When did God EVER send a minister to placate the listeners after the flesh? WHEN???

To speak life to the spirit, is to speak death to the flesh, how can you build your carnal church or social kingdom with that understanding??? The goal of God your Father is Christ being formed in you so you can fulfill the will of God IN Jesus Christ. All other *'supposed ministries'* are detractions from the work of the Holy Ghost.

Neither did the Holy Spirit *'mis-speak'*. The ministry gifts were *'until'*. The only gifts mentioned going forward are the foundational gifts of the Apostle and Prophet.

As the Apostle described the one who planted and the one who watered, they were not worthy of receiving the honor that belongs to God who gave the increase (1 Corinthians 3).

We are to give a *'Man of God'* who delivers the Word of God the honor due him. This is our giving attention to the Word of God, while respecting the anointing of Christ on him. Seeking to *'please'* him or gain favor with him is idolatry. A true man of God does not desire your praise.

His desire is that you grow up into Christ.

> "And they shall teach no more every man his neighbor, and every man his brother, saying, Know the LORD: for they shall all know me, from the least of them unto the greatest of them, saith the LORD: for I will forgive their iniquity, and I will remember their sin no more."
> Jeremiah 31

And also...

> "Be ye therefore perfect, even as your Father which is in heaven is perfect." Matthew 5
>
> "In this was manifested the love of God toward us, because that God sent his only begotten Son into the world, that we might live through him.
> Herein is love, not that we loved God, but that he loved us, and sent his Son to be the propitiation for our sins.
> Beloved, if God so loved us, we ought also to love one another.
> No man hath seen God at any time.
> If we love one another, God dwelleth in us, and his love is perfected in us.
> Hereby know we that we dwell in him, and he in us, because he hath given us of his Spirit." 1 John 4

Loving God, is recognizing God our Father as providing us His righteousness IN Christ, cleansing us of ALL sin.

Loving God is personally thanking Him that this is HIS word.

Our part is to believe His word and return to Him, cleaving to Him, through abiding in His Holy Spirit.

This is our building Him a house of rest, a sanctuary to abide, our being His Temple through the tangible Holy Spirit.

MENE, MENE, TEKEL, UPHARSIN

TITHES

In this chapter we will dethrone the false King and discharge the False Priest. We are also going to see two houses, clearly and distinctly identified as separate, not combined, not merged, not even closely resembling one another.
We will see tithes in scripture for its intended purpose, which was to support a king's house, and be the source of his provision to his servants, his support staff.
When we read of the Israelites desiring a king, we will also get an accurate description of the tithes, of the 10% and its purpose is detailed in 1 Samuel 8:11-18.
Here we see 10% was the standard way kings supported their rule. This was not scripturally separate from what any king would warrant. Each king warranted the 10%, as they would also impose this percentage on nations they would conquer. The tithe, the 10% rule applied also to God as Balaam had prophesied there is a King among them.
So tithes were the way the kings of men, and God's house, the tabernacle and the temple were supported under the Old Covenant.
But now that the old is done away with, we have a 'different' house, amen?
There is no longer a need to have servants stand before the King in his house on behalf of others.
There is no longer a need to support people standing in our 'stead.'
There is no longer a need to support a *'temple'* made with hands...
Babylon will say Jesus is the King of Kings, and Lord of Lords,

and that he is entitled to the tenth.
I would agree with that wholeheartedly if I were not part of the Body of Christ!
Isn't the Church bone of His bone, flesh of His flesh? Will a wife pay tithes to her husband?
Did Abram collect tithes of Sarah?
Or are they 'One,' as in one flesh?
Isn't the Body of Christ supposed to take care of itself, the Body of Christ in love?
Is not this the purpose of the fivefold ministry, the Apostle, Prophet, Evangelist, Pastor and Teacher, to bring about this… caring?

> "For the perfecting of the saints, for the work of the ministry, for the edifying of the body of Christ:
> Till we all come in the unity of the faith, and of the knowledge of the Son of God, unto a perfect man, unto the measure of the stature of the fulness of Christ."
> Ephesians 4

Is there something here the body is to grow into?
Understand this, this present day '*Minister/King*' kingdom finance system is over.
With the following understanding, when a church leader preaches tithes, he is building his illegitimate kingly portfolio, HIS house.
And most likely, the prince in the kingdom, the pastor's son, is being groomed to take over the rule when his dad, the king, steps down from his throne.
Per the Word of God, this illegitimate man is operating as an faux abolished Levitical Priest in his own man built 'temple' apart from the Old Covenant. He is also declaring he is a God's servant with no home ownership, no retirement plan having only God as his reward. He is falsely operating as the King's servant fulfilling the Law's commandment and…

> "has a commandment to take tithes of the people according to the law…"

This charlatan is also pretending to stand before God on your behalf, in your stead. Any collector of tithes on behalf of God today is maintaining his Babylonian kingdom, even as he has been taught by the Great Whore as she maintains her kingdom.

Too much?

Men teaching men, have passed down this tradition, their theology of men even with honest hearts, good hearts. But that in itself does not make it right. If God told you to collect tithes, then do so. But ask Him where under the New Covenant His word supports this.

> *In the mouth of two or three, let everything be established.*

Jesus told those <u>under</u> the Law,

> *"Woe unto you, scribes and Pharisees, hypocrites! for ye pay tithe of mint and anise and cummin, and have omitted the weightier matters of the law, judgment, mercy, and faith: these ought ye to have done, and not to leave the other undone." Matthew 23*

When the disciples were asked about the temple tax, Jesus did not dig into the monies given to Him for the poor, or their daily needs. Instead, He instructed Peter on who actually owed the tax.

The children of God would not owe the tax, as it was their Father's house.

The children were free!

Nevertheless to avoid offense, Peter would return to his trade, and bring the first fruit from his fishing task to pay the temple tax. He told Peter to go fish, and bring up the first fish he caught and take the coin from that fish's mouth, and pay the tax.

Being redundant, the tithe belonged to the '*King*' so there would be a provision in the King's house and, under the Law, provision in God's house, the earthly temple.

If a man is collecting a tithe for his '*ministry*,' he is acknowledging his own kingdom, not even '*The House*' that Moses was faithful in…as it has been declared to be done away with.

He is definitely NOT acknowledging Christ as the Son over HIS Own house... whose house are we...

> "Howbeit the Most High dwelleth not in temples made with hands; as saith the prophet..."

How ridiculous to think a house built with hands can fulfill or hold the creator, the presence of God? Is this not absolutely the most flagrant foolishness before God that can be imagined?

The *'Temple made without hands'* is God's focus and the essence of the apostles teachings.

Man's pride makes *'building his ministry, his work,'* with his name and his image at stake. The tithes are collected for his *'ministry,'* for the support of HIS House, for the church building built under his tenure, for salaries, for vehicles, for vacations, for children's education, for retirement investments, etc., etc.. Tithes have been used to support mistresses, and other special *'needs'* ministries for the king himself.

> *(Some Pastors and so-called apostles actually have servants working in THEIR house as "handmaidens of the Lord."*
>
> *The "king" mentality is the belief you are "special" before God and warrant special treatment.*
>
> *This is the devil's work with sexual exploitation, abuse often being associated with these 'harlot daughter' ministries).*

None of these items were ever to be the purpose of the tithes. If we think the tithes had to be adapted to fit our 'culture,' that would be the culture of unbelief, faithless and not holding the Head of the church.

But go ahead. Pay your *'tithes'* to the ministry.

But now your finances are in jeopardy if you are paying tithes in disobedience. Before the Living God of whom I stand, this corrupt system of *'kings'* taking money from the Body of Christ building personal kingdoms is finished.

Babylon's days are numbered. Her kings have been *'weighed in the balance and found wanting.'*

As stated prior, *'The beast'* that Babylon rests upon? As she does not acknowledge his rule, God has put it in his heart to consume her. The beast is going to consume her, beginning with her elders, her pastors. When you see her pastors put out, pursued and punished by the beast, these words will ring in your ears.

When the beast has finished with them her supporters will be his next target.

Babylonian Leaders and Preachers are teaching '*tithing*,' as that is the message they have been taught to teach, not hearing from God.

This was addressed earlier. Jesus stated to Peter after Peter received the revelation of who Jesus was,

> "Upon This Rock, I will build my church and the gates of hell will not prevail against it."

This is not a house built with brick, or '*fired*' clay. It is not built with man-hewn stones, it is built on living stones, those whose faith in God is unshakeable as they are built on the Rock, the Chief Cornerstone being the Head of the Corner!

It is not built on theology, traditions, theory, or knowledge. The Government?

> "...For unto us a child is born, unto us a son is given: and the government shall be upon his shoulder." Isaiah 9

The revelation of Jesus Christ by the Holy Spirit IS the Rock upon which the individual living stones are built.

On this rock, the power of God is manifest as opposed to those who build on '*their service order*,' their '*politically correct*,' socially adaptable ministries and giftings.

Divorce, premature death, sickness, ministerial affairs, strife, and hypocrisy are rife in these assemblies as men teach what they have been taught, devoid of the Holy Spirit and unable to receive revelation from God. Men are paid mammon/money to teach men, giving approval to each other, devoid of the approval that comes from God.

Never in the new Covenant is there a covenant right for part of our income, or even a part of your life...

INSTEAD...

The whole of our world has been bought at Calvary. We are not our own, we are bought with a price that covers our entire world, 100%. We have been bought with the precious blood of the Lamb. For us to give 10% of our finances as a Law-based tithe into a system that is corrupting the Gospel of Jesus Christ for financial gain will cost us tremendously financially.
Why?
Because we are supporting a system that is stating what Jesus did at Calvary was inadequate. This same system was abolished in His resurrection. This is especially true if our mentality is 10% is for the Lord, and 90% is ours apart from God. That HAS been preached,

> "Give God only 10%, and God tells you the remaining
> 90% is yours to please yourself!"

Let me rephrase that. Paying tithes under the law is supporting a man's kingdom that is not of God. Our responsibility before God is a personal relationship. Our responsibility is to get to a place IN CHRIST where we fellowship with HIM.
Remember that sweet church couple who sold their property, promising the resulting finances to God? Ananias and Sapphira? Recall what Peter said by the Holy Spirit?
This is critical to comprehend. By the Holy Spirit, Peter said this,

> "While it was your own, was it not yours to do with as
> you pleased?"

Their attempted deception had deadly results. Just as Balaam thought God did not see him, Ananias and Sapphira promised something to God then held back a part of the committed thing for themselves.
Have we given our life to Christ?

> *Do we understand when it was our own life,*
> *it was ours to do with as we pleased?*

But before God, we are now not our own.
We are those who are bought with a price...have we deceived ourselves?
This is on YOU and ME. Paying 10% will not release us. It will

not pay God off. And, in fact, it is offensive to Him.
Paying tithes to please a Pastor is being a 'man pleaser.' Again, we are asking for ruin.
Giving is an act of obedience out of a relationship and a love for the Lord Jesus Christ from our heart. It is not an obligation to '*your church.*'
You ARE the church.
You are to be the Temple of God.
Giving is to be done in obedience to our head, which is the Lord Jesus Christ. You and I are members of the Body of Christ, and it is to function as a body, a family, not a business, or based on the Law. It IS the Body of Christ!

> *"From whom the whole body fitly joined together and compacted by that which every joint supplieth, according to the effectual working in the measure of every part, maketh increase of the body unto the edifying of itself in love." Ephesians 4*

Again, we are to be the House of God, His place of rest, His Habitation. We are HIS HOUSE HE is FAITHFUL over. We are His house as we hold fast the confidence and the rejoicing of the hope firm unto the end!
If we are bone of His bone, and flesh of His flesh, He is OUR provider, and He takes care of each of us using each of us as members of the Body in the Body to the Body!
As Spirit-Filled believers, we ARE the Temple built without hands, the Body of Christ. This body is to function in relation to its Head, our Lord Jesus Christ, in love. If one member suffers, the whole body is affected, and I am affected, as well as you.
Taking financial care of those who minister the things of God is handled as the Head of The Church knows what is needed in the Body, and able to move in and through the body supplying each need through its members. Remember, this is why the Apostle, Prophet, Evangelist, Pastor and Teacher gifts were given to the Body?
If we are compelled to '*support*' a ministry to '*keep it going*,' keep

in mind the Lord Jesus Christ is the Head of the church.

He is alive and more than capable of maintaining HIS ministry! Does *'guilting'* a believer into supporting a ministry sound like the ministry of the Holy Spirit?

At the risk of being redundant, the Temple of God is the Body of Christ, us. We are to be filled with the Holy Spirit, and we are to be HIS place of rest. This is not about works. It is about obedience following the leading of the Holy Spirit and fellowshipping our Father. Everything related to our time here in this wilderness Earth is about walking with God.

When we walk in a way pleasing to God, God can bless us IN HIM so we can be a blessing to the Body beyond our wildest dreams.

When To Pay Tithes

If the Lord instructs you by the Holy Spirit to pay tithes, pay tithes in faith, in obedience.

> *A young man staying with relatives was seeking the Lord. At one point the Lord instructed him to do three things, one being to pay tithes. After about two weeks, he was confronted by an individual accusing him of not doing the three things that his Father had instructed him to do. Of those three accusations, one was that he had not been paying tithes. The young man was able to answer truthfully in the affirmative to being obedient in all three accusations of disobedience.*

Another time to pay tithes, is when it would be offensive, or cause a brother to stumble if you did not pay tithes. The Apostle Paul spoke of not eating meat as long as the world stands in 1 Corinthians 8 if it would be an offense to a brother. All things are lawful, but not all things are expedient. God's Provision I have stories of how God provides as you walk with Him. When you seek to walk in His Spirit, and you please God by following Him, heaven and earth seem to be tools He uses just to *"do for you."* God is like that.

> *"Seek ye first the Kingdom of God and His*

> *Righteousness, and all these things shall be added unto you. Matthew 6*

Jesus is responsible for those He called, from Noah to Abraham, Jacob, John, Peter, John G Lake, Smith Wigglesworth, Watchman Nee, and Reese Howell. Of late there is a country preacher Thurman Scrivner who never requested a dime from anyone as he fulfilled God's plan. There are stories of how God provides for those He has called.

The life we are called to live by faith?

The true ministers of the Lord Jesus Christ will lead the way living IN THAT FAITH. God is responsible for those He calls. Faith is based on hearing what God is telling you and being obedient to His Word. Am I saying not to give?

NO! Give from your heart, literally and liberally, as to Jesus Christ personally, as HE directs, not as unto men, or as a result of men's *'pressure.'*

When you give, do it as Paul stated, as you have purposed in your heart. Give to the one who gave His all for you, and as you do, God will bless you abundantly, with Him and in Him. Let God direct your giving. Help a brother, a sister, in the Lord as directed...

Do so anonymously, if at all possible per Matthew 6.

Do not give to get a tax deduction. Give as unto the Lord, as HE directs, and you will never lack. If a *'minister'* takes this understanding and requests you *'give'* any amount, advise him you will take it under consideration.

God always confirms HIS word. Your obedience is to be to the Head of the Church, Jesus Christ personally. It is not about you *'keeping'* anything. It is about obedience.

Recall what Samuel told King Saul when Saul had been disobedient blaming *'the people?'*

> *"For rebellion is as the sin of witchcraft, and stubbornness is as iniquity and idolatry. Because thou hast rejected the word of the LORD, he hath also rejected thee from being king.*
>
> *And Saul said unto Samuel, I have sinned: for I have*

transgressed the commandment of the LORD, and thy words: because I feared the people, and obeyed their voice." 1 Samuel 15

The excuse did not work then, nor will it now.

Final thought: If the social meeting place was disbanded, and their weekly meetings discontinued, would your home be a convenient place for the Body of Christ to meet?

In Acts, they went from house to house, the widows were not neglected, and the ministry of Christ flourished. Give from your heart, literally and liberally, as to Christ.

Giving to God is ministering to the Body of Christ.

EQUALITY IS NEVER WHOLENESS

Wholeness contains the promise of ALL the united whole contains, while individual equality contains the limitation of the individual part. This is not more evident than when the individual part is identified in contrast to, or in opposition to the unified whole.

Division is the bane of equality. When parts of a whole identify themselves as equal, wholeness cannot exist as each part in its equality establishes itself as a separate *'whole'* in itself.

Teamwork, as in making the *'dream work'* is where equal parts contribute to a common or shared goal. Contributing their *'part'*, each contributor retains an identity separate from the others, as achieving the goal is their purpose in participating. Wholeness is not an aspect of the individual's cooperation.

Beginning of Wholeness: The Separation
When God created man, God separated His life into the body of clay, and man became something that had not existed prior, a living soul. Man now possessed the very substance of God as his life.

What God performed in Adam, in separating the woman from him, God had first performed in separating His own spirit, *TO* Adam.

God sent forth His spirit into Adam, with Adam now possessing the very life of God. In this, man was capable of becoming one with God, being God's place of rest in the earth. God would be fulfilled in Adam with Adam completed, or made whole in God in returning to God, what he had received. Adam was to be God's place of rest in the earth. When Adam sinned,

God's place of rest was lost.

God's place of *'wholeness'* in man was lost. God was never fulfilled, completed, or did He become *'One'* with man until Jesus Christ, His Son exited the wilderness.

Abstract?

God's Ways are Being Revealed

As it was not good for man to be alone, God in creating man in His image gives us a picture of *'who God is.'*

God created man in His image, male and female created He *'them.'* God, being One God and yet *'plural'* now possessed His image in the created *"Them."*

God, the *"Us"* had created man for an awesome purpose. Man sharing the very subs

tance of God in their spirit, was to become *'One'* with the Godhead.

This can never occur in the corrupt flesh and blood soul of man. As touched on previously, through Jesus Christ the end of all flesh has come before God, just as in the days of Noah. God has condemned sin in the flesh. Those who will walk with God will do so in His Holy Spirit having received the gift of His righteousness.

Back on track..!

Just as God had breathed, or separated His life to man, God separated the woman from the man.

When God separated the woman from Adam, Adam was missing part of himself. This will sound wrong to the man-taught, but God also in breathing life into Adam, separated something of Himself, His very life to Adam. In this, as Adam, God in entrusting Himself to another became reliant on the one who possessed His life, to become 'One' with them, or to have a place of rest.

If this offends your intellect, let this break your heart.

> *"Heaven is my throne, and earth is my footstool: what house will ye build me? saith the Lord: or what is the place of my rest?*

Hath not my hand made all these things?"
What CANNOT the Creator, *create?*
Just as the woman drew her substance, and her life from man, man had drawn his life from God. The woman received her flesh, blood, and bone from her husband Adam, the source of her substance. The woman's flesh contained the blood, the soul, or life of Adam in her flesh. Adam, the living soul likewise in creation possessed the very soul of God in his physical bloodstream. He lived by God's word, which contained the life of God on it.
Having the very life of Adam, the woman being apart from Adam, meant Adam was missing something of his-self. The woman now possessed Adam's life, apart from him having power over it.
Possessing the very life of God, the man being apart from God, meant God was missing something of His-*self*. Adam possessed God's life, apart from Him, having power over it. Wow...
This should impact our heart, we have the power to complete God through a relationship where our heart to Him, becomes His home, the place His heart can safely rest.
Again, that will sound in error to man-taught intellectuals who have their god defined, boxed, and tied off.

Opportunity for Wholeness
When God presented the woman back to Adam, that was Adam being restored. Restitution was taking place. What had been removed from Adam was being returned to him. Adam had previously searched through all of God's creatures, and a help-meet was not found.

Adam could never accept less than him-
self as a help-meet.

The woman that was returned to him, was literally Adam. She WAS bone of his bone, flesh of his flesh; she was his equal in sharing his substance and identity.
She was his match, being of his flesh and bone, she was

compatible to be joined to him, becoming *'one flesh'* as his help-meet. Their being *'one flesh'* is exactly how the *'Us'* in God saw *'them.'*

Even their name, their identification was also singular as the Lord our God is One God, amen?

Their name was Adam, Genesis 5:2. Their identity was a shared name until sin entered.

God restored to man, that which had in a deep sleep been removed from him. Adam had a help-meet for him just as God had man, as His established place of rest.

God took care of Adam needing a help-meet... first.

Love is like that.

> *"Charity suffereth long, and is kind; charity envieth not; charity vaunteth not itself, is not puffed up,*
> *Doth not behave itself unseemly, seeketh not her own, is not easily provoked, thinketh no evil; Rejoiceth not in iniquity, but rejoiceth in the truth;*
> *Beareth all things, believeth all things, hopeth all things, endureth all things." 1 Corinthians 13*

Love puts its desires on a back-burner as it ensures the object of its love is taken care of first. God gave man the desire of his heart, before God would address the desire of His heart in man. Yet, we must keep in our heart that God had created man as His place of rest, His habitation in the earth.

God had created the heavens and the earth, and a place of rest was not found. Likewise God had placed man in the earth, and a help-meet for him was not found in all creation. Again, God took care of His son's needs, first.

> *"And the LORD God took the man, and put him into the garden of Eden to dress it and to keep it.*
> *And the LORD God commanded the man..." Genesis 2*

God placed him in the protected environment of His Garden, and put him on the path to ruling the earth. Adam just needed to stay *'true to God.'*

Adam in the image of God the Father, shared the word of God with his wife. As the head of his home, God would not divide

asunder what God had joined together.
>*This is a principle in God's Kingdom.*

Adam needed desperately to watch over his heart, his wife, and God's Garden in patience for *'them'* to inherit the promises of God.

The issue would be manifest in this.

Adam knew loneliness, Adam knew what it was like to be alone.

His wife?

Not at all.

Would Adam risk conflicting with his own flesh and blood, his wife's desires, if those desires conflicted with God's word, to HIM?

A choice, a decision would need to be made

> *(Would you, or I prefer our own flesh and blood soul, if it conflicted with... God's word? Or would we, count it dead to please the One who gave His all, for us?)*

Adam's wife, from her heart, would need to return her entirety to her husband in love, living by the same word of God, for them to experience wholeness.

Note, for them to be complete, it would be the heart of love in the woman, returning her all to her husband. *Hold that thought.*

The woman is vital to wholeness in marriage, in creation. While identified as being the *'weaker'* vessel, the woman holds the key for wholeness. This may sound in error, but we will see that it remains true from Genesis, through Revelation.

Remember God had created all things in six days, and on the seventh day God rested? The sixth day was when the final act of creation was completed. Man had been created in the image of God, male and female created He them. God indwelt Adam in his very bloodstream *(Leviticus 17:11)* and had a habitation.

The Fall

Then a tragedy occurred, sin entered. Man sinned, and God's place of rest was removed. As a result, we do not see the end of the seventh day, yet.

All of the days that were concluded, had similar language;

> "And the evening and the morning were the first day."

Except, on the seventh day.

That language is not used... yet.

Instead we find God dealing with man, striving with man, then ending all flesh with the exception of Noah through the flood. We see death reigning from Adam to Moses, and then God's word is delivered through His servant Moses. God's word was the law of God a man could *'live by'* if taken in faith, from the heart. It did not happen.

In Isaiah 66, we hear God again calling on man to understand Him and hear His heart.

> *"Thus saith the LORD, The heaven is my throne, and the earth is my footstool: where is the house that ye build unto me? and where is the place of my rest?*
> *For all those things hath mine hand made, and all those things have been, saith the LORD: but to this man will I look, even to him that is poor and of a contrite spirit, and trembleth at my word..."*

Wholeness for God, seemed to be on par with Hosea finding his place of rest. God had created heaven and earth, but God's place of rest He could not create. Remember that thought I requested you hold?

> "...for them to be complete, it would be the heart of love in the woman, returning her all to her husband."

The genius of God is found in this. Love is the ONLY way to experience wholeness.

Any self-centeredness will destroy the opportunity for wholeness. Love does not seek its own. For wholeness to be found, the lesser must return seeking the greater's fulfillment. If the *'greater'* sought to be made whole in the lesser, or weaker vessel, it could be construed as domineering, controlling, or an abuse of power.

God shows His love, He draws us by the Holy Spirit, it is on us how we respond from our free will.

Now we can understand the tragedy of sin as being adultery. Trusting another with all you are, everything, is entrusting your heart to them. Adultery can shred that heart.

For those who have lived it, there is only wholeness in forgiving. The pain must be 'lived through' as God endured making the path back to Him.

In seeing that we all have as sheep gone astray, we find there is NO one that is innocent of adultery before God. God sent His Son, to redeem us who have lived an adulterous life after the flesh, so that we can walk pleasing to Him in the Holy Spirit. This is the ONLY p[ath that God accepts.

Adam literally belonged to God possessing His life, just as the woman possessed Adam's life. Possessing God's life, receiving his all from God, *it was only in God that Adam could be made... whole.*

In striving for ruling, to be as a god, Adam took another's word, and the spirit on that word, was death.

God now could never, would never be fulfilled, or joined to man through a life lived fulfilling that flesh and blood soul.

(This and other items are addressed in the chapter, 'Obtaining God's Soul, Personally'...).

Wholeness Offered to Man

God sent His Word, His Son, our Lord Jesus Christ who had been with Him before creation. The plan of God, instituted when man fell, had been prophesied and now?

The body was being prepared.

The angel delivered the word of God to Mary, who believed God's word through God's messenger and the Holy Spirit performed it. The body was being formed in her womb that would be the spotless Lamb of God.

At about thirty years of age, this Son of God being found in fashion as a man, a servant, humbled himself, was baptized by John and became obedient unto dying to the body prepared Him.

That flesh and blood soul took a back seat to the *'flesh and blood of God.'* That different soul would be the *'first-fruit'* of that generation, singular as those born of God will never die. This soul would be <u>God's word</u> made living by God's <u>Holy Ghost.</u>
Being led by the Holy Spirit, Jesus walked out each and every one of His teachings on dying to the old soul, and finding the New Soul.
God at this point had His Son in whom He was well pleased. *God had His habitation, His place of rest.*
Jesus stated, *'I am my Father are One.'*
For the first time since Adam's sin, God had a place of rest.

> *Jesus is the picture of God made whole in the son of man, and the son of man who is made whole in God.*

In Jesus, God had a place of rest upon the earth. This place of rest is where the Kingdom of God and Earth were joined. God is able to perform His will in the earth through His Sons.
Per Hebrews 1, Jesus is the express image of God.
We are to be transformed into HIS image, amen?
All that God possessed in His wholeness now belonged to His Son. All that the whole contains is released through their shared living, Jesus walked in that *'wholeness.'*

> "...All things that the Father hath are mine: therefore said I, that he shall take of mine, and shall shew it unto you." John 16:15

God's plan is a bit more extensive than one Son.
God desires a family.
A family in the image of His Son, who represented His express image! A family in the image of God's Son, would be a family that loved Him, more than their little temporal flesh & blood soul life in this wilderness called this... world.
The way of God's creation?
The life of the seed is in itself, a seed must die in being buried, in order to rise again in new life. But in this new life, the result would be *'much fruit.'* The much fruit would result in MANY seeds that in dying would also produce new life.

> "The hour is come, that the Son of man should be

> *glorified.*
> *Verily, verily, I say unto you, Except a corn of wheat fall into the ground and die, it abideth alone: but if it die, it bringeth forth much fruit.*
> *He that loveth his life shall lose it; and he that hateth his life in this world shall keep it unto life eternal.*
> *If any man serve me, let him follow me; and where I am, there shall also my servant be: if any man serve me, him will my Father honour." John 12*

If a man loveth his life in this world, he will lose it. If a man hates his life in this world, and will serve God, let him follow Christ in being crucified in Him, buried WITH Him, and where Jesus is, at the right hand of God, there also shall His... *'servant be.'*

Not the believer, not the 5,000 or the 70.

Not the presumptuous self-called uncorrectable 'man of God'. But the servant of God.

Man? He is a servant. Jesus took upon him the form of a servant, and was made in the likeness of men, amen?

That tells us that man was created by the Creator to serve. Jesus being God in the flesh, washed his disciples filthy feet.

Man was not created a god, regardless of what your favorite teacher tells you, your choices are who you serve. Who you yield your body to obey, his servant you are. Choose your lord, wisely.

This servant, this Son of God died to the flesh and blood carnal soul, its loves, affections, desires to please God in the tangible Holy Spirit ONLY.

Remember that thought I asked you to hold, again?

> *"...for them to be complete, it would be the heart of love in the woman, returning her all to her husband."*

That would be returning all that God had given her, through him...

Wholeness; Godly Restitution

In being transformed into the image of God's Son, it is our love

that is key.
Not love for our earthly family, or those outside the family of God, but our love for God that is key.
Jesus upon exiting the wilderness in the power of the spirit, led by the Holy Ghost delivered a message that angered everybody at the Nazareth synagogue to the point they tried to kill Him.
Jesus at the wedding in Cana, addressed May as woman, not mother.
When teaching inside a house, His mother, brethren and sisters called from outside.
We know what He said.
Where Adam failed, hearkening to the voice of his wife, his flesh and blood, Jesus drew a line. Jesus revealed a love for God that transcended a love for His own flesh and blood soul.

> *"Till we all come in the unity of the faith, and of the knowledge of the Son of God, unto a perfect man, unto the measure of the stature of the fulness of Christ: That we henceforth be no more children..." Ephesians 4*

 The purpose of those servants of God, those called of God are to bring us this point in our love for God. If they are not, they are liars if they say they are of God. They have another spirit, a different word, and are Satan's ministers of righteousness.
The servants of God, are to speak what God is telling the church.

> *The church, as the woman spoken of in Titus 2:4, is to be taught by those that love the Lord, to love her husband.*

This is restitution, restoring to God our Father in the Holy Spirit what He separated to us from His Son. Just as the woman was in Adam when God formed him from the dirt, our life was hid in God in Christ BEFORE creation. So now we know, the 'Who' God has sent into our hearts, amen?

> *"And because ye are sons, God hath sent forth the Spirit of his Son into your hearts, crying, Abba, Father.."*
> *Galatians 4:6*

Just as God breathed His life into Adam, and Adam died to

God preferring his flesh and blood. So we have the opportunity to give God what He desired from creation. We have the overcoming life of Jesus Christ. It is by the Holy Spirit He walked out the plan of God on this earth. We will succeed by walking out God's plan the very same way Jesus did, or not at all.

> *We cannot walk in the tangible Holy Ghost and follow ANY man, other than Jesus Christ.*

Those whom God has sent, who minister by the Holy Spirit, will also point you to Jesus Christ in and through the Holy Spirit on God's word.

Let me be clear. In our not fellowshipping God in His word, living by His word in the tangible Holy Ghost we also make a choice.

> *"If we suffer, we shall also reign with him: if we deny him, he also will deny us.." 2 Timothy 2:12*

Restitution

Wholeness exists for you, for me when we find our life in the One from whom we drew life from. When we see that God's words are spirit, and they are life, we have clarity as to how to live. We also have clarity for marriage.

In Hebrews 1, we find that God;

> *"..Hath in these last days spoken unto us by his Son, whom he hath appointed heir of all things, by whom also he made the worlds..."*

Before the woman was separated from the man, God had given Adam instructions for the Garden. Adam was told the entire Garden was his to enjoy, and the fruit of every tree was his, with the exception of the Tree of the Knowledge of Good and Evil. It was then his wife was separated from him, and restored to him.

Adam was the one who spoke these words of God to his wife.

Likewise, God has spoken to us by His Son, Jesus Christ.

This word we hear from the spirit and the bride calling us to find our life in Him, to be fulfilled in Him, precedes our being made whole in Him, amen?

The marriage is pending between Christ, and that which was separated from Him, amen?

In Acts 3, we find Peter speaking of our Lord,

> *"Whom the heaven must receive until the times of restitution of all things, which God hath spoken by the mouth of all his holy prophets since the world began."*

The bride of Christ will live by His word, as revealed by the same Holy Spirit Jesus lives by. Jesus will never accept less than him-self as His help-meet.

It will not be a dead word the bride believes, a theological discourse as the Pharisees and scribes. Jesus' words are her spirit, and her life.

Radical? Extreme?

Jesus at one point asked His disciples, *'Will you also go away?"* Jesus will not receive, or accept to Himself, any less than who He is.

How does that fit the Churchianity's doctrine of grace approved fleshly living? That is Satan's mute donkey, his *'minister of righteousness'* braying, again.

Marriage

A Godly marriage will have the husband acknowledging Christ as his head. He will walk in faith towards God, and as he walks with God in the Holy Spirit, He will acknowledge NOTHING can enter his life unless God allows it. In this, he will entrust God with his everything being obedient to the Holy Spirit's leading.

A Godly marriage will have a wife walking yielded to her husband, with faith towards God. It will not be faith in her ability to mouth her religion and manipulate her husband. She yields as unto Jesus Christ with each word being acceptable to Jesus Christ.

Jesus receives her heart attitude *personally*.

Both mates will have their faith in God, not relying on the other mate to determine their faith, or their resulting obedience to God.

Wholeness occurs as they live by the same word of God.

Satan's agenda is to divide, split and conquer. If the husband goes to church to keep his wife happy, to avoid hell at home, there is a change needed.

The wife needs to follow her husband.

Satan's ministries cater to the soul, appeasing, placating the soul. Frankly, they appeal to the woman's soul, her mind, her will, and her emotions. Satan places the false ideal of a man of God to destroy her. The misrepresentation of a man of God falsely portrayed is Satan's tool.

A husband that loves the Lord may not be comfortable in church, and that uneasiness may be Christ in him not accepting the liar's presentation.

The *'ministry'* accusing him of being convicted of sin, or as avoiding God's word, forsaking the assembling together will be Satan using God's word as manipulations.

The wife may be the tool Satan uses to override the Holy Spirit telling the man to get out.

The wife needs to be in faith towards God, and follow her husband as unto the Living Lord Jesus.

God knows those who are His, amen?

> *"There is neither Jew nor Greek, there is neither bond nor free, there is neither male nor female: for ye are all one in Christ Jesus."* Galatians 3:28

Satan has used this scripture to strip the man from having authority in his own home. The pastor's Jezebel, or Vashti through the unhindered, unrebuked work of Satan has *'neutered'* her husband as Jezebel ruled Ahab.

God's order established in creation has been attacked, and has destroyed the home, the church and the nation beginning in the pastor's bedroom.

God's people have been deprived of the protection and security of God's divine order. This scripture has been twisted to create a gender-free environment where *'before their god'* men can marry men, women marry women just as a wife can use it to

tell her husband he has no rule, no headship.
Nice, right?

> *"But from the beginning of the creation God made them male and female.*
> *For this cause shall a man leave his father and mother, and cleave to his wife;*
> *And they twain shall be one flesh: so then they are no more twain, but one flesh.*
> *What therefore God hath joined together, let not man put asunder." Mark 10*

Jesus identified male and female.
Jesus also noted those that God had put together, male and female, no man should put asunder.
Never do we find a reference that gender will be done away with, ever. Why? Because the servant is not greater than the master.
It is not a gender issue, it is a *'who are you going to serve'* issue. Having a *'Creator'* is our also having a *'created purpose'*. Why was the woman separated from the man? Let us look at one more scripture.

> *"...And it shall come to pass in the last days, saith God,*
> *I will pour out of my Spirit upon all flesh: and your sons and your daughters shall prophesy, and your young men shall see visions, and your old men shall dream dreams:*
> *And on my servants and on my handmaidens I will pour out in those days of my Spirit; and they shall prophesy..." Acts 2:17-18*

In the *'last days'* does God still identify His servants as male, AND female?
Hmmmm... Pastor? Your wife is to yield to you as unto the Lord, she is not to be your Jezebel, or Vashti. But being a weak lily-livered miscreant, pilgrim, you would not want to endure her wrath, amen? It is easier to have a *'happy wife, happy life'*...
If you desire to please God, and walk with Him, you must intercede for her and then follow the direction of the Holy

Spirit. Why?

> She is to be to you, what you are to be to our Lord.

Is Jesus your head? Or is that foul spirit that rules your obstinate wife your master?

All Flesh?

This scripture likewise has been taught that the Holy Spirit has been poured out on all flesh indiscriminate of their being a believer or non-believer.

One of Satan's messengers states God's Holy Spirit 24/7 is being poured out on all flesh. So when the Holy Spirit was poured out, those mocking in the street was the result of being under the influence of the Holy Spirit? The silliness of man's reasoning, man's theology is exposed.

Again, we hear the *'dumb ass'* braying.

God's word, 2 Peter 2:16 (KJV)

In John 14, Jesus stated that the world cannot receive the Holy Spirit.

> *"..And I will pray the Father, and he shall give you another Comforter, that he may abide with you forever; Even the Spirit of truth; whom the world cannot receive, because it seeth him not, neither knoweth him: but ye know him; for he dwelleth with you, and shall be in you."*

If the world cannot receive the Holy Spirit, how then can the Holy Spirit be poured out on all flesh?

The understanding of God's word is simple, once known. Who comprises the *'ALL flesh'* in Acts two?

When we read it we see God makes no distinction between the son, the daughter, the young man and the old man. Let us look at what Peter told his hearers on the day of Pentecost, it lines right up with what Jesus told His disciples above in John 14.

> *"And we are his witnesses of these things; and so is also the Holy Ghost, whom God hath given to them that obey him."*

Being disobedient, and claiming to have received the Holy

Spirit is now revealed as living a lie.

Is there any other reason your issues continue, your prayers bounce off the ceiling, and you pay some tucked or untucked miscreant to pacify you?

This distinction is also revealed in verse 18.

The Holy Spirit will be poured out on God's servants, and God's handmaids. Those that serve God and receive the Holy Ghost are both male and female, they are one in Christ. God is not making a distinction between male and female in receiving the gift of Christ!

If you are a man serving God, you have Jesus Christ as your head, and doing His will is your will. If you are following man, not Christ, you cannot please God, and you are not *'In Christ.'*

In serving *'another'* you have alienated the tangible Holy Spirit by choice, He does not abide *'with you'* and cannot be in you.

If you are a wife serving God, you are God's handmaiden. If you are carnal, self-willed, and concerned about your equality with your husband, you are not accepting God's word. In not accepting God's word, you are following the voice of another.

You have alienated the tangible Holy Spirit by choice, He does not abide *'with you'* and cannot be in you.

In both cases, this knowledge removes God's grace that covers ignorance.

God's grace belongs to those with a heart after God. Otherwise God's patience is stupidly misunderstood as... grace.

As for those in ministry, if equality is your message, with this understanding the grace of being ignorant is departed.

As broad as your sin, should be the breadth of your repentance, or not. Willful sin has no sacrifice, but a certain looking forward to of judgement, God's word.

Distasteful and wrong?

God is God.

When we think God must accept our sacrifice with our excrement, we have our peers in Malachi 2:3.

There is no wholeness with God, or our mates when we strive for equality. What we do is place ourselves in a corporate group whose end we will share and not enjoy.

> "And the King shall answer and say unto them, Verily I say unto you, Inasmuch as ye have done it unto one of the least of these my brethren, ye have done it unto me. Then shall he say also unto them on the left hand, Depart from me, ye cursed, into everlasting fire, prepared for the devil and his angels..." Matthew 25:40-41

Another Spirit Over The Church

While the pastor may claim to do the '*work*' of God, their employment of service planners, maintaining a system of worship, reveals the man pleasing, soul manipulating spirit that pleasures him as the head of that church.

This is itself denying the Lord Jesus Christ.

If, IF it was God's house, God's word and His spirit would set the order.

Men, women go to the cultural church NOT to come before God, literally, but to make a showing before man. If God's presence was there, His holiness would convict of sin, of righteousness, and of coming judgement.

Instead it is the Whore's sons/lovers detailing the grace they need to cover their sin, in their living after the flesh.

Declaring either the death of Christ, or His absence, they forge ahead as Eli's sons making this message clear by their activities.

In this they deliver another gospel.

As a church group, individually they follow a head other than Christ.

This is falsely identified as the '*body of Christ*' to achieve the common goal of church growth, '*doing a work for Jesus.*'

This is ignorance as they falsely identify themselves as the body of Christ... but in not following Jesus Christ personally, it is another spirit they follow.

Does this sound so very wrong?

Did not God ordain churches, pastors, their schemes, their

oratories and personalities to win the world to Jesus???

Had not God ordained the Levites as His ministers?

And yet the scribes, Pharisees, the Levites took God's vineyard as their own. Of those sent to them, they beat some, mocked some, and killed others. The church today is no different receiving honor one from another, and not the honor that comes from God, alone.

How could this be... *wrong?*

Religiously, Babylon has not changed, as it is the same spirit with a different temple, a different name over the door, exercising the same rule.

> *"Woe unto you, scribes and Pharisees, hypocrites! for ye compass sea and land to make one proselyte, and when he is made, ye make him twofold more the child of hell than yourselves..."*

Consider the unique Gospel of Jesus Christ and the Body of Christ.

This gospel has the pre-existing Son of God, King of Kings as its only Head.

He is the One with the scars in His hands, feet, and side.

He is the One who came as a servant, who was beaten, crucified, and then buried.

He is the Man who in being raised from the dead with victory over death, hell, and the grave that is to be our head, and the head of His Body.

Being the very first-fruit from the dead, there is no man capable of taking His place, amen?

This man had discipled men through being the servant of God by the Holy Spirit to follow Him in and by the Holy Spirit. Those who learned of Him, learned to lean on Him, and learn from the Holy Spirit are His disciples. These are the men who were sent to make disciples.

The seventy, the five thousand, those taught of men, those learned of the religious rulers apart from the Holy Spirit?

They were not part of this commission.

They have NEVER been part of this... commision.

It is in our abandoning all we have relied on after the flesh, leaving all our soul requires for validation and personally following this Jesus in and by the Holy Spirit that we are made whole.
Is that not what our Lord told us?
Jesus is the One who purchased us to Himself, to be our Lord, not a secondary fallback when we have personal difficulty.
He is our Master, and our Lord so we as servants of God may identify with Him.
We see Him as taking our place at Calvary.
Going a step farther, we also take up our cross and identify with Him in our being crucified with Him, our first-born soul also being poured out at Calvary.
We, being dead, do not have our life in this world at all. We who are redeemed from death, born of His word, and having received His spirit, walk in the Holy Ghost and are raised in Him.
To not abide in the Holy Spirit, hating our life in this world (John 12) is to live counting the pleasing of the physical creature, our body as our life.
In this lifestyle, we are dead, but not buried.
Dead, but not crucified with Christ.
Dead with another master we obey. We endeavor to find our *'wholeness'* in the god of this world, satisfying and fulfilling the desires of our living cadaver, and its mind.

Sons of God

As children of God however, the death we acknowledge, is the death of the cross we have taken up. We willfully participate in this death through our laying aside anything, everything that God's Holy Spirit will not witness with His presence. This is *'abiding in Christ.'*
We must abide in Him, before He can abide in us. John 15:4-7.
This is our choice to suffer with Him, that we might be resurrected and reign in Him. If we do not remain in Him, we have chosen not to follow Him. If we do not choose the

tangible Holy Spirit as our life through abiding in Him, we have taken another's word, and are following another.
The faux Babylonian gospel of grace says,
> "All is done, sit back, relax, thou shall not surely die..."

The spirit and the bride however have a different message,
> "Come out of her, my people, that ye be not partakers of
> her sins, and that ye receive not of her plagues."

Can we hear Jesus warning His followers to leave Jerusalem to not participate in her judgement?

One message contains an invitation to wholeness, the other an eternity apart from God. The message of paying the price to depart her comes at a cost, the other requires no effort at all. The false gospel presents a false grace presented by the harlot, her ministers, who are her lovers drunk with the *'wine of her fornication,'* God's word, not mine.

Too hard? Too direct? Is that why Jesus stated narrow is the way, strait is the gate that leads to eternal life and few there be that find it?

This is all about God having a place of rest IN us as we abide in the Holy Spirit. It ceases to be about us, but understanding the will of God so we can walk pleasingly before Him. Being present in the body, how do we live before God? Paul in Romans 8 details the 'how-to' in the first two verses, and then throughout the chapter.

> "So then they that are in the flesh cannot please God.
> But ye are not in the flesh, but in the Spirit, if so be that
> the Spirit of God dwell in you. Now if any man have not
> the Spirit of Christ, he is none of his."

To believe we have the spirit of God indwelling us as we savor the things of the world is an error.

We have been given the power to become the sons of God. We retain the power of choosing what we meditate, dwell on, and focus on. We HAVE been delivered from the Kingdom of Darkness. It then is our choice to be involved in the realm of darkness enjoying murder, deceit, lust and pornography. It is our choice to invite this swill into our home through the shows we watch, the video games we stream. To believe for one second, that God's grace covers spiritual adultery is asinine.

Eternal life comes at a price, the cost is this very soul, this life we told God we buried so we can enjoy the fellowship of Jesus Christ in and through the Holy Spirit. If this is too much, keep in mind we choose who we follow, and that choice is honored. If we choose not to follow our Lord?

Note that Jesus did not chase down the 5,000 that walked away, nor the 70. Being born of God, experiencing the Holy Spirit drawing us to Him should not make us believe we have *'it made.'* Let us recall God in Genesis 6:3 (NIV),

> "Then the LORD said, My Spirit will not contend with humans forever..."

Pre-flood, the inhabitants of the world knew the presence of God as He contended with each one of them. That sense of God's presence did not ensure their salvation, amen?

The only ones who heeded the call of God was Noah, and his family. Their lives were consumed with following God's instructions and that obedience was the result of faith in God. That same faith was used by God to judge the world, Hebrews 11:7.

God has again used the faith of one man to judge all flesh this day, the faith of His Son, Jesus Christ our Lord.   All who follow Him, will be saved.

This is the wholeness with God that is available....

And our heart is to see the seventh day concluded with God our Father, at rest...

CHURCH MINISTRY

As stated before: There is an unmatched anger, a zeal, that is pending and will impact every *'church minister'* in their house, behind their closed doors.

When I say this is personal to my Head, the Lord Jesus Christ, I am saying it is extremely personal with each and every church minister/leader, intentionally or unintentionally operating as the Head of the Church, it is intimately personal, no exceptions. *"Mene"* means *"numbered,"* God has numbered the days of your reign and has brought it to an end. *"Tekel"* means *"weighed,"* you have been weighed on the balances and have not measured up. *"Upharsin"* means *"divided,"* In this case, *"YOUR kingdom,"* YOUR rule has come to an end.

For those walking *"In Christ,"* in the life of Christ, pleasing the Lord…only with your eyes shall you behold these things.

There is no easy conclusion to this book, every attempt I have made to *'offer a path of reconciliation'* or of redemption is not accepted before the Lord. I cannot change that, nor will I.

The Judgment of God, when delivered, is always warranted and typically occurs after repeatedly ignored warnings. Imputed sin, is judgment. Imputed sin, occurs when God's warnings are ignored, and God's grace has reached its end. We have two examples in Matthew, the first being in chapter 5,

> *"Agree with thine adversary quickly, whiles thou art in the way with him; lest at any time the adversary deliver thee to the judge, and the judge deliver thee to the officer, and thou be cast into prison.*
> *Verily I say unto thee, Thou shalt by no means come out thence, till thou hast paid the uttermost farthing."*

The second example is in chapter 18,
> *"So likewise shall my heavenly Father do also unto you,*
> *if ye from your hearts forgive not every one his brother*
> *their trespasses."*

Our Old Testament example is Job who had ignored God warning him in dreams. In the New Testament, the Apostle Paul warns of both the severity of God, and the terror of the Lord.

What can we take away from these instances? God's word is true, once sin is imputed, once judgment begins, there is a price the unrepentant and hard hearted will pay.

> *This helps us understand why; "Noah did not offer a*
> *boat building course."*

www.ingramcontent.com/pod-product-compliance
Lightning Source LLC
Chambersburg PA
CBHW051748040426
42446CB00007B/263